UNDISCOVERED
DUNDEE

UNDISCOVERED DUNDEE

BRIAN KING

BLACK & WHITE PUBLISHING

First published 2011

by Black & White Publishing Ltd

29 Ocean Drive, Edinburgh EH6 6JL

1 3 5 7 9 10 8 6 4 2   11 12 13 14

ISBN: 978 1 84502 338 6

Typeset by Ellipsis Digital Limited, Glasgow

Printed and bound by MPG Books Ltd, Bodmin, Cornwall

CONTENTS

For my parents and all my family in Dundee

Introduction

Stand in the middle of Dundee High Street facing south and you will be looking at the pillars of the eighteenth century Town House. Behind the Town House, a warren of ancient buildings known as The Vault meanders its way down to the thriving dock area. To your right is the house General Monck reputedly occupied when he took the town for Oliver Cromwell in 1651. Beyond this, the bustling Overgate and its assortment of shops and houses winds away into the distance. You will require only one thing to take in this view – a very good imagination.

The Town House was the first to go, crashing into a heap of rubble in the 1930s almost exactly two hundred years after it was built. Despite a campaign for its retention and suggested sites for its rebuilding, this William Adam-designed landmark was cleared to make way for the City Square. The Vault, containing the fine town house of the Laird of Strathmartine, also came down around this time. Monck's house and the Overgate lasted until the 1960s when a soulless shopping centre took their place. The city centre docks were filled in to accommodate the landfall of the Tay Road Bridge, and in the process separated the town from the river – the very thing that had drawn the earliest settlers to the location. Stand in the middle of Dundee High Street and you will see a city cut off from its past.

History in Dundee, then, is not a visible thing as it is in other cities such as Edinburgh or York. There are not many places in Dundee today where it is possible to stand and take in a view that would be instantly recognisable to a visitor from another century – decades of wanton destruction in the name of progress have seen to that. As the dust clouds from the demolitions have cleared, however, they have left behind a keen interest in the city's past. This is undoubtedly a sense of nostalgia for some, mourning the town that they loved and lost. For younger generations, though, there remains a curiosity about the past and a feeling that they have somehow been cheated of their civic inheritance. Indeed, interest in the history of Dundee seems to have increased precisely because it is not there in a tangible sense.

Just as the few remaining historic sites in the city centre, such as the Old Steeple or the Howff graveyard, grab the attention of the visitor, so the same few themes inevitably recur in works of local history. There are stories of the traditional industries of Jute, Jam and Journalism or of the city's modern totem, the *RRS Discovery*, the story of the Tay Bridge Disaster of 1879 or of that tragedy's chronicler – the chronically tragic poet William McGonagall. All of these will undoubtedly find their way into the following pages in some form, but it is not the purpose of this book simply to repeat the old stories.

Undiscovered Dundee is, rather, an anthology of unknown and forgotten Dundee. It is an attempt to bring a lost past to life and to piece together the clues of the half-remembered stories that have been handed down to us. Many of the people and events described would have been well known in the city in their day but they have drifted from the collective consciousness with the passage of time, while some others were always less familiar. A hidden history lies buried in the debris of the demolished city and some stories need to be fully excavated while others simply require the accumulated dust of decades to be removed. Where possible this has been done by returning to original documents and in the process bringing to light new information. It is hoped that there will be something to surprise even the weariest student of 'Auld Dundee'.

By its very nature such a history will tend towards more offbeat characters and stories but these will often bring forward details of everyday life that give a clearer picture of their time than many of the major figures and happenings. Where more mainstream people and events have been featured, they have been approached from a new and hopefully hitherto undiscovered angle. Where the terrain of living memory is entered into it is hoped that blurred memories will be brought into sharper focus by new details.

For the most part, though, this is the story of the unknown – forgotten events such as the disaster that propelled Dundee into the headlines around the world more than a decade before the fall of the Tay Bridge, or the riot that broke out in the town following a boxing match in England. It is the story of harmless eccentrics and brutal murderers, of heroes and villains, of strange events and everyday landmarks. It is the story of the forgotten Dundonians who stayed and made a difference to their city and of those who left and made an impact on a larger stage. Sometimes the story will take us far from Dundee itself and sometimes it will be the story of what happened when the world, in the form of everyone from writers to royalty, from presidents to pop stars, came to Dundee. It is always Dundee itself, however, which binds the story together.

Stand in the middle of Dundee High Street and have another look. You are standing in the middle of a city that is alive with history.

1
Time and Chance

Sometimes the whole course of history can be changed by a single action or decision. This is not only true of the actions and decisions of kings and presidents but also of those whose names are not recorded by historians. If some long-forgotten individuals had not decided that the area around what was to become known as the Black Rock, on the north bank of the river that we call the Tay, provided shelter and was easily defended, then the city of Dundee as we know it would not exist.

Sometimes things happen in a way that leaves a tantalising 'What if?' question behind. Dervorguilla of Galloway, the mother of John Balliol, King of Scots, established the long-since vanished Greyfriars Monastery in Dundee and co-founded Balliol College in Oxford. It has often been speculated as to what might have happened if she had done these things the other way round.

There are also times when things seem to come together in a way that is hard to imagine was not decreed by fate. It required the shipping, textile and whaling industries to come together in nineteenth century Dundee for another now forgotten individual to discover that the rough fibre of jute, shipped from the Indian subcontinent, could be spun by machine when softened with whale oil, in the process building the foundations of Dundee's most famous industry.

The following stories bring these twists of fate to a more human level. They show how one person's life can be transformed by forces beyond their control, such as the slip of a pen or the turn of a card, and how even the simplest of choices can have devastating consequences – as two teenage boys found out in 1865 when they decided to head off for a night out.

Fearful Catastrophe in Dundee

There is a spring in the step of the McConnell brothers as they make their way down Scouringburn towards Bell Street this evening. The streets are still buzzing with the New Year atmosphere. It is Monday, 2 January 1865 – but it is not just the holiday that has the brothers excited. Like all teenagers they enjoy the thrill of heading off somewhere without their parents' permission. Not that these are teenagers in the sense that the world will come to know them a century later – that word won't even be coined until the 1930s. These boys are already hardened by years of working in the jute mills. Alexander, the elder brother, is now around sixteen years old. His brother, William, is around fourteen. Ages are not so precisely calculated in the world that the brothers inhabit, nor are names so readily shortened. Alexander still works in the mill; William in the grocery shop their father runs. They belong to the first generation of their family to be born in Dundee or even in Scotland. Like so many of those that the brothers pass on the way down Scouringburn tonight, the McConnell family is Irish. The Scouring Burn itself, now piped underground, gushes far beneath the boys' feet. It provided power for many of Dundee's earliest jute mills. The water brought the mills to this area and the mills brought the Irish fleeing the Famine that has afflicted their country in the wake of the failure of successive potato crops in the late 1840s. This area is now mainly inhabited by Irish people. The McConnells are unusual, though, in that their family is Protestant – the vast majority of immigrants to Dundee are Roman Catholics. Their family comes from County Antrim. Their mother is dead and their father has remarried. They live with their father and stepmother and their older sister Sarah in Lower Pleasance.

The boys hurry on their way, eagerly anticipating what the evening is to bring. They are setting out on an adventure but the adventure of their adult life is also just beginning. For Alexander this will mean two marriages. He will live to see the Tay Bridge built, fall and rise again; he will see the new century dawn and a new King on the throne. He will work as a blacksmith and will learn a trade, ending his days as a mechanic in a factory. Not for him, though, the hot, oppressive, dusty air of the jute mills – his lungs will be filled with the sickly sweet air of a confectionary factory. For William, on the other hand, there will be nothing. His life will end in Bell Street tonight.

The Sweeney family is also heading to Bell Street. They are more typical of the Irish immigrants who have come to Dundee in the last few years. They live in the Hawkhill in a crowded backland entered through the pend known as Isles Lane. Joseph Sweeney is forty-eight years old and works as a weaver. He is with his wife Mary and their thirteen-year-old son Peter. Like Alexander McConnell, Peter has been a mill worker since he was young. Peter has been asking his mother all day if they can go to Bell Street tonight. Finally, when he asked again during their evening meal, she relented, on the condition that his father came along too to look after him. As they near Bell Street, they notice that everybody appears to be heading to the same place as they are. The Sweeneys can tell that it is going to be busy. There is an excitement in the air.

Mrs Mary Springthorpe is pleased with the success of the last few days. Her special presentations over the Christmas and New Year period have drawn large crowds to her music hall. Mrs Springthorpe and her husband have rented the premises in the basement of the Bell Street United Presbyterian Church since 1858 when they moved to Dundee from Aberdeen. Before that they toured the country with their waxwork show – 'consisting of the most noted Kings, Queens, Statesmen, Warriors, Poets, Eccentric Theatrical and other eminent personages' and 'grand cosmoramic views'.

They also established successful exhibitions in Liverpool and Hull. This recent success is tinged with sadness though, as Mr John Springthorpe – 'artist and modeller in wax' – died almost a year ago. His obituary in *The Era*, the main theatrical newspaper of the day, describes him as 'upright and gentlemanly in his dealings' and notes that 'the slightest hiss from the audience would make him resolve to part at once with the unpopular performer rather than risk losing the good opinion of his patrons'. The name Springthorpe has until now been associated in Dundee with excitement, fun, enjoyment and above all escape from the grim living and working conditions that most people have to suffer. After tonight the name will be associated only with tragedy, suffering and death before it fades from the collective memory altogether.

Robert Keillor is nineteen and lives in the Perth Road. He is an upholsterer like his father. By the time he arrives at the hall there is a crowd gathering. He decides to see if he can push his way through the crowd and get nearer to the entrance. John Kinnison and his friends are already there. They are all aged between about thirteen and sixteen years old. Some of them have come along with John and some he has met by chance. He is with two brothers David and Andrew Nicoll, Robert Bruce, Arthur Kelly and a young boy called Douglas Macdonald.

It is now almost seven o'clock. The performance doesn't begin until quarter to eight but the doors are being opened because of the large crowds expected. The gates at the top of the steps leading down to the basement hall are being kept closed – with one half only being opened to let in two or three people at a time. John Jones, who is employed by Mrs Springthorpe, is in charge of the gate. The crowd is by now spilling out over Constitution Road but the system is working well. Jones opens one half of the gate and lets a few people enter. They then walk down the flight of steps to the small paved area with the ticket booth and then into the hall. The hall is filling up this way and will soon be about a third full. The McConnell brothers have reached the gate.

Nobody knows how it begins. The crowd has been becoming impatient for some time. Alexander McConnell thinks that someone deliberately knocks out the bar that holds the other half of the gate – others think that the pressure of the crowd simply becomes too much. However it happens, the gate is breached and people are driven forward into the stairwell. John Jones the gateman is swept down the stairs first and onto his knees but somehow manages to get out of the way in time. Someone loses their footing at the bottom of the stairs and the surging crowd becomes a heap of bodies in the stairwell.

Robert Keillor is one of the first to fall. He is carried off his feet. He sees an old man fall first and others fall on top of him. Keillor is trapped 'in a slanting position' on the second step from the bottom. The old man beneath him is crushed to death as the crowd continues to surge forward. Keillor and others plead with people to stop pushing forward but they are, he thinks, 'seized with panic'.

William McConnell is swept away from his brother. Alexander finds himself in a heap with several people on top of him. He manages to get his head free and to breathe. He cannot move otherwise and can just hope he will be rescued. He cannot see William.

John Kinnison and his friends are also swept forward. Kinnison sees an old man – a sailor he believes – falling with them and tries to grab hold of him to stop himself but they are all dragged down together. Later, the body of a sixty-year-old sailor, James Knight of Doig's Entry in the Overgate, is one of those recovered. Douglas Macdonald jumps onto Kinnison's back in an effort to save himself. They land near the bottom of the stairs. Arthur Kelly is beside them. Andrew Nicoll and Robert Bruce who were behind them are now above them. There is no sign of David Nicoll.

A man by the name of John Beat is also among the first to fall. He lands around the third step from the bottom. He is unable to move his arms. He hears a woman who had been standing near to him say that her child is dead but he does not know if this is true. 'I could hardly describe the scene,' he will later recall, 'people were lying some heads up, some feet up – some one way and some another. There were none of those in front of me who were on their feet. The whole of them were lying in one mass – just like a heap of straw, and then the rest on the higher part of the stair were hanging over with their whole weight on the top of them.' Beat shouts to tell people to stop pushing but his voice is lost in the screaming and confusion. People at the back of the crowd, unaware of what has happened, keep pushing forward. John Kinnison is also shouting. He is asking for the hall door to be opened to relieve pressure at the other end. He shouts until he is tired but no one pays any attention. He almost manages to get himself free but his legs are trapped. Douglas Macdonald still clings to his back.

There may now be anything up to one hundred people crushed into this pit with no means of escape. For those lying in what has become a twisted heap of bodies it seems that the ordeal lasts forever. Eventually, though, people realise what is happening and after around twenty minutes, the crowd begins to clear from the top of the stair. It is far from over, though – removing both the dead and living from the pit will take a long time; bodies lie awkwardly twisted together, living and dead limbs are entwined and the forces of panic and helplessness hamper the rescue effort. Slowly, though, bodies are removed and pressure is relieved. John Kinnison is able to escape. Douglas Macdonald, still clinging to Kinnison's back, gets out too. Their friends Andrew Nicoll and Robert Bruce will be found among the dead.

A man named Alexander Bertram who was in the hall early leaves by the back door and runs to get a doctor. Some of the injured will be dead by the time he returns from the Murraygate with Doctor Smith. Smith is the first medical man on the scene. It is now half past seven. He is brought to the body of a young man but can do nothing for him. Nearby lie around a dozen bodies, which have been pulled from the scene, all bearing the signs of suffocation. The hall has been largely cleared of the living now, but it acts as a temporary mortuary. The bodies are all laid out in the main hall and various side rooms. Some of the injured await treatment; their exhausted faces show only a vacant stare. John Beat has managed to escape the crush and is helping with the dead and injured. When he recovers the body of one young girl, he finds that she has a deep mark round her throat. The fastening on her cloak has been pulled tight round her neck in the crush and killed her. It seems to Beat that she was hanged.

Some of the most badly injured survivors are sent by cab to the Royal Infirmary. Among them is a thirteen-year-old message boy named John Holland who hails from the West Port. He is severely injured. He was found lying unconscious at the top of the steps. He is found to be dead on arrival at the infirmary. Attempts are made to revive him with a 'galvanic battery' – an early form of electric shock treatment – but to no avail.

News of the accident spreads quickly through Dundee. Most people live within walking distance of Bell Street. Many are out and about tonight celebrating the New Year holiday – people who would be accounted for any other night of the year. There is uncertainty over the whereabouts of lots of young people in particular. The anxious and the curious begin to congregate outside the hall. Those who fear they have lost friends or relatives are led into the hall to view the bodies.

Alexander McConnell eventually finds the body of his brother William among the dead. Their father is still unaware that his sons were at the music hall. Some become hysterical on finding the body of a loved one. Mary Sweeney searches the hall for her husband Joseph and son Peter. She is inconsolable when she discovers their lifeless bodies. She finds Peter first and then Joseph in a different part of the hall. A reporter will later say that her 'expressions of grief went to the hearts of all who were present'.

Gradually, the hall begins to clear. Permission is given for the bodies to be removed by grieving friends and relatives. By eleven o'clock there are only five bodies remaining. These are taken round the corner to the mortuary or Dead House at the Howff. The Dead House is then closed up for the night, leaving many anxious families to an uncertain night.

Twenty people died in the disaster at Springthorpe's Music Hall. They were mainly young working people out seeking cheap entertainment and some respite from their drab lives on a rare holiday. The Springthorpes had a long established admission price of 6d admission for 'Ladies and Gentlemen and persons in trade' but 3d for 'working classes and children'.

The event caused shockwaves throughout Dundee and was widely reported elsewhere. Many people recognised they had been in similar situations and that a potential disaster awaited in many of their own cities. A correspondent to the *Irish Times* bemoaned the condition of 'many of our places of public assembly in Dublin' and feared that one theatre in particular 'could be the scene of sufferings as terrible as those at Dundee – the recital of which has sickened all readers'. Such worries were not without foundation. Four years later eighteen people died in an almost identical accident in Bristol when attempting to gain entrance to a Boxing Night pantomime.

There was no general review of safety at public gatherings in the wake of the Springthorpe's disaster – indeed the Music Hall itself re-opened soon after the accident. The Procurator Fiscal, John Boyd Baxter, had carried out a local investigation the day after it happened but concluded that no blame was to be apportioned. Nevertheless, this did not stop some people seeking to do so. The Reverend Taylor of the Free Gaelic Church in Meadowside thundered in a sermon delivered the following Sunday that the 'excessive and godless love of pleasure' was to blame. 'God, foreseeing the madness of our folly, determined to read a lesson to the inhabitants of Dundee and through them to the country at large,' he said.

Springthorpe's revival after the tragedy was short lived in any case. In early February 1865, the church authorities announced that they would not be renewing the lease when it expired at the end of April.

The building that housed Springthorpe's Music Hall and the United Presbyterian Church still stands at the corner of Bell Street and Constitution Road today. Appropriately, it is now the Bell Street Music Centre and is still concerned with popular entertainment. It is an eerie feeling to stand and look over the railings and into the pit where so many people were crushed to death while around you people continue with their daily lives, unaware of what happened there. There is no memorial plaque on the wall to those who died and the tragedy is little known in Dundee now. It was to be overshadowed by an even worse accident – the collapse of the Tay Bridge – a few years later.

Sadly, disasters at public gatherings continue in our own time – most notably at football matches. In the tragedy at Hillsborough stadium in Sheffield in 1989, ninety-six people were crushed to death. Scotland's worst such event was the Ibrox disaster of 1971, which claimed sixty-six lives. Like the tragedy at Springthorpe's, at Ibrox there were many young people among the dead – young people who had been out seeking entertainment. Like Springthorpe's, the tragedy took place on a stairway. Indeed, the Ibrox disaster happened on 2 January – the anniversary of Dundee's forgotten tragedy at Springthorpe's Music Hall over a century earlier.

The Dead

James Knight, 63, seaman of Doig's Entry in the Overgate

Joseph Sweeney, 48, weaver of Isles Pend, Hawkhill and his son **Peter Sweeney**, 13, a mill worker

Margaret McLean, 13, mill worker of 25 Bucklemaker Wynd

William John McConnell, 13, shop boy of 42 Lower Pleasance

Lillias Urquhart, 17, mill worker of Ireland's Land, Chapelshade

Robert Bruce, 14, mill worker of Smithfield, Mains Road, Dundee

James Mudie, 60, weaver of Union Street, Maxwelltown

Andrew Nicoll, 16, mill worker of Smith's Land, Smithfield

Agnes Hamilton, 12, mill worker of Milne's East Wynd, Scouringburn

Elizabeth Gowan, 13, of Speed's Land, Perth Road

Mary Robertson, 9, of 35 Todburn Lane

Jane Mitchison, 12, mill worker of Dallfield Walk

Alexander Campbell, 20, mill worker of Gray Street, Lochee

Mary Ann Findlay, 17, mill worker of Borrie's Land, Dallfield Walk

Andrew Low Smith, 7, of Springhill

John Holland, 13, message boy of 18 West Port

Jean Smith, 13, power loom weaver of 47 Wellgate
Alexander Davidson, 16, apprentice mechanic of Dallfield Walk
Elizabeth Dow Hodge, 12, mill worker of 9 Joint Stock Buildings

The Cut of the Cards

It was 5 May 1967 – the beginning of the so-called Summer of Love and the month that 'San Francisco' by Scott Mackenzie entered the American charts. In Dundee City Chambers that evening at around 7pm another Mackenzie was wondering if his time had come. Alex Mackenzie had been nominated to be Dundee's new Lord Provost but so had his rival, the sitting Lord Provost Maurice McManus. The meeting was deadlocked. The stakes were high. McManus had held the position throughout the sixties. If Mackenzie was successful he would become the city's first Progressive (the equivalent of Conservative) Lord Provost since 1954.

Legislation stated that in the event of a tie in the vote, lots should be drawn in the form of cutting playing cards. Before the meeting one of Mackenzie's colleagues had advised him that as the cards were new he should cut well down the pack. The colleague had then almost immediately withdrawn the advice, as he did not wish to take the blame for any failure. Mackenzie was also said to have several superstitious tokens with him.

Maurice McManus was first to cut the cards. He drew the five of Spades. There was tension in the air as Mackenzie drew his card. It was the seven of Hearts. Order papers were waved and a cheer went up from his supporters. There was, of course, dismay from McManus's side. It was a sad way to end the term of office of a popular Lord Provost but the moment was Mackenzie's. He took the oath and was moved into the chair thus gaining the casting vote that tipped the balance in favour of the Progressives.

Meanwhile, Mackenzie's wife was at home when the telephone rang. It was the Lord Provost's official chauffeur. As soon as he addressed her as 'Lady Provost', Mrs Mackenzie knew that her husband had won. It was a

Mackenzie draws the winning card

strange way for her to have found out – but then it was a strange way to select a Lord Provost.

Mention of the way that Mackenzie became Lord Provost will normally invoke in Dundonians a response such as 'only in Dundee' or 'of course it wouldn't happen nowadays'. However, such a method of decision-making does not belong exclusively to Dundee or to the dim and distant past. A similar deadlock occurred in South Ayrshire Council in 2003 with Conservative and Labour votes tied in the choice of Provost. On this occasion the Labour Party candidate was successful with an eight of Spades compared to his opponent's two of Clubs. The victor was one Mr McKenzie.

April Next to Come

The verdict was guilty. It fell to Lord Deas to pronounce the sentence. In the Dundee of 1873 there could only be one punishment. The jury's recommendation to mercy would have to wait for due process. He donned the black cap:

> In respect of the verdict of the Assize against the panel, Lord Deas and Lord Jerviswood discern and adjudge the said Thomas Scobbie, panel, to be carried from the bar back to the prison of Dundee, therein to be detained, and fed on bread and water only, until Tuesday, the 29th day of April next to come, and upon that day betwixt the hours of eight and ten o'clock forenoon, within the walls of the said prison to be hanged by the neck upon a gibbet by the hands of the common executioner, until he be dead, and ordain the said body thereafter to be buried within the walls of the said prison, which is pronounced for doom.

In the dock, Thomas Scobbie remained composed as he heard the sentence. He was subsequently led away to what had become a condemned cell.

Seven months earlier, on 24 September 1872, at Kingennie near Murroes, a woman named Jane Spalding was washing some shirts outside the cottage that she shared with various members of her extended family. Between ten and eleven o'clock in the morning Jane took the shirts to nearby Kingennie Woods where she hung them to dry on a rope. The shirts were still there at one o'clock but when she went back a little later she noticed that they were missing. She returned to the cottage and told her forty-two-year-old brother George what had happened. George went out to see if he could see anyone. He was accompanied by Jane's young son, also named George, who had been out herding.

Shortly afterwards, the boy came back and said that his uncle had 'found someone'. Jane went out and met her brother in the company of a man. The stranger said that he did not have the shirts and had not stolen them but added that he knew where to find them. He led George Spalding and his nephew to where the shirts were hidden under a hedge. Spalding told his nephew that he was going to take the man to the police at Monifieth, a forty-five minute walk away. The two of them set off down the road accompanied by Juno, Spalding's retriever. It was around four o'clock.

Around half an hour later they were seen by two slaters, David Molison and Melville Suttie, who were on their way home from working at the nearby farm of Laws. It seems that Spalding's prisoner had made a bid for freedom but Juno had grabbed him by the coat and Spalding had managed to re-capture him after a scuffle. Molison said he heard the man say to Spalding that he would 'do for him'. Molison and Suttie discussed whether they should go after the two men but they concluded that there was no real danger. Instead they watched them disappear down the road to Monifieth.

At about half past nine that evening the dog returned to the cottage alone. The family were not unduly worried that George Spalding had not also returned. He worked as a gamekeeper and this meant that he sometimes kept strange hours. Concern grew, though, when he had still not returned the next morning. Another sister, Susan Spalding, took young George and the dog out to search for him. Juno led the way along the path to the main road. Young George Spalding later told the court how the dog had seemed uneasy when they reached a certain spot; how it had run forward and stopped, looking back at them and then gave a howl when they walked past the place where it waited. The boy was sent back to see what was wrong with the dog. It was then that he discovered his uncle's body lying under a bramble bush.

The accurate descriptions that witnesses were able to provide of the man last seen with Spalding meant that suspicion quickly fell on one Thomas Scobbie. It does not appear that Scobbie was the most handsome of men. A newspaper report at the time said that his face was 'deeply pitted with the pox' and he was said to have been given the ironic nickname 'Bonnie Scobbie'. There was a rare moment of laughter at the trial when one witness, Ann Henderson, who testified that she had seen Scobbie as she walked home from work on the evening of the murder, said that she was so startled by the look of his face that she could not answer when he asked her the time. With such distinctive features it did not take the police long to identify their chief suspect.

Thomas Scobbie was around thirty-five years old at the time of the Kingennie Murder as the case became known. He was a native of Crossford in Fife and the son of a shoemaker. He had been involved in some petty crime as a youngster but enlisted in the army at eighteen and was sent to India with the 92nd regiment at the time of the Indian Mutiny. He transferred to the 79th regiment in order to stay in India after the mutiny had been quelled. In 1865, he was invalided home and stationed in Aberdeen where he met and married a mill worker named Ann Rough. Around 1867 he left the army and returned to the only other life he knew – crime. He seems to have lived the life of a wanderer and accumulated convictions for theft throughout the country. As the number of his crimes increased so did the length of the sentences dispensed by the judiciary, until in October 1869, he was sentenced to a year in Perth Prison.

On his release he came to live in Dundee where he held down several conventional jobs. It is not clear if his wife had followed him in his wanderings but they were certainly together in Dundee – perhaps in an attempt to make a new start after his release. In 1871 their daughter Elizabeth was born but her father was to play little part in her upbringing. She was barely a year old by the time Scobbie was arrested for George Spalding's murder and by that time he was already being described as a 'tramp' and was not living with her mother at her house in Cotton Road. It was also reported he had not contributed to his wife's maintenance for a long time. Ann Scobbie eventually returned to Aberdeen with her daughter.

It was a Constable McIntosh who recognised Scobbie's description and led his superiors to the Model Lodging House in the Overgate. The proprietor told them that Scobbie had indeed been staying there but had been absent for the last two nights. He did return that night at about eleven o'clock to find that the police were waiting for him. He was taken to Kingennie the next day where he was identified by the members of the Spalding family and other witnesses. It was said that Juno the dog had growled and sprang at him.

The police used pawn tickets found among Scobbie's possessions to recover some clothes from a pawnbroker's shop in the Overgate. The pawnbroker, Edward Rowan, said that they had been handed in on Tuesday, 28 September – four days after the murder – by a man giving the name of John Young. Rowan later identified Scobbie as the man who had handed in the clothes. There were some burrs and seeds on them and there were tears on the coat and the trousers. Was this where Scobbie had been attacked by the dog?

A piece of ribbon had been found at the scene of the murder. When Scobbie was arrested his Balmoral bonnet was found to have only one ribbon and that matched the one found at the scene. The evidence against Scobbie was mounting up but it was all circumstantial. There were no eyewitnesses to the actual murder but this did not seem to concern the jury who only took ten minutes to come back with a guilty verdict – albeit with a recommendation to mercy.

The trial had been due to be heard in Edinburgh early in 1873 but had to be postponed when Scobbie became seriously ill. It was thought that he had deliberately poisoned himself by eating the lime off the walls of his cell. The delay had given the circumstances of the murder a chance to seep into the public consciousness and the passing of the death sentence then split public opinion further.

Some felt that the murder was not pre-meditated and only arose out of the high-handed approach of George Spalding in making what was, in effect, a citizen's arrest. Others were appalled that public sympathy appeared to be with a murderer as opposed to someone who had merely attempted to carry out his public duty. A petition organised in Dundee in favour of clemency for Scobbie attracted 4321 signatures. This was sent to the Home Secretary by Sir John Ogilvy, Member of Parliament for Dundee, but as 29 April approached there was no sign of a reprieve. Scobbie was visited in his cell by the Bishop of Brechin among others and was said to be restless and prone to weeping bitterly.

On Saturday, 26 April 1873, a man arrived in Dundee who had killed many more people than Thomas Scobbie ever would. William Calcraft had been the public executioner since 1829 – known for his 'short drop' hangings, which meant that the victims died of strangulation. Calcraft brought with him only one carpetbag – which reputedly contained a new rope and a white cap. He took up residence at Dundee Prison with his meals being brought in from the Royal Hotel.

Calcraft was to leave Dundee later that evening in front of a large crowd who came to gawp at him at the railway station, but without having carried out his official function. The reprieve that saved Scobbie arrived in Dundee so closely behind the hangman that *The Times* said 'it might have saved the cost of postage if Calcraft had been allowed to bring it in his pocket'. When the news was conveyed to Scobbie he was understandably relieved and thanked all those who had appealed for clemency. He would spend the next twenty-two years in Parkhurst Prison on the Isle of Wight.

It appears, though, that it was not just the jury's appeal for mercy or the strength of public feeling that saved Scobbie's life; it may, in fact, have been a clerical error that prevented him from having to face the hangman's rope. It was said that Lord Deas had made an error in referring to 'Tuesday the 29th day of April next to come'. This would have been acceptable wording if the trial had taken place, as it was supposed to, prior to April 1873, but as April had already started when the sentence was pronounced, then 'April next to come' would be April 1874, which did not have a Tuesday the 29th. Indeed, there would not be a Tuesday 29th April until 1879 – six years in the future. In the circumstances, it was felt that the sentence could not be legally carried out.

Scobbie was released on licence in 1894. After his release he claimed that he was innocent of the crime. His unlikely defence, given his distinctive appearance, was one of mistaken identity. He had, he said, been in Dundee on the day of the murder. He returned to Fife where he died three years later.

The landscape around Kingennie has changed much in the years since the murder as roads and housing have made their mark on the place, but to generations of Monifieth children a small clump of trees at the junction of Victoria Street with the main Arbroath Road was known as Scobbie's Roundie. This was said to be the area where the murder had taken place and where young George Spalding, when bringing the police back to the spot to recover his uncle's body, found the cause of so much suffering. Some way from the body lay two abandoned shirts.

A Journey to Dundee

The Dundee-bound train pulled in to Leuchars Station with its plume of white vapour billowing in a ferocious wind. It was seven o'clock in the evening but already dark. William Thomas Linskill peered anxiously out of the window of his first-class compartment into the winter blackness but could see no sign of the coach that was due to take him to St Andrews. There would normally be a connecting train but today was Sunday and so he had had to make his own arrangements.

Linskill was not a native of St Andrews although it was where he would come to belong. He was, in fact, an Englishman. His father had been Mayor of Tynemouth. Linskill had first been taken to St Andrews as a boy by his parents and had fallen in love with the place and with the game of golf. He became a competent golfer and was a friend and pupil of the legendary young Tom Morris.

All Linskill wanted to do now was to get back to St Andrews but the coach was still not in sight. It was a stormy night – had some accident befallen it?

Linskill was educated at Cambridge where he was responsible for introducing the game of golf to the university. He had also instituted the Oxford versus Cambridge Golf Match and was captain and later honorary secretary of the Cambridge University Golf Club. A contemporary said of him that he was 'one of the very finest putters that ever put a ball into a hole'. Linskill wrote an instruction book called simply *Golf*. Reviewers praised it for its clarity and simplicity and over one hundred years later it is much sought after by collectors.

Where was the coach? Linskill got out onto the exposed platform but could see no sign of it. He now felt the full force of the wind and rain. He exchanged a word or two with the stationmaster.

Linskill had a drooping moustache and booming voice. That voice proved useful when he took to the stage, as he frequently did in plays and panto-mimes and concerts organized for charity. He was a humorous man and sang comedy songs – some of which he had written himself. A friend once said that it was hard to remember Linskill without a smile on his face.

What if the coach did not appear? He could not walk through the dark country roads in this weather. His thoughts were interrupted by the sound of a carriage-examiner's hammer tapping the wheels of the train.

Linskill became a well-respected member of the community in St Andrews. He was a member of the Town Council for more than a quarter of a century and Dean of Guild. He helped bring about improvements in the street lighting and the fire service.

It was clear now in his mind that the coach was not coming. Something must have happened to prevent its arrival at the station.

Linskill became interested in local history. After visiting the catacombs in Rome he became convinced that such a network of tunnels existed under St Andrews. The discovery of a mine and countermine at St Andrews Castle in 1879 seemed to vindicate him but no more such discoveries were made.

He would continue to Dundee and spend the night there. He would get back to St Andrews in the morning.

Linskill had another hobby – ghost-hunting. He always wanted to encounter a ghost but was unsuccessful. His own explanation was that he was not psychic. He once wrote, 'I have spent days and nights in gloomy, grimly haunted chambers and ruins and even a lonesome Hallowe'en night on the top of St Rule's ancient Tower (my only companions being sandwiches, matches, some cigars and the necessary and indispensable flask) yet, alas! I have *never* heard or seen anything the least abnormal, or felt the necessary, or much-talked-of mystic presence.'

He climbed back on the train and settled back down in his seat. They would be moving soon. Before long the train would be in Dundee.

Linskill's stories were gathered together in a book – *St Andrews Ghost Stories*. The first chapter is 'The True Tale of the Phantom Coach'. The story tells of an unearthly carriage whose appearance is a portent of death and disaster.

Everything was in order. The train was being readied to leave. Next stop – Dundee. The stationmaster took one last look down the road.

Thomas Robertson, the stationmaster, helped William Linskill from the train with his luggage that night. Robertson had spotted the lights of Linskill's coach in the distance. It had simply been delayed by the bad weather. A journey to Dundee would not be necessary. The coach making its way to Leuchars Railway Station was not the phantom coach of St Andrews coming to claim Linskill or to foreshadow his death but rather this was the coach that would save his life. Another half century in this world lay ahead for him but death and destruction were not far away.

The train that Linskill had left carried on its way to Dundee, but it was never to reach its destination. It was the evening of 28 December 1879 – a date that would become infamous in Dundee's history – the day that the Tay Bridge collapsed, taking the train and all its passengers and crew to the bottom of the river.

The coach wound its way back to St Andrews buffeted by the storm. Inside William Thomas Linskill was still unaware of how close he had come to losing his own life.

Linskill was to spend years searching for the supernatural. Perhaps what

The collapsed Tay Bridge

he was really looking for was proof that there was some higher meaning that would explain the seemingly random nature of his survival and the deaths of so many others on that stormy winter's night.

2
Hidden Depths

Language proved to be a barrier when a French contractor turned up at the Garden Mills flax works in Benvie Road one day in the 1960s. Even a native French speaker who worked there was unable to fully comprehend the visitor's particular dialect. The solution came from an unlikely source. From the factory's dust extraction section – known as the stoorhoose – emerged a stooping figure covered from head to foot in dust. This human dust bag proceeded to conduct a fluent conversation with the Frenchman.

The name of the unlikely linguist was Robert Fox. Fox had spent some time living and working in France after fighting there with the Scots Fusiliers during the First World War. Such was his proficiency with the language that he was employed as a sub-editor on a French publication. Here he was reputed to have dispensed with the services of a journalist by the name of Vladimir Nabokov – the man who would go on to write *Lolita*.

Returning to Dundee in 1939, Fox wrote articles for the local newspapers including many reminiscences of life in the city in the early years of the twentieth century. These would appear under the by-line R. D. Fox or simply with his initials R. D. F. (Robert Duncan Fox). He also wrote many letters to the local press, which grappled with the issues of the day in an intelligent and witty manner.

When he died in 1972, the *Evening Telegraph* said of him that he was 'a man whose extensive reading built on his early education an edifice of knowledge and a grasp of current questions which men in high places could envy'. There was clearly much more to Fox than would have been apparent to anyone seeing him at work in the stoorhoose. Indeed, it is a foolish person who judges the intelligence of anyone in Dundee by their station in life. Dundee is a city of the self-taught and the self-depreciating, and appearances, as in Robert Fox's case, can certainly be deceptive. The subjects of the following stories might on first sight have been dismissed as commonplace – the down and out, the railway signalman, the lowly town official or the quiet man walking his dog along Carnoustie beach – but there is much more to each than the casual glance could ever hope to capture.

The Caveman of Ballantrae

The caves around Bennane Head on the Ayrshire Coast have a murky history. It was here that Sawney Bean and his family of cannibals are supposed to have spent several years feasting on the flesh of unfortunate travellers before being captured by the authorities and put to death in Edinburgh. It is now thought unlikely that Sawney Bean ever existed – his gruesome exploits are probably just the stuff of legend – but there was a much more recent (and much more real) cave-dweller in this vicinity. He was as harmless as Sawney Bean was supposed to be deadly and his name was Snib.

The road to Snib's cave has now been closed and by-passed to cope with increased traffic, but it was at one time the A77 coastal route – the main road to and from the Irish ferries at Stranraer. Bennane Cave was once used as a smiddy and its entrance partially bricked up. This provided a measure of shelter and meant that a fire could be safely lit for warmth. It was to be home to Snib for many years.

Snib was a familiar figure in the Ballantrae area from the early 1950s, with his wild hair and unkempt beard. In winter he would be wrapped in several layers of coats tied up with a piece of rope. Even his name was second hand. He seems to have inherited this from an earlier local worthy known as Snib Scott.

Snib was an odd, solitary figure and could perhaps appear menacing to anyone who did not know him but he posed no threat to anybody. He was a very private man though he would sometimes chat for a while if approached. Gradually, the local people came to accept him as part of the landscape. He was often to be seen on the beach collecting pieces of wood for his fire or bottles to take to the local shop.

People were also impressed by his integrity. He was fiercely independent and largely self-sufficient. He would accept no charity directly given but would take things that people left for him to 'find'. He always returned any valuables he found at the nearby picnic site and expected no reward. He never left any litter and to anybody who did engage him in a brief conversation he proved himself to be an intelligent and well-educated man. So who was this gentleman cave dweller?

Henry Ewing Torbet (known to his family as Harry) was born in Dundee on 11 May 1911. Harry's grandfather had been a flax dresser. He and his family had left their native Dunfermline in the early 1860s – no doubt seeking improved circumstances – and had ended up in Dundee. This search for betterment came to fruition in Harry's father who started out as a mill worker but later became involved in the insurance industry, eventually becoming an inspector. The transition to a more middle class lifestyle was practically complete when the family moved to the aptly named Prospect Place in 1933 and many of the family went on to have successful careers.

Young Harry seemed destined to continue his family's upward trend. He appears to have been successful in his education and on leaving school took up a job in a bank. He was to remain at the bank for a decade or more and looked set for a successful career and a conventional lifestyle. He is said to have been engaged to be married at one point. His future seemed secure. One day, however, he walked out on everything and took to the road.

The thought of opting out of the rat race has probably occurred to many of us at one time or another, but few have the courage to follow it through and live with the consequences and the loss of the comforts of modern living that we all take for granted. It is not clear what exactly caused Harry to leave everything he knew for a life of poverty and uncertainty – or indeed exactly when this occurred. It could have been triggered by some event in his life – the break-off of his engagement perhaps? The death of his mother in 1951? Did these things make him re-evaluate his life and give everything up? These are possibilities, yet events such as these happen to most people without causing them to give up their former lives. It seems more likely that he just wanted to opt out of conventional society and the things that restricted him – a desire he probably always had whatever actually triggered him to act on it.

For some time Harry is reputed to have wandered about in the West Highlands before settling in a derelict miner's cottage at Waterside in Ayrshire. From there he came to settle in the cave at Bennane Head and his life as Snib began. From then on, even when he left on his travels for days on end, he always returned 'home' to the cave.

In these early days, he was almost entirely self-sufficient – the lifestyle, perhaps, that he was seeking when he left Dundee. He claimed no benefits and accepted no charity. He would catch rabbits or fish and cook them on his driftwood fire. The former bank clerk, who had handled hundreds of pounds on a daily basis, would now save up coppers he had found on the ground and buy a loaf of bread from the baker's shop in Ballantrae.

As time went on, however, local people began to help by leaving things out for him. In later years the owner of the land around the cave would take him the occasional cooked dinner and at Christmas, he would receive a full Christmas dinner together with all the trimmings. Surplus food and clothing, cigarettes and newspapers, would find their way to the cave – but always left outside to spare Snib the indignity of accepting charity.

Living so close to the main road, the traffic was always a hazard for Snib and this began to increase over the years. On one occasion he was run over by a speeding car. He escaped with a broken leg, but was probably lucky to do so. He was taken to Ayr County Hospital. This was his first contact with the medical profession since he had left Dundee decades before. Considering his lifestyle, this was quite remarkable, but then the Torbets were a hardy lot – three of his siblings lived into their nineties.

Snib's stay in the hospital was also his first time sleeping in a bed since his time in Dundee, but it would not be for long. He discharged himself and hobbled on his crutches back to the cave more than thirty miles away. A doctor had to come to the cave to cut the plaster cast off, as he would not return to the hospital.

After this incident, Snib began to slow down and become more dependent on the generosity of the locals. His travels had come to an end too – perhaps he had begun to fear the traffic – for he then stayed in the vicinity of Ballantrae. The wintertime must have been particularly hard for him. At that point, when many of his contemporaries from the bank would be retired and spending their time on the golf course or in the garden, Snib still had to suffer the hardships of cave-dwelling. The effort involved in tasks such as collecting firewood and gathering food could only have become more arduous as he got older but still he resisted all attempts to get him to move into a house.

One day it was noticed that there was no smoke from Snib's fire rising over the bricked-up entrance to the cave. Snib was found suffering from the effects of hypothermia. An ambulance was called and he was taken to Heathfield Hospital in Ayr. Weakened by the effects of the hypothermia and also suffering from pneumonia, he died there on 8 March 1983. He was seventy-one years old.

Snib had been such a fixture of the area around Ballantrae for so long that people then began to miss him, perhaps more than they had thought they ever would. For many younger people, Snib had been around as long as they could remember. Some locals attended his funeral and many thought that there should be a permanent reminder of this remarkable and unusual man. It was decided to erect a cairn on the beach near the cave. The cairn was made of stones recovered from the beach where Snib would gather his firewood. A fitting inscription was added to the front of the cairn. It reads:

HENRY EWING TORBET (SNIB)

OF BENNANE CAVE

1912(SIC)–1983

RESPECTED AND INDEPENDENT

There are not many retired bankers whose death could move a community to erect such a memorial.

The Drummer's Tale

In the early part of the nineteenth century a visiting professor came to Dundee with the intention of delivering lectures in the Hebrew and Persian languages. While walking with one of the local ministers to the Town House to secure use of a room for his lectures, the professor was introduced to Dan McCormick, the Town Drummer. The Town Drummer's job was principally to make proclamations 'by tuck of drum'. On hearing of the nature of the professor's visit, Dan pulled a Psalter out of his pocket and started questioning the would-be lecturer on the finer points of the Hebrew language and how he intended to teach it. The professor is said to have left the town soon after – reckoning that if the Town Drummer knew more about the Hebrew language than he did, there was no need of his services in Dundee. Some versions of the story have him declaring as he left that the town must be a colony sprung from one of the lost tribes of Israel.

Dan McCormick was not just an expert in Hebrew, however. He also had knowledge of Gaelic, Arabic, Greek, Latin, French and German as well as other languages. He studied literature and science and had an extensive collection of books. He was a skilled musician and, according to an obituary in the *Dundee Advertiser*, 'While in the vigour of life his performances on wind instruments were considered excellent.' He also gave music lessons. Who, then, was this learned man that occupied the relatively lowly position of Town Drummer?

Daniel McCormick was born, not in Dundee, but in the east end of London around 1760. His family, though, originally hailed from Lochaber. His father was in business as a dyer – probably in Fort William – but had moved to London a year or two before Dan's birth. Dan himself was said to be reticent about revealing the reasons for this move.

A. H. Millar, the historian and at one time Dundee's City Librarian, presents a very plausible explanation for this mysterious move in his book *Haunted Dundee*. Dan's father, Millar suggested, had been 'out in the '45' as a Jacobite rebel. There were six McCormicks from Fort William among the followers of Stewart of Appin on the side of Bonnie Prince Charlie. Five of these were killed at Culloden, but one was only wounded. Was Dan McCormick's father the one that survived? If so he seems to have managed to return to his previous occupation for a while. Six years after the battle, though, things were becoming difficult for Appin's men in the aftermath of the murder of Colin Campbell of Glenure (known as The Red Fox) whose loyalties lay with the Hanoverian monarchy. A fictionalised version of the events surrounding Campbell's murder appears in Robert Louis Stevenson's *Kidnapped* but the repercussions for the McCormick family appear to have been all too real.

After their flight to London, Daniel McCormick's parents were never to return to Scotland as they both died while their son was still young. Following their deaths, Dan returned to Lochaber and attempted to take up his father's business but without success. He was soon on the move again – this time bound for Glasgow seeking employment. Here he was able to devote his spare time to his academic pursuits. There was talk of the priesthood, which seems a natural course for a young Catholic so devoted to study, but this was a path he did not pursue.

Instead, Dan joined the 5th or Argyllshire Regiment of Fencibles. On

16 October 1798 he would have marched into Dundee with his regiment and up Burial Wynd to the barracks at Dudhope Castle. (In 1807, the residents of the morbid-sounding Burial Wynd would successfully petition the council to have their street's name changed to Barrack Street.)

The 1790s were a time of fear for the authorities in Britain – fear of revolution as had happened in France and fear of invasion by France. A volunteer force was raised and Dundee's Provost, Alexander Riddoch, became the Colonel of the 2nd or Light Infantry Dundee Volunteers. Riddoch himself arranged for Dan and some of his comrades to be discharged from their regiment and installed as Drill Instructors in the Volunteers. So eager was the Provost to secure Dan's services in particular that in 1801 he was officially made one of the Town's Officers. In 1810 he was appointed Town Drummer and also became the Town's Billet-Master.

These relatively minor official roles would have provided Dan with time for his studies and money to amass his impressive collection of books. His reputation as one of the keenest minds in the town also continued to grow. The story is told of a candidate for the Professorship of Greek at St Andrews University coming to seek the support of Dundee's Provost. The Provost told the candidate that he was not qualified to judge his suitability for the post. One can only imagine the look on the would-be professor's face when the Town Drummer was sent for, or when the Town Drummer proceeded to quiz him on the intricacies of the Greek language – or indeed when the Town Drummer proceeded to pronounce him unfit for the position he was seeking.

Dan clearly enjoyed his time in Dundee. One obituary refers to him using his proclamations as 'a safety valve to his super-abundant humour and wit to the great amusement of the citizens'. Described by this time as a stout, square-built man, he was often to be found sitting on the wall at the City Churches in the Nethergate surrounded by schoolboys from the Grammar School – putting questions to them about Latin and Greek and helping them with their studies. The boys clearly respected him and his fellow Town Officers, too, as one writer recalled: 'When any mischief was going on the cry of "There's Dan McCormick" or "Willie McKay" was enough, and the delinquents skedaddled in "deil tak the hindmost" style.' This was good enough for Dan – such minor wrongdoers were rarely pursued and captured.

Dan also became widely known outside the town. The pioneering English educationalist Samuel Wilderspin in his book *Early Discipline Illustrated* used Dan as an illustration of 'the well-instructed in humble stations': 'The town drummer or crier of Dundee has the reputation of being the best classic[ist] within thirty miles of that town.'

Daniel McCormick died on Friday, 14 December 1832, having spent over thirty years in Dundee. He had never married but, intriguingly, his *Dundee Advertiser* obituary said of him – 'He was not indifferent to the attractions of the fair. He has left behind him a daughter.' It is not known what happened to the daughter – but was it his susceptibility to the 'attractions of the fair' that put paid to his thoughts of entering the priesthood?

Even those who thought they knew the extent of Dan's learning must have been astonished when they read the following advertisement in the press a few months after his death, inserted on behalf of an Edinburgh Auction House:

LIBRARY

OF THE LATE

MR DANIEL MCCORMICK

TOWN DRUMMER OF DUNDEE

JOHN CARFRAE & SON beg to intimate that they will SELL by auction in their Rooms 3, Drummond Street, on Monday next, 1st of April and four following days at one o'clock, the Valuable LIBRARY of the late Mr Daniel McCormick, Town Drummer of Dundee, consisting of Books in Divinity, Oriental and Biblical Literature, Classics, Philology and General Literature, Ancient and Modern, comprising also several Rare Works in Gaelic, Irish and Welsh.

The extent of Dan's library was astonishing. There were 795 lots in the auction and the sale, as the advertisement implies, took five days to complete. An article in *The Scotsman* reflected the sheer incredulity that met the sale:

> We have seen a catalogue of his books which would do honour to a bibliomaniac of the second and third magnitude. There are upwards of – what do you think? 1500 volumes, and these are not made up of Tom Thumbs, Blue Beards or Little Glass Slippers; but of the most classical, scientific and valuable tomes in the living and dead languages. There are a great number in Latin and not a few in Greek, Arabic, Syriac etc. Nor were these books selected for show alone as many are; for Daniel McCormick was a man of much reading and an excellent linguist withal.

At a time when illiteracy was rife, Daniel McCormick's learning would have surpassed that of most people in Dundee including many of those who did not share his 'humble station' in life. Indeed, yet another version of the story of the visiting Hebrew scholar that Dan frightened out of delivering his lecture sees the professor reflecting on the ill-divided nature of things. He says with reference to a local minister of religion – probably the one who accompanied him at his meeting with Dan – that the Town Drummer would have made a first-class Doctor of Divinity and the Doctor of Divinity was more suited to being the Town Drummer!

Dear Diary: John W. Hazel

Pub arguments are not nearly as much fun as they used to be. Internet access has meant that a dispute which might have raged for weeks can now be resolved instantly by anybody with a mobile phone or a laptop, but what did people do in days before the technological revolution if they wanted to know when Dundee United adopted the tangerine strip or when the last tram ran in Dundee? Often the burning issue would appear a little less urgent in the cold light of sobriety, but if they were still interested in finding the answer they might send a letter to the local press and wait for a reply to be published. In Dundee, however, there was a quicker way – ask John W. Hazel. Hazel was not a journalist, a librarian or an archivist but a railway signalman who had access to a unique fund of knowledge – his own diaries which he kept meticulously for over half a century.

John Wood Hazel was born 17 February 1900 at St Mary's Lodge, Kinoull Hill, Perth. Though he did not play football or cricket as a child, he was a keen fan of both. He was a lifelong supporter of St Johnstone FC and for many years acted as a representative for various junior football clubs including the Perth team Jeanfield Swifts and Alyth United, keeping them supplied with players. He was also a cricket umpire for more than forty years and was at one time a member of the Thistle Harriers athletics club in Dundee.

Leaving school at fourteen, he started work with the Caledonian Railway Company Limited at Perth Station. As the years went by, it would often be John Hazel who settled arguments between his work colleagues with his encyclopaedic knowledge, particularly of sporting questions. There came a point though, he said, when he simply could not store all the information in his head and the written word had to take over.

It was on 1 January 1925, while he was working as a signalman at Errol Junction, that Hazel began to record things in his diary, such as all the scores in the Scottish First and Second Divisions, the scorers and the attendances as well as the weather, local events and other things that interested him. He took a particular notice of the teams from his adopted hometown of Dundee, as well as his beloved St Johnstone. So fond was he of Dundee that from 1934 when he was transferred to the Ninewells Junction Signal Box, until his retirement in 1965, he turned down offers of promotion elsewhere on the railways so that he could continue to live in the city. Prior to this, he had worked at various places including Comrie, Auchterarder, Kinfauns, and Ballinluig.

In 1932, when he was working in the signal box at Connel Ferry near Oban, Hazel began a new aspect of his diaries. Watching all the people go by on a train, he began to think about the number of people he knew. From then on he began to keep a record of all the different people he met each day and where and when he had met them. In years to come he would amaze people by giving precise details of their previous meetings years before. So meticulous was he in this that he would take a note of all the guests at any wedding he attended and even of the mourners at a funeral.

As the years went by his fame as a diarist spread and he would often be contacted by journalists to help answer their readers' queries or even by members of the public who would stop him in the street or knock at the door of his house in Abbotsford Street with their questions. This could quite easily have become an irritant, but Hazel enjoyed helping people and meeting the varied people whose disputes he settled (always remembering to note down the details of their meeting, of course).

His letters to the local press were always worth reading. He wrote regularly to the papers for more than half a century and his letters covered all sorts of subjects from sport to politics, from the weather to questions of morality. Where other correspondents merely had their opinions, though, John Hazel had decades worth of recorded facts in his diaries.

As they grow older, many people like to look back on the events of their younger years. John W. Hazel was able to do this in greater detail than most and he had even recorded the names of the films he had seen with his wife Mary in their courting days. The couple would spend many hours reliving past events in the years before Mary's death in 1974.

In 1977, John W. Hazel's *Book of Records* was published. It was a compendium of the sort of facts and figures that would in later years be called trivia but which hold a fascination for people and which, when the subject of a dispute, become for a short time the most important things in the world. The book was said to be a source of great pride to him.

John Hazel with his numerous diaries

Hazel's story was to have a tragic ending. At around midday on 15 October 1986, a body was found on the Dundee–Perth railway line close to Invergowrie station. The next day Tayside Police confirmed that it was that of John W. Hazel. The eighty-six-year-old had been struck by the 11am Aberdeen–Glasgow express train not far from the Ninewells Junction Signal Box where he had worked for so many years. It was a sad conclusion to a long and interesting life, yet there are not many people who leave such a fascinating legacy behind them or have the vast majority of their days accounted for as John W. Hazel did in those famous diaries.

And in the End . . . Iain Macmillan and the Most Famous Road Crossing in the World

Every day, people from all over the world risk their lives by standing in the middle of a busy London road to have their photograph taken. Luckily, the point on which they stand is a pedestrian crossing. The photographer, however, may have to stand well back into the road if he or she wants to take in the whole of the crossing including the cars parked by the roadside – which they invariably will want to do. They do this because on 8 August 1969 a man from Dundee took a picture of four men using this crossing. The men were called John Lennon, Paul McCartney, George Harrison and Ringo Starr, the photographer's name was Iain Macmillan and the photograph was to become the front cover of the Beatles' *Abbey Road* album.

Abbey Road was the last Beatles album to be recorded. By this time the individual band members had grown apart and their enthusiasm for group activities had begun to wane. The Beatles' lives were changing – Lennon and McCartney had each married in March 1969. Lennon and his new wife Yoko Ono had spent their honeymoon engaged in the famous 'bed-in' for peace while McCartney – the last bachelor Beatle – had become a family man and stepfather to wife Linda Eastman's daughter Heather. Tensions had been high during the recording of their previous album. Ringo had left the group at one stage but was coaxed back by the others.

In an effort to turn the clock back to earlier, more carefree days, they had embarked on a film project called *Get Back*, which was to show the group rehearsing new songs and end with a live concert filmed at an exotic location. In the end the film was given the more sombre name of *Let it Be* and the 'exotic location' turned out to be the roof of the Beatles' Apple organisation offices in Savile Row London. None of the Beatles was entirely happy with the project and the film was shelved. It was decided that they should record another album – the one that was to become *Abbey Road*.

Abbey Road had not been the first choice of name. It had been suggested that the album be called 'Everest' (after the brand of cigarettes smoked by engineer Geoff Emerick) but in a fading of enthusiasm similar to that which afflicted the plans for the concert at the end of *Let it Be*, the Beatles were not prepared to head off to the Himalayas. In fact, they were only prepared to go outside the EMI Studios in Abbey Road, St John's Wood, London. Thus, the album was given its name – and Iain Macmillan was given about ten minutes to shoot the cover photograph. The Beatles were anxious to get the image captured as quickly as possible. Lennon in particular did not want to hang around. If word got out, a crowd would soon gather. In addition, there was only so long that they could hold up the traffic. Taking a photograph in a strict time frame, with less than enthusiastic subjects and in the middle of a busy road would be challenging conditions for any photographer. Macmillan only took six shots. The result, though, was to be an iconic image that would almost develop a life of its own in the years to come.

Iain Stewart Macmillan was born in Dundee in 1938 and attended Dundee High School. His family lived in Lawside Road and later Tullideph Road before moving to Downfield in 1953. On leaving school in 1954, he became a trainee manager for Jute Industries Limited. He was keenly interested in photography, though, and in 1958 moved to London where he attended Regent Street Polytechnic. After graduating, and a spell as a cruise ship photographer, he worked as a freelancer and gained numerous commissions for newspapers and magazines.

In 1966, Macmillan took the photographs for *The Book of London* – a portrait of the capital at the height of the swinging sixties. One person whose image he captured for this collection was the little-known Japanese conceptual artist Yoko Ono. Through Ono, Macmillan met John Lennon, which is how he came to find himself in the middle of Abbey Road that hot August day in 1969.

Almost as soon as the album was released, fans began to scrutinise every detail of the cover. A bizarre rumour originating in the USA around this time stated that Paul McCartney had died in a car accident in 1966 and had been secretly replaced by a lookalike. This rumour spread far and quickly but it is unlikely that many people took it seriously. There were supposedly clues to McCartney's death scattered throughout the Beatles' song lyrics and album covers (although the songs sometimes had to be played backwards before these 'clues' could be heard). The *Abbey Road* cover was interpreted as a funeral procession with John (dressed in white) as a clergyman, Ringo (in a dark suit) as the undertaker and George (in working clothes) as the gravedigger. Paul McCartney was out of step with the others, held his cigarette in the wrong hand (the real Paul was left handed) and was barefoot (a sign of death in ancient Greece and Rome it was said). In fact, McCartney had been wearing sandals but had slipped them off immediately before the photo shoot. Lennon himself only realised that McCartney had been barefoot when the album came out.

The biggest 'clue' to the supposed death of Paul McCartney, however, was the registration plate of the Volkswagen car (a *Beetle* of course) parked by the side of the road – LMW 281F. This allegedly stood for Linda McCartney Weeps and showed that Paul would have been 28 – IF he'd lived. McCartney was, in fact, only twenty-seven at this time. It is also difficult to see why Linda McCartney would be weeping for Paul if he'd died in 1966 – she'd clearly met and married the lookalike! Such nonsense, nevertheless, only served to enhance the iconic status of every element of Macmillan's picture. The Volkswagen, which had simply been parked there by a local resident in 1969, became familiar to millions of music fans. Years later, Peter Gent, the proprietor of a musical instrument shop in St Albans, spotted it in a car showroom. Realising the car's importance, he promptly bought it. It was sold at Sotheby's in 1986. The car then reportedly went to the United States and ended up in the Volkswagen Autostadt Car Collection in Wolfsburg, Germany.

If some eagle-eyed record-buyers had spotted the car number plate on the left hand side of the picture, then they would also spot the man in the dark glasses standing to the right. Paul Cole was an American salesman visiting London on holiday and who just happened to be standing in the right place at the right time to make it onto one of the most famous images of the twentieth century. He was waiting for his wife who had gone to a museum and was passing the time of day talking to a policeman who was sitting in the black van at the side of the road. He saw the Beatles being photographed crossing the road 'like a line of ducks' but didn't know who they were and thought no more about it. It wasn't until around a year later, when his wife Marion was learning to play George Harrison's song 'Something' on the organ and had a copy of the album, that Cole spotted himself. When he died in 2008 at the age of ninety-six, Paul Cole's death was reported around the world because of his association with Iain Macmillan's picture. The conspiracy theorists may like to note that Mr Cole resided latterly in the town of Barefoot Bay.

The *Abbey Road* cover was not the end of Iain Macmillan's association with the Beatles. He photographed the cover of John Lennon's album *Live Peace* in Toronto and later spent time with Lennon and Ono in New York. He attended the session for the recording of their Christmas classic 'Happy Xmas (War is Over)' and took the photograph that adorns its picture sleeve as well as the photographs of John and Yoko morphing into each other, which featured on their record labels at this time. His most bizarre assignment, though, was for Ono's Fly project – where she wanted to release hundreds of flies into the air and have Macmillan follow them round New York photographing them where they landed. When this proved somewhat impractical to say the least, Macmillan instead went into a polythene tent filled with flies. The photographs he took were later superimposed onto pictures of New York landmarks for a book. It was a long way from the illustrated career guides and other textbooks that had characterised his work in the early sixties.

In the seventies, Ian Macmillan moved into teaching photography. In the eighties he moved back to Dundee – or rather, to Carnoustie and to the house his parents had bought in 1960. Meanwhile, the *Abbey Road* cover continued to assume its iconic status adorning tee shirts, posters, mugs, key-rings, fridge magnets, jigsaws, clocks and almost any other surface imaginable. The album itself was re-released as a picture disc.

Macmillan said that the appeal of the image was in its simplicity. This simplicity meant that it could easily be imitated or satirised. Many people had imitated Peter Blake's psychedelic masterpiece that was the cover of the Beatles 1967 album *Sgt. Pepper's Lonely Hearts Club Band* but with its numerous elements this was difficult to stage. All you needed for a pastiche of the *Abbey Road* cover was four people and a zebra crossing. It didn't even have to be *the* zebra crossing, as the image was by then so strong in people's minds that the reference was clear. Over the years many albums were released that referenced Macmillan's picture. Albums by such diverse artists as the Shadows and Booker T and the MGs parodied the cover, but perhaps the most famous version in recent years was the cover of the Red Hot Chilli Peppers' *The Abbey Road E.P.*, where the band walk over the famous crossing naked apart from some strategically placed socks.

The cover was referenced in other media too – from a scene in the film

Fans re-create Iain Macmillan's famous shot

Trainspotting to the television series and accompanying book of *Grumpy Old Men*. The image has been used for numerous publicity pictures. Everybody from *The Simpsons* to Margaret Thatcher has made their way over those famous black and white stripes.

Iain Macmillan himself was associated with two recreations of the scene at Abbey Road. One was for the album *Hinge and Brackett at Abbey Road* and the other was with Paul McCartney for his album *Paul is Live*. The legendary status of the cover was then assured as a former Beatle named an album making reference to the mythology that surrounded it. In this new version of the cover, the registration plate of the Volkswagen reads 51 IS – reflecting McCartney's age in 1993 when the album was released.

Iain Macmillan died from cancer in Dundee in May 2006. He is remembered as a modest and unaffected man who loved photography but not the celebrity merry-go-round or cut-throat media industry that too often accompany it. At the time of his death his agent Raj Prem said, 'Iain was too gentle for the industry in which he worked and eventually he preferred to teach photography instead. He was a much better photographer than many of his contemporaries but he never said a bad word about them and was always modest.'

In 2010, the first major retrospective of Iain Macmillan's photographs went on display in Dundee at Discovery Point. As well as some of his most famous images, the exhibition included some evocative pictures of Dundee that he had taken in 1959.

The crossing at Abbey Road is now surveyed twenty-four hours a day by a webcam. People from around the world can now watch as others try to recreate Macmillan's photograph. On 8 August 2009 – the fortieth anniversary of the photo shoot – hundreds of people turned up to walk across the zebra crossing, resulting in traffic being stopped for an hour. In 2010, the crossing was given Grade II listed status being recognised for its 'cultural and historical importance' following advice from English Heritage. What has been called 'the world's longest photo session' shows no sign of stopping. It may have only taken him ten minutes, but there can be few photographers who have ever created an image so imitated and admired as the modest man from Dundee.

The Wheelbarrow Man

As James Gordon left his home in Blackness Road one day in the 1880s to start his new job at one of Dundee's busy railway stations he must have thought that his luck had at last changed. He had been in his previous job for twelve years but this new job held better prospects. Gordon himself later recalled what happened when he arrived at the station: 'When I presented myself to commence my duties, I was coolly told that the old man was to be kept on and that for the present there would be no opening. I was thus thrown out of my old place and deprived of the new.'

Born in Glasgow in 1843, Gordon had spent most of his life in his parents' hometown of Dundee, first coming to the city as a child. At the age of fourteen he went to Greenock to start work at an engineering firm but an accident there left him with only the little finger and first joint of the fourth finger on his right hand. Finding employment became difficult after this and Gordon tried a number of jobs back in Dundee, working as a baker, a painter and in a brewery but found them all difficult due to his disability. Working as a porter seemed to be the only thing suitable. In 1865, Gordon married Wilhelmina Guthrie and the couple went on to have twelve children. By 1886, four of their children had died and one had gone to live in New Zealand. This still left seven children to be fed – and now their father found himself without a job.

Gordon took out a licence as a street porter but found it tough to make a living. Sometimes his weekly earnings were only four or five shillings. The family began to sink deeper and deeper into debt. It was difficult to see any way out of their situation – difficult to most people that is, but James Gordon, sitting contemplating his future one night by the fire after a particularly disappointing day, managed to come up with a plan. He remembered that he had some old wheels and wood and, with help from a friend, began to construct a two-wheeled hand barrow. On top of the barrow he placed a large biscuit box for storage purposes and two empty cigar boxes with holes cut into the lids suitable for placing coins. Two uprights held a sign that read: 'From Dundee to London and Back'.

A letter to the local press fully explained his intentions:

Sir,

I am to leave Dundee on Tuesday November 2, with a two-wheeled barrow, and travel with it to London, and from London back to Dundee. I intend to accomplish the double journey in sixty days – that is, land in Dundee on January 1, 1887. No work on Sunday. By making the above known through your wide-spread and valuable paper, I have not the least doubt but it will do me a vast amount of good on the road as I am and will be entirely dependant on the public.

I am etc
James Gordon, Street Porter
239, Blackness Road Dundee, October 14 1886

N.B. – this is to try and get a little support for my family as I go along. I have no wager, nor nothing of that kind on it.

Gordon's wife, Wilhelmina, thought her husband's plan was a foolish one and feared that he would die in the attempt. Nevertheless, he was determined to make the journey and on the morning of 2 November, with oversized boots stuffed with horsehair to protect his feet, he set off for his starting point at Dundee East Station. Any doubts that James Gordon had about the wisdom of his undertaking must have vanished almost immediately. A large crowd lined the streets around the station and he had difficulty in moving forward with the barrow. His son accompanied him as far as Invergowrie where his collection boxes were emptied for the first time and found to contain the sum of £1 – around four or five weeks' wages.

He was able to send his son back home with more money than the family had seen in some time.

That evening Gordon reached Perth. He had with him a small notebook, which he intended to get stamped at every local post office. He later abandoned this when he realised the detours that would be involved to get to some post offices and instead got his book stamped wherever he stayed for the night.

The second day's journey took him to Blackford, a small village outside Auchterarder. After the euphoria of the first day, Gordon was faced with the grim reality of what his journey would involve as he struggled uphill with the barrow in the rain. Indeed, it rained every day for the first eleven days of his journey. Nevertheless, Gordon is said to have attracted considerable attention in Auchterarder itself and the money continued to pour into his collection boxes.

The reception that Gordon got at Auchterarder or the next day at Falkirk was nothing compared to that which awaited him in Edinburgh where crowds of people turned out on Princes Street to see him. Their numbers increased as he approached the General Post Office to get his notebook stamped. Gordon later recalled, 'I got frightened, and was beginning to think that my journey was at an end, for one of the blue-coats was about to lug me away to their jail as an obstructionist, when a gentleman, apparently of some authority, came to my aid and told the policeman that it was not the man with the barrow who was causing the obstruction but the crowd and that it was his duty to clear the crowd away and not the man.'

Gordon left Edinburgh with 'a good deal of bronze coin' and made his way to Haddington where he rested the next day as he refused to travel on a Sunday. He appears to have been a man of strong religious conviction. Throughout his journey, the end of his barrow bore the inscription, 'Jesus saith: he that believeth in me hath everlasting life.'

On Monday, 8 November, he set off for Cockburnspath and the next day he crossed the border. It was the first time in his life that he had left

Scotland. His first stops in England were at Berwick, Belford, Alnwick and Morpeth. He gathered little money in the English rural areas, though, as news of his undertaking had not reached them. In some places he was greeted with enquiries as to whether he was carrying a peepshow or was a 'hokey pokey' [ice cream] man.

Newcastle, though, was quite a different story and here Gordon was given what *The People's Journal* called 'his greatest ovation'. A Dundee man living in the town wrote of Gordon's visit, 'Gladstone or the Queen could not have created much more excitement than this man and his barrow. When he came into town there were thousands after him, and when he passed a place where a menagerie is exhibiting, the band played "See the Conquering Hero Comes". The coppers rattled into his barrow like hailstones.'

Gordon was able to send £6 back to his wife from Newcastle and left the town with a sponsorship deal – his cart now bore an advertisement for a Newcastle tobacconist on its side. His overwhelming reception meant that he left Newcastle two hours behind schedule. He was accompanied all the way to Durham and two miles out from that town he was met by a local concertina player who heralded his arrival to another large crowd. As he settled down to sleep that night in the home of a Mr Marley, Gordon could afford to feel pleased with his progress so far. In the short time he had been in Durham, he was able to send his wife a further £1.

Gordon's journey continued through Darlington and Thirsk before he reached York on 18 November. He made little impact there, though, as he arrived after dark. The next day took him to Selby and he then proceeded to Doncaster where he was warmly received by a large number of Scottish people. He rested in Doncaster on the second Sunday of his journey. The next day he set off for the village of Tuxford, Nottinghamshire before arriving at Grantham on 23 November.

It was from the Black Dog Inn in Grantham that Gordon replied to a letter he had received via his wife. The letter was from a Dundee man named McCulloch who was the proprietor of a hotel in Holburn Circus,

London. McCulloch had read of Gordon's adventures in *The People's Journal* and was willing to provide free board and lodging. He promised to do everything in his power to make Gordon's visit to London a success. Gordon gratefully accepted and demonstrated his knowledge of the value of publicity – asking McCulloch to contact the London papers and tell them of his arrival.

London was still a long way off, however, and Gordon carried on to Stamford before setting out for Huntingdon. This was the longest leg of his journey; a distance of twenty-eight miles. He had some difficulty in getting to Huntingdon as a problem had developed with the wheels of his barrow, but this was resolved with the help of a friendly blacksmith. On the evening of 26 November, he arrived at Royston, Hertfordshire, where he met his benefactor, Mr McCulloch, for the first time.

McCulloch was as good as his word and went out of his way to make Gordon's time in London a success, proving himself adept at publicity. He had Gordon's photograph taken at Royston and had a pamphlet printed telling his story so far. He had also arranged that Gordon should spend three days at The Royal Aquarium in exchange for what McCulloch called 'goodly sum' from the management as well as securing further advertising on the barrow.

A tough journey to Waltham Cross followed and Gordon rested there on the Sunday. The next day he set out on the final leg of his journey to London. McCulloch sent a man to meet him at Dalston Station and guide him to central London. Gordon later recalled the scene that met him there: 'By the time I got to Regent Street, I was perfectly dazed. A great crowd was following me and there were so many carriages and cabs on the street that I hardly knew whether my head or heels were uppermost. The crowd seemed to think that it was a matter of life and death my arriving at the Aquarium by four o'clock, and running before me, cleared my way amongst the heavy traffic, so that I got on without difficulty, arriving at the Aquarium where the streets were lined by thousands.'

The Royal Aquarium, which had opened in 1876, was famous for everything except, it seems, fish. All sorts of novelties were presented there – from a woman called Zazel, the world's first human cannonball, to Mr Pongo, one of the first gorillas seen in Europe. James Gordon and his wheelbarrow were on display here for three days in a temporary enclosure, where he sold copies of his pamphlet for three pence each.

The journey had been a great success but for Gordon there was now the small matter of the return leg to contend with. He left London at around ten in the morning on 3 December and once again faced a long trek through bad weather conditions and, in much of rural England, little money in his coffers. He remained in good shape, though, and despite twice wearing the heels off of his boots, maintained that he had never had a blister or pain in his joints – something he ascribed to bathing his joints in whisky every other day. He was not averse to using whisky for its more traditional purpose either, it appears, and having started out with the

FROM DUNDEE TO LONDON AND BACK WITH A WHEELBARROW:
JAMES GORDON LEAVING THE WESTMINSTER AQUARIUM ON HIS RETURN JOURNEY.

A sketch of James Gordon's triumphant moment before the long journey back notion of not drinking on the journey, eventually concluded that 'a wee drop' would do no harm. He remained confident of making it back to Dundee by New Year's Day.

The return journey certainly had its ups and downs. After leaving Huntingdon, Gordon was caught in a great storm and ferocious winds, which at one point blew him over injuring his shoulder and ribs. On another occasion his barrow broke down three times and he had great difficulty in fixing it. In Doncaster, though, he was given accommodation and food at the Green Dragon and received a hearty welcome from the general public who replenished his collection boxes. In York, where he managed to arrive during daylight hours this time, he took up a spot on Coney Street where he soon attracted a crowd.

The north east of England was once more to provide a great reception for Gordon. Crowds gathered to welcome him to Newcastle on Saturday, 18 December. Unfortunately, the biting cold delayed his arrival and also caused much of the waiting crowd to disperse before he got there and it was a smaller but nonetheless enthusiastic crowd that saw him arrive. He was given accommodation at the Waterloo Hotel as he had been on the first leg of his journey and all weekend large numbers turned out to visit him there. Gordon's two visits to Newcastle entered local folklore when they were commemorated by Tommy Armstrong, 'the pitman poet' from County Durham in his song 'Th' Wheelbarrow Man'.

A snowstorm hit while Gordon was in Newcastle and it was feared he would be unable to continue, but nevertheless he set out for Morpeth as planned, pushing his wheelbarrow through what was described as a good depth of snow on the road. When he finally arrived in Morpeth he was met by the town's mayor and entertained at the Queen's Head hotel. The weather was so bad by this stage that some suggested Gordon take the train for part of the way but he would not hear of it and set off along the slush covered roads the next morning.

On Christmas Day, Gordon arrived at Berwick where a large crowd turned out to see him. An idea of the conditions in which he was then travelling can be gained from the fact that the newspapers at the time were reporting the deaths of several elderly people from the effects of the cold in nearby Coldstream. Later that week, a severe storm halted his progress from Dunbar to Haddington. When attempting to find a place to stay in East Linton he was turned down by one establishment where he was told that they 'did not put up tramps'. His protests that he had stayed at some of the 'principal hotels' on his route went unheeded.

Scotland's capital, however, afforded Gordon a warmer welcome. His journey from Haddington, some seventeen miles away, had taken him ten hours and he arrived in Edinburgh after dark. When it became known that he was in town, a large crowd gathered at the General Post Office to see him and the proprietor of a fair that was going on at the nearby Waverley Market engaged him to appear on a platform there.

Gordon left Edinburgh on 29 December. Bad weather was now hampering his progress at every turn and it was not clear if he would make it back to Dundee on New Year's Day as intended. He trudged on, though, travelling to Falkirk and then Stirling where he made an impromptu appearance at the Arcade Theatre. A particularly arduous day's journey from Stirling followed, broken, at least, by stops for refreshments in Blackford and Auchterarder and aided by the spikes that the blacksmith at the mining village of East Plean had put in his boots. He arrived at Perth at twenty minutes past midnight on New Year's Day 1887 and stayed at Pembury's Hotel in Hospital Street where he was able to grab a few hours of sleep before setting out for Dundee.

His experiences in some places north of the border, particularly in East Linton, when compared to the reception he had received in the north east of England, had left Gordon with a somewhat jaundiced view of some of his fellow countrymen, but he could not have been very far along the road from Perth when he realised things would be different on the road to Dundee as well-wishers turned out to greet him, slowing his progress.

Gordon reached Inchture at around two o'clock and from that point onwards, crowds lined the roads, many people having walked out from

Dundee to meet him. By the time he reached Invergowrie, he could scarcely manoeuvre his barrow through the throng. In Dundee itself, the police cleared a way for him until they too were swept away by the crowd who had grown impatient for Gordon's arrival. There were around 10,000 people in the High Street where the crush became so great that the barrow was overturned and damaged and Gordon had to be bundled into the Theatre Royal in Castle Street where he appeared later to full houses. It was estimated that between 40,000 and 50,000 people in all turned out to see him in Dundee that New Year's Day.

Gordon had clearly achieved what he set out to do and raised some much-needed money for his family. Nor was his period in the limelight over. He embarked on a tour of the locality being enthusiastically received at Forfar, Kirriemuir, Alyth and Blairgowrie. He even became the subject of a children's street rhyme:

> Have you seen Gordon the Wheelbarrow Man?
> On his way to London with his caravan.

The success of Gordon's trip led many to copy him. Even before he had reached London, a rival, John Martin of Newcastle, known as 'Sawdust Jack', set out with a heavier barrow. Another Dundee street porter, John Cochrane, wheeled a one-wheeled barrow to London and back in only forty-seven days. James Gordon had started a national craze but new participants began to find returns diminishing in a field crowded with competitors and were forced to play on disabilities or resort to gimmicks. A one-armed man named Spark pushed a barrow from John O'Groats to Lands End; a Dundee whaler named James 'Toshie' McIntosh who had lost both legs to frostbite went from Dundee to London on a tricycle; another Dundee man, Alexander Adams, made the same journey on stilts, while a man from Newcastle, John Welsh, set out for London with four bricks on his head.

This increasing absurdity and desperation came back to haunt the man who had started it all and when James Gordon set out to make a trip to Lands End in July 1887, it does not seem to have generated the same interest as his previous venture. Gordon, it seems, had been unable to use the success of his first trip to find himself a more permanent source of income but instead had become reliant on the money generated by what was only ever going to be a passing fad. In August 1888, increasingly desperate, he was sent to prison for five days for stealing barrow wheels and axles – no doubt for his next undertaking – from the East Railway Station in Dundee.

In 1899, Gordon, who had once been greeted by crowds wherever he went, died in the poorhouse in Dundee at the age of fifty-six. During his initial trip to London, the *Illustrated Police News* had criticised the venture saying, 'A more childish expedition was never undertaken. Any man with health and strength could wheel a barrow twenty miles a day.' The point was, though, that it was only James Gordon who had had the initiative to use this simple method to generate income for his family. Gordon understood people's thirst for novelty and, like any modern Internet sensation, his journey caught the imagination of people up and down the country. Even in the 1880s, though, fame could be a fleeting thing and as James Gordon discovered, the public's attention soon turned elsewhere.

3
Forgotten Days

In the last days of December 1879, people gathered on Dundee's esplanade to look at the ruptured remains of the Tay Bridge. One of Victorian engineering's proudest achievements had been shattered by a gale with the loss of more than seventy lives. In Dundee's streets and closes, in the workplaces and schools, and in the pubs and shops, there was little talk of anything else. There could have been no one in Dundee who was unaware of what had happened.

Seventy years later, in December 1959, there could have been no one in Dundee who was unaware that the Broughty Ferry lifeboat, the *Mona*, had been lost with all of her crew, after going to the aid of the North Carr Lightship which had come adrift from her moorings.

Over the years, there have been many days when Dundee has woken up to find a single local story dominating the news. Some of these, like the Tay Bridge Disaster or the loss of the *Mona*, have become etched in history and remain well known many years later, but there were other days when local events preoccupied the city. These events were known across the whole city at the time but, for some reason, have faded from the collective memory. The following pages recall some of these days in Dundee's history which have left a lighter footprint behind.

The Dark Day

Dundee woke up on the morning of Tuesday, 12 August 1884, to what promised to be a fine, if unremarkable, summer's day. There was not a cloud in the sky as people trudged to their factories, mills and schools in the early morning light. On the railways, heavy freight traffic was causing delays – a frustrating prospect for those gentlemen heading north for the Glorious Twelfth. The prospect for grouse shooting was said to be excellent with the birds being plentiful, strong and free of disease. For farmers gathering to sell their livestock at Dundee's Cattle Market that day, strong demand was expected to push up the price of cattle, if not sheep. In the most noteworthy incident of the morning, a schooner ran aground in the Tay at Harecraigs, West Ferry, but was later refloated. There was nothing to indicate that this day would be talked about for decades to come.

Around nine o'clock clouds began to gather in the sky accompanied by a light breeze. A heavy shower of rain fell in the late morning and the sky cleared once more. The sun even made a tentative appearance – but not for long. Around noon, the breeze died away and the sky grew darker and darker until a blackness enveloped the whole town. As the *Dundee Advertiser* later put it, 'All Nature seemed dead. An unnatural stillness prevailed and from the bright noon of a Summer day the town was almost without warning plunged into the darkness of a Winter midnight.'

Almost every report of what happened that day refers to the darkness as resembling that of a winter's night. The streets became deserted as people sought refuge indoors. Gas lamps were lit in shops and offices and an eerie atmosphere descended on the town. It was said that hardly a word was exchanged in the darkness and there was a terrible anxiety hanging in the air about what natural catastrophe was about to befall Dundee.

Work stopped in many mills and factories and the Cattle Market was suspended when the auctioneers discovered that they could no longer see either animals or the buyers. The horse-drawn tramway service lit its lamps and was disrupted when the terrified animals dragged a car off the rails.

Not surprisingly, many people were terrified too. In some mills, when they lit the lamps, they found that people had fainted. Six girls were found unconscious at their looms in one factory alone. Others left their machines and cowered in the passages. In South Tay Street, one machinist, Marjory Smith, ran into the street where she is said to have collapsed with fear.

Children were naturally fearful and a newspaper report of the time noted the difficulty that many mothers might have in calming their 'little ones' while 'being themselves in a state of terror'. It is easy to sympathise with adults such as teachers who found themselves in charge of large groups of panicking children. Rehearsals were underway at the Dundee Music Hall in the Exchange Buildings for a forthcoming 'Juvenile Naval Spectacle' called 'Trafalgar'. The production was advertised as starring 'The Famous Fothergill Family and 100 Dundee Children'. Most of these 100 children were being drilled on stage when the darkness fell. It was reported that it was 'with the utmost difficulty that they were kept free from panic'.

The darkness held a greater anxiety for many adults. The religious teaching of the time laid a great emphasis on Judgement Day and many feared that this darkness was heralding the end of the world. That the air began to be filled with sulphurous fumes did nothing to alleviate the situation in any way and people began to pray – often out loud – with some dropping to their knees wherever they were. Others bade their farewells to loved ones.

The Bible states that a trumpet blast will herald the Day of Judgement. In Cat's Close, a narrow passageway that ran between Blackness Road and Scouringburn, a rag and bone man announced his presence with a blast from a tin trumpet, which reverberated in the otherwise silent air and caused some terrified residents to flee from their homes.

After around a half hour of the silent darkness, things moved on to a new and equally terrifying phase. At around 12.30pm there was unleashed one of the most violent and relentless thunderstorms that Dundee has ever seen. An *Evening Telegraph* correspondent described the scene: 'The darkness still deepened and the lightning came with an ever-increasing intensity and the thunder rumbled with increasing loudness, until it burst in a terrific and awe-inspiring storm right above the town. Flash followed flash and peals which seemed to shake the earth reverberated through the sulphurous air. Down came the rain in deluging torrents and as the rain increased the darkness slowly passed away, but heaven's artillery only rolled the louder, until the town seemed to be suffering the horrors of a bombardment which filled the mind with awe and fear.'

The lightning was said to be particularly spectacular and many accounts describe brilliant fireballs exploding just over the earth. It seems that Dundee may have been visited by ball lightning that day. Ball lightning is still a controversial phenomenon to this day, with many scientists still disputing its existence. Its fleeting appearance, if it exists at all, makes scientific examination difficult, but there were certainly reports of ball lightning elsewhere in the country that day.

Reverend Alex Jeffrey, a visiting minister from Ipswich was travelling back across the Tay from Fife on the 12.30pm boat when the storm broke. He told the *Advertiser* of his view from this unique perspective: 'Long jagged lines of electric light were perpetually flashing out and in some cases shooting up like flames from the crater of a volcano. In one case the lightning flash showed a central belt having all the colours of the solar spectrum; while in another the colour was a bright mauve. The stillness that reigned in the intervals of the thunder peals was remarkable; but even more so was the unprecedented darkness. It was certainly a new experience . . . to see from the river lights gleaming in Newport and Dundee within an hour of noon on 12 August.'

At Dudhope Castle at one o'clock, the time gun was not fired. Not only might its sound have been lost in the other explosions which rumbled across the sky but Sergeant-Major Ponton who was in charge of the gun had decided that it was too risky to open the gunpowder magazine while the storm continued.

The rain was then said to be so heavy as to make it almost impossible to go out in it. There was a great deal of flooding particularly in low-lying districts. Basement houses in Foundry Lane were among the worst hit, with some families losing furniture, bedding and clothes under two or three feet of water. Similar scenes were enacted in nearby Whale Lane and Mary Ann Lane with some families who lived on the ground floor having to move in with their upstairs neighbours. Many shops, cellars and warehouses in the vicinity of the docks were also flooded.

In Lochee, water cascaded down the High Street and blocked gratings at the top of Bank Street, which meant that it too became a flowing stream – adding to the woes of the low lying areas in South Road in whose direction the water now flowed. A bolt of lightning exploded at Rollo's bakehouse, causing one man, David Adams, to be thrown off his feet, though he later recovered. A fireball was also seen to explode at the nearby farm of Menzieshill.

For a storm that was so spectacular, the amount of serious damage done and injuries suffered was relatively minor. Lightning struck a house in Fairmuir and the manager's house at Douglas Bleachfield lost a chimney when it too was struck. The German barque *Concordia* on the Tay had part of its mast destroyed when it was hit by lightning. Two houses in Broughty Ferry were also struck and in one of these perhaps the most serious incident of the day in the locality occurred to one of the most unlikely people.

Twenty-seven-year-old John Bremner was housebound after having damaged his spine in an accident some years earlier. His father Alexander, a builder and contractor, had come up with an idea to keep his now disabled son in touch with the outside world. Only five years after Alexander Graham Bell had made his first phone call (summoning his assistant from the next room) in 1876, Bremner had installed a telephone in his house in Brook Street. The phone was only connected to the West Free Church around one hundred yards away, but John Bremner was said to be able to hear 'distinctly all that is said in the pulpit', which must surely rank as Dundee's first live broadcast of a public event – even if it was to an audience of one.

John Bremner was found unconscious in the afternoon. It was supposed that he had been holding the rudimentary telephone when the lightning struck the building. So bad was his condition that it was reckoned that he would not survive. By ten o'clock at night, however, he had regained a degree of consciousness and he eventually recovered. Neither his original injury nor the lightning strike had affected Bremner's mental capacities and in the years to come he earned a steady income by entering chess tournaments by correspondence and composing chess problems for newspapers throughout the country.

There were further serious incidents elsewhere in the district as a result of the storm. In Carnoustie, a young boy named William Tosh was struck by lightning while visiting a neighbour's house but later recovered with only a black mark on his face to show for the experience. In Forfar, the lightning tore away part of the ceiling of the house of a family named McGregor. A jug was knocked off the kitchen table and Mrs Mary McGregor was said to have narrowly escaped injury. Though no one was physically hurt, the effect on the family's nerves must have been shattering. In the house that day lay the body of the McGregor's twenty-one-month-old son, Alexander, who had died suddenly two days earlier.

The storm had not only raged in Dundee but throughout the country with much damage being done by flooding. People were killed by lightning strikes in Norfolk and Middlesbrough and storms were reported as far away as Yarmouth. On the farm of Broadshawig near Lauder, Charles Maitland, the twelfth Earl of Lauderdale, was struck while out shooting. The pony he was riding was killed instantly. Lauderdale was taken to the house of a shepherd where he subsequently died. His watch and chain were reported to have been melted by the blast.

As night fell in Dundee, the storm, which had eventually died down earlier, underwent a revival and rumbles of thunder were said to be heard throughout the town until long after midnight. It had been a day that people were glad to see disappear into history although it was one that would be long remembered. The town woke up to a brighter day in every sense the next morning when news began to spread that two men from the

Dundee whaler *Chieftain* who had previously been reported as lost had turned up safe and well at Peterhead[1].

Forty-six years later, on 29 August 1930, Dundee was once again plunged into darkness in the middle of the day. At around 11.30am, for about twenty minutes, the sky was said to be as black as midnight. The storm that subsequently broke out and raged for several hours caused flooding throughout the city. In Victoria Road, the force of the water burst through a dividing wall between two rooms in a basement. Houses in Broughty Ferry were again struck by lightning. No doubt many were terrified by the darkness and the severity of the storm, but it is easy to imagine the knowing looks on the faces of Dundee's senior citizens. As a *Scotsman* reporter put it, 'the storm was a phenomenon to which only elderly people could find a parallel in the historic Dark Day of August 1884.'

The Fight That Became a Riot

Boxing was a brutal business in the days before the rules published by John Graham Chambers (and endorsed by John Sholto Douglas, 9th Marquess of Queensberry) in 1867. The fights were usually in the open air and the boxers – or pugilists, as they were known – were bare fisted. Each round would continue until one of the fighters was knocked down and each fight would continue until one of the parties could not go on any further. Fights of eighty or ninety rounds were not uncommon. There was little concern for the welfare of the competitors and the whole thing was steeped in gambling and corruption.

It was against this background that Sandy McKay, billed as 'champion of Scotland', fought Simon Byrne, an Irishman, at Salcey Green near Hanslope (in the modern borough of Milton Keynes) on 2 June 1830. The prize money was £200 a side, an unimaginable sum to most people at that

---

[1] One of those recovered was James 'Toshie' McIntosh, who, despite having lost both legs to frostbite, made a journey from Dundee to London and back – see the previous chapter, 'The Wheelbarrow Man'.

time. The fight lasted for forty-seven rounds and it was McKay, the Scotsman, who came off worst. The *London Examiner* described his condition at the end of the fight: 'he received many heavy blows about the left temple and his face was so frightfully cut and disfigured that his features were lost in a confused mass of gore and bruises.' The *Morning Chronicle* said, 'Sandy's face was opened up in all directions and almost tattooed like that of a New Zealander.' The paper also noted that his opponent Simon Byrne's left hand was 'cut to the bone with McKay's teeth'.

Sandy McKay received medical attention and was 'bled' while still in the ring. He was taken to the Watts Arms in Hanslope by carriage – a bumpy ride that could not have helped his condition. A doctor kept two fingers in his mouth throughout the journey to prevent him choking. He was then carried up the stairs with his head hanging down, which, again, would have exacerbated his problems. In all likelihood, though, McKay never stood any chance of recovery. He died at around 9.30 the next evening. He was twenty-six years old. He was buried in the churchyard at Hanslope, where his tombstone bears the epitaph:

Strong and athletic was my frame
Far from my native home I came
And bravely fought with Simon Byrne
Alas, but never to return.
Stranger take warning from my fate
Lest you should rue your case too late
If you have ever fought before
Determine now to fight no more.

Simon Byrne was arrested three days later aboard a ferry to Ireland and taken into custody at Liverpool. He was charged with manslaughter.

A tragedy such as this would be a major talking point around the pubs in Dundee if it happened today and it was no different in 1830. A broadside leaflet distributed at the time tells how on Monday, 5 July, a local man named Heron was involved in just such a conversation. Also in the pub at this point was an Irishman by the name of Thurrel and the two soon became embroiled in a heated argument. The exact nature of the men's argument is not known, but over the days since the fight, rumours had spread that the unfortunate McKay had been poisoned. Others suggested that Byrne had not fought fairly. The differing nationalities of the two fighters meant that national pride had also become involved and senti-mental, nationalistic poems were published about McKay:

> Still tae his country's honour true,
> And wearing still a bonnet blue,
> He strove for Scotia through and through,
> To fight, to bleed!
> But sad's the news we've gotten noo,
> Poor Sandy's dead.

Nationality certainly seemed to be a factor in the Dundee pub argument and Heron and Thurrel, followed by crowds of their supporters and the curious, then decided to proceed to the Law to fight it out. Heron, it seems, was knocked down right away and Thurrel continued to kick him while he was down. This so enraged Heron's supporters that they began to attack Thurrel and his Irish supporters with sticks, stones and anything else that came to hand. The broadside described the 'truly alarming' scene that ensued as involving 'many men, women and children being lying, trampled under foot, much cut and bruised, and unable to make their escape'.

The broadsides were, in some ways, the sensationalist press of their day and so it is not clear if Heron and Thurrel ever actually existed, but what is certain is that fighting did break out on the Law that night between Scottish and Irish factions as a result of the Byrne/McKay fight. The rioting soon spread and later that night houses in the vicinity occupied by Irish people were attacked and their windows broken.

There were underlying resentments against the Irish in Dundee that the Byrne/McKay controversy had ignited. The number of Irish people coming to live in the town was steadily increasing. A witness told a government committee around this time, 'They have come over from Ireland in great swarms within these twelve years.' This was certainly an exaggeration – the Irish population of Dundee at this time was probably between three and four thousand and many of these would not have been permanent immigrants. However, the immigration was by this point on such a scale as to be perceived as a threat by some native Dundonians. They accused the impoverished Irish of driving wages down. A newspaper report from the time suggests that the trouble on the Law was pre-empted by a group of Irishmen coming from Aberdeen, where they had lost their jobs, and offering to work for lower wages in Dundee.

There was also a strong anti-Catholic element in the town, which now seized the chance to take action. In the sixteenth century, Dundee had enthusiastically embraced the Reformation – becoming known as the Geneva of the North. By the 1780s, the Catholic population of the town was said to number less than a dozen. That number had been growing recently, though, and the Catholic Emancipation Act of the previous year had given Catholics greater freedom. They worshiped in a meeting house at Meadowside, having moved from smaller premises in the Seagate. The new chapel held between 350 and 400 people. The growth in the number of Irish then threatened to revitalise further Catholicism in the town.

Things did not die down the day after the skirmish on the Law – indeed they got much worse. That evening a mob roamed the town looking for Irish people to attack. Any Irishman recognised or discovered in the street was set upon. Such police as there were claimed to be unable to intervene due to the size of the mob. On one occasion, however, the Procurator Fiscal, Mr MacEwan, bravely mounted a barrel and made a speech to a mob which had gathered at the foot of the Hilltown, somehow persuading them to disperse.

A contemporary newspaper report described one of the tests the mob used in their witch-hunt: 'The watchword for putting down an Irishman is trying him by the pronunciation of the word *guinea*; and the schoolboys on the streets are amusing themselves by acting, in miniature, the part of the rioters, and testing each other by the golden shibboleth, a guinea.' It was no game, however, for any unfortunate Irishman unlucky enough to be caught out.

Being off the streets was no guarantee of safety either. Houses known to be occupied by Irish people, particularly in the west end of town, were attacked with what one report called 'tumultuous violence'. The Irish were dragged from their houses – sometimes from their beds – and beaten. Windows were smashed and the rickety wooden staircases leading to upper houses were set on fire. Two small houses were said to have been pulled down completely.

The Catholic Chapel was attacked – all its windows were smashed and the interior was desecrated. The home of the priest, Constantine Lee, was also attacked. Lee, the first of many Irish-born priests to be stationed in Dundee, was in no doubt that it was anti-Catholicism, rather than any question of wages, which inspired this attack. In a letter to the *Advertiser*, he described the aftermath of the attack: 'The next day (Wednesday), large groups of the populace surrounded my premises gloating over the work of destruction, with evident marks of satisfaction and complacency – sometimes expressing their disappointment that the whole building had not been levelled with the ground. I could not pass in or out of my own house without being insulted. I sought the protection of the police but they were too much occupied to afford me any assistance.'

On the Wednesday evening an angry crowd numbering several thousand assembled in the centre of town determined to continue the persecution of the Irish and indeed drive them out of town altogether. The authorities belatedly began to take some action and around 300 special constables were sworn in. Placards were put up forbidding public assembly and some of the ringleaders arrested – but the attacks on the Irish continued. One Irishman told how he narrowly escaped with his life on Thursday, 8 July, having been chased for over a mile out of town, along with three others.

The mob, he said, were 'parading the streets in every direction, in a riotous unruly manner, and swearing aloud they would not leave a single Irishman in Dundee'. He met many of his fellow countrymen on the way out of town. The *Advertiser* reported that 'great numbers of the poor Irish have been so alarmed by the riots, that they left their dwellings and remained all night in the fields or in the Hill of Balgay.'

In the aftermath of the rioting, some found themselves before the courts, but this would have been only a fraction of those involved. Most were fined or given the alternative of sixty days in prison. Three people – a baker named William Robertson and John Adamson, a weaver, both aged twenty-two, together with a thirteen-year-old boy named Nathan Croll, were given sentences of six months in prison for mobbing and rioting at various locations in Dundee and in particular for their part in the attacks on William Coyle in Bucklemaker Row and Andrew Savage in Blinshall Street.

It does not appear that anyone was killed in the rioting, although one report lists three dead. There were certainly many people injured – some of them seriously. There would have been psychological scars too. Could the Irish ever trust the native population again or was a powder-keg of hatred always there just waiting for some spark such as the Byrne/McKay fight to ignite it?

Resentment remained in the Scottish psyche too. In 1888, nearly sixty years after the riot in Dundee, an Aberdeen newspaper wrote bitterly that the Irish in Dundee 'should not be allowed to forget . . . that in the early part of the century when the textile trade increased by leaps and bounds in Dundee the Irish descended upon it in swarms like locusts, reduced the wages of the native workers by working at a lower rate, and generally made themselves so obnoxious that the inhabitants rose upon them *en masse*, drove them out of the town, and compelled them to fly to the fields where they camped out for weeks, till, on the promise of good behaviour for the future they were allowed to return'.

It is difficult to imagine the victims of such brutal attacks meekly promising better behaviour. It is more likely that many of those Irish who had fled the town simply drifted back when the worst of the trouble had died down. In any case, the Irish were not driven from Dundee for good. In fact, they and their descendants would help to shape the history of the city from this point onwards. Their numbers began to rise sharply from the 1840s due to increased emigration from Ireland in the wake of the failure of the potato crops when the Dundee jute mills provided a reliable source of work. In spite of – or perhaps because of – their increased numbers, there was never any anti-Irish trouble on the scale of the 1830 riot again.

The Catholic Church also experienced a resurgence, boosted by the Irish influx. Six years after the ransacking of the old meeting house, a magnificent new Catholic chapel was opened in the Nethergate – and is still in use today as St Andrew's Cathedral. In the years to come, other Catholic churches would be built across the town, but anti-Catholicism never again appeared on such a scale in Dundee. Further waves of immigration would also come to Dundee over the years, most recently from the Indian sub-continent and Eastern Europe, but whatever economic or cultural tensions have arisen there has never again been a disturbance like the one which followed the Byrne/McKay fight.

So what of Simon Byrne, the man whose accidental slaying of Sandy McKay had inadvertently led to the trouble in Dundee? His trial for manslaughter took place in Buckingham on 22 July 1830. His wealthy backers rallied to his cause, providing his legal team. Character witnesses declared Byrne to be a good and kind man who had been reluctant to fight McKay in the first place. The jury took around ten minutes to decide their verdict and Byrne was declared not guilty. Earlier, even Sandy McKay's mother had said that she sincerely pitied Byrne's situation and knew that he had no enmity against her son.

Three years later, Simon Byrne fought James 'Deaf' Burke at Nomansland Common near St Albans. This time, Burke emerged victorious after a fight extending to ninety-nine rounds. Byrne was taken to The Woolpack inn in St Albans 'in a state of great debility and distress'. On Sunday,

2 June 1833, Simon Byrne, 'The Emerald Gem' and the man who had unwittingly caused Dundee's only race riot, died from his injuries.

15 John Street – 15 August 1893

Anyone walking into the tenement at 15 John Street, Dundee, as the time approached three o'clock in the afternoon on Tuesday, 15 August 1893, would have noticed nothing unusual. They would have seen a message boy climbing the stair to deliver some bread; they would have seen mill workers Mary Farley and her daughter Ann leaving their attic flat to return to work as their dinner hour drew to a close, and they would have seen three women – Isabella Norrie, her daughter Catherine Millar and neighbour Barbara Leckie – standing gossiping at the door of one of the flats on the third floor.

There was a change in the atmosphere a few minutes later, however, when someone else emerged from the Farleys' attic flat and passed the three women on his way downstairs. This was Mary Farley's unemployed husband, James. With him was the couple's four-year-old son, also named James, whom Farley used to take out for a long walk each afternoon. The women were suspicious of Farley, a large and powerfully built man, whose behaviour had been growing increasingly eccentric. He would sometimes jump down the stairs one step at a time or perform a strange jumping motion on the pavement whilst talking incoherently. He would threaten his neighbours after accusing them of persecuting him. Another neighbour, a Mrs Mitchell, would keep her door firmly shut whenever he was about. Local children would taunt him, calling him 'Jack the Ripper' much to his annoyance. He had never actually done anyone any harm, though, and when he made some comment to the women as he passed on this particular day, they gave little in the way of reaction apart from mumbling something about being allowed to stand at their own door if they wanted to.

A few minutes later, however, Farley had returned to the building in a rage. Accounts of what happened next are confused but it seems that a young girl named Robina Chaplin who had been playing outside, came in to the tenement ahead of Farley and shouted to warn the women of his approach. They may have already retreated indoors by this point but in any case, Farley and his son simply carried on up to the attic floor. Almost immediately though, he emerged from his house once more and headed back down to the third floor. Isabella Norrie was now on the landing, possibly having come back out of her house to see what the commotion was. James Farley produced a revolver and shot the fifty-one-year-old widow in the abdomen. At the sound of her mother's screams, Mrs Norrie's daughter Catherine Millar rushed from her mother's house carrying her two-week-old son, Wilson, in her arms. Farley swore at her before calmly aiming and shooting the younger woman twice. Farley then returned upstairs to his house.

John Street formed part of the densely populated area known locally as The Crescent after the area's main street, Dudhope Crescent. It did not take news – or panic – long to spread through an area like this. John Street was soon filled with a mixture of the curious and the terrified. Others rushed to nearby Bell Street to alert the police but some local beat officers – Constables Anderson, Dickson and Clark – arrived at the scene first. The three officers, together with local men John Wishart and Andrew Coyle, made their way up to the attic landing. Farley shouted and swore at the men through the locked door. As they reached the landing, the door opened slightly and Farley opened fire once more. One by one his potential captors fell: John Wishart was hit and blood began to pour from his arm, Constable Anderson was shot in the face and collapsed backwards into the arms of Constable Clark, who himself narrowly missed being hit, and Constable Dickson received a wound to his shoulder.

In the street, the crowd watched in horror as each victim emerged or was carried from the tenement, the blood still pouring from their wounds. The most seriously injured were bundled into cabs and taken to the infirmary. All were still alive when they were brought out but each was a potential murder victim – and Farley had not yet been taken into custody.

Farley remained locked in the house with no means of escape, but at the same time the police were now aware of what his response would be if they approached the door again. There was also the fact that he had a young child in the house to be taken into consideration. So far as the officers could make out, the boy was unharmed. The attic had only one window, which faced Cochrane Street. By now a large crowd had also gathered on that side. At one point Farley removed several flowerpots from the windowsill and opened the window slightly, causing widespread panic that he was about to start shooting randomly into the street, but he only shouted abuse. He would reappear at the window periodically and each time he did, a similar panic spread through the crowd.

The police from Bell Street Station were now on the scene. Lieutenant Lamb sent for Farley's wife, Mary, who was allowed to go into the flat to try to reason with her husband. The police had also given her instructions to grab the revolver and throw it out the window or bring it out with her. Like so many other aspects of the police handling of this case, this sounds incredible to modern ears. Not surprisingly, Mrs Farley was unable to secure her husband's surrender or the gun. Farley merely promised to 'slay as many of them' as he could. Mary Farley emerged after a short time with nothing except the unrealistic proposal that if the police withdrew, her husband might go to Bell Street and give himself up.

Next, Farley's landlord, a Mr Walker, was allowed to let himself into the flat with a spare key in order to talk Farley into giving himself up. Farley expressed reluctance to shoot Walker but made it clear that he would do so if the landlord proceeded any further. After this attempt at negotiation failed, the decision was made to storm the flat.

A large piece of wood was found with which to burst open the door. The police also collected wooden chairs, which they would hold in front of them as protection should Farley fire on them. When the door was burst open, Farley was seen to be standing in the middle of the room, revolver in hand. The police charged at him, led by Inspector David McBey holding a chair in front of his face. Farley did not have time to fire the gun but seemingly from out of nowhere produced a large knife, which he thrust with all his strength into the policeman's body. The other officers were able to overpower Farley as he slashed wildly at them with the knife. McBey could only murmur, 'I'm stabbed,' as he collapsed to the floor.

The news soon spread through the crowd outside that Farley had been captured and that McBey had been stabbed. People strained to see Farley as he was brought out, shackled to two policemen, with blood running down his face from wounds received in the struggle. He was led in the direction of Bell Street to jeers from the crowd and calls for his lynching. All the way, Farley ranted and raved while large numbers of people followed in procession to the Central Police Office.

Meanwhile, Inspector McBey had been carried to the second-floor house of the Chaplin family where a bed sheet was used in an attempt to stop the bleeding. At around five o'clock he was brought out on a stretcher to be taken to the Infirmary. He was conscious but ominously the blood was seen to be continuing to seep through the dressings on his wounds.

The background of James Farley now began to emerge. He was an Irishman, born in County Cavan around 1847, although, like so many others in the Famine period, he left Ireland at a young age. He had worked as a stoker in various places, reportedly including Russia and America. In 1866, he was working in Manchester when he married Mary McDonald, a native of the same county in Ireland. The couple moved to Glasgow where they lived in the Gorbals. It was here that their two children were born. It was here, too, that Farley was reputedly left traumatised while acting as one of a rescue party following a gas explosion. The Farleys moved to Dundee around 1890 and lived at Clepington Street before moving to John Street two years later. Farley was said to have been unfit for work for around five years.

At the Dundee Royal Infirmary, the wounded were being looked after. Inspector McBey and Catherine Miller were the worst affected. Some newspaper reports said that neither was expected to live. Though unharmed, Miller's two-week-old son was admitted to the hospital to be beside his mother. The child's grandmother, Isabella Norrie, had a bullet lodged in the lower part of her abdomen but was not thought to be in danger. John Wishart, who had been one of the two civilians who attempted to gain entry to Farley's house, had been shot in the arm, the bullet having passed right through. The bullet that penetrated Constable John Anderson's face, leaving a ragged wound, had hit his jawbone – a fact that probably saved his life. Constable William Dickson's shoulder wound was said to be the least serious injury sustained.

As the week drew to a close, all the victims were making progress – all except Inspector McBey. He had seemed to rally at times, but on the morning of Saturday, 19 August, he took a turn for the worse and at 10.30am, he died. He was forty-four years old and left behind a widow and four children.

David McBey had joined the Dundee Police force in 1872 at the age of twenty-one. He was born in Kincardineshire, the illegitimate son of a cook in domestic service. It may have been to escape the shadow of illegitimacy that he made his way to Dundee to work or he may have simply been looking for an escape from his job as a farm labourer. Whatever the reason, he soon found that police work suited him and he was promoted to the rank of sergeant in 1878.

McBey was one of Dundee's earliest detectives and one of the city's first plain clothes policemen. He was stationed for a time at the Western District office in the heart of the Scouringburn area – an area with more than forty licensed premises (and many more unlicensed shebeens) and where, despite being only around half a mile from the central station, the divisional police made around a thousand arrests a year. In 1892, McBey had been given a reward of twenty-five shillings for his part in the rescue of some women and children from a fire in Wilkie's Lane. On that occasion he had shown the same sort of disregard for his own safety that had now cost him his life. The charge against Farley would now be murder.

The charge of murdering Inspector McBey together with that of the attempted murders of Isabella Norrie, Catherine Millar, John Wishart and Constables Anderson and Dickson was put to Farley at Edinburgh on

Inspector David McBey

10 October 1893. It was clear from the start, though, that he would not be considered fit to plead. Doctor Templeman, who had seen Farley in Dundee Prison on the day of the incident, testified that Farley had said on that occasion that his neighbours were backed by the police and by Parliament and had the power to kill him. Doctor Littlejohn, who saw him in Edinburgh, said that Farley was suffering from 'acute melancholia'. He would give a loud howl every now and again and when questioned by Littlejohn as to why, he answered, 'My inside is cold.' Farley was declared insane and was sent to Perth Prison 'during Her Majesty's pleasure'. He

died at Liff Hospital in 1930.

Other than Inspector McBey, all of Farley's victims survived. It is likely, though, that the two women in particular would have been left with some form of disability and Constable Anderson with disfigurement. In a sad post-script to the events at John Street, Wilson Miller, the two-week-old baby held in his mother Catherine's arms as she was shot by Farley, died of pneumonia at the end of October 1893.

It is easy from a twenty-first-century perspective to look disparagingly at the way the events in John Street in August 1893 were handled and to look down on a society in which someone like James Farley is shouted at in the street by children rather than treated for his mental illness; where unarmed police and members of the public attempt to tackle an armed and dangerous man; where civilians are sent in to negotiate with or capture such a man and where a crowd is allowed to gather immediately below the window of a man who has already shot two people. To do this, though, ignores the fact that modern procedures have emerged from the lessons learned from the past and ultimately from the bravery of men like Inspector David McBey.

School's Out

At the beginning of September 1911, Gwilym Harries, headmaster of Bigyn School, Llanelli, Wales, was suffering from a cold. He did not attend school on Monday, 4 September, nor did he feel well enough to return to work the next day. He was, he later recalled, barely able to leave his room. The other teachers would surely cope without him for a couple of days, he must have imagined. It is easy to speculate as to the nature of his reaction, then, when he was told on the Tuesday afternoon that a number of boys from Bigyn had walked out of the school and were marching up and down Murray Street in the town centre and singing noisily.

The incident made the local press and was used as a stick with which to beat the then increasingly militant Trade Unions: 'The strike epidemic now prevalent has infected the rising generation at Llanelly and in order to be in the "fashion" the schoolboys decided on a "down tool" policy. The origin took place at Bigyn School on Tuesday when the scholars in sympathy with one of their colleagues who was punished for an offence deserted their classrooms and paraded the streets to the accompaniment of singing and booing.'

The school strike in Llanelli was, in truth, a small-scale incident where a few boys had taken advantage of the headmaster's absence and the leniency of other teachers. They were out of school for a relatively short time and were all punished on their return. Nevertheless, a fire had been lit in the late summer of 1911 that would rapidly spread. Within days, school strikes had broken out in Liverpool and Manchester. Over the next couple of weeks they would spread to places as far apart as Glasgow, Portsmouth and Dublin. The nature of the strikes varied from place to place. Some children simply fancied an afternoon off school but others produced coherent lists of demands – abolition of corporal punishment, more holidays and less homework being among the most popular. In Glasgow, a demand was made for a penny a week pay; in Arbroath they asked for cushioned seats – presumably they did not foresee success with regard to the abolition of corporal punishment!

Just over a week after the incident at Bigyn School, the trouble came to Dundee where, in the words of the local press, it 'took on a more serious face'. The year of 1911 was a time of industrial unrest in Dundee. It began with the Jute and Flaxwokers' strike which closed Cox's jute mill in Lochee and ended with the carters' and dockers' strike which effectively paralysed the city in December – but one of the biggest demonstrations in Dundee that year was to involve not mill workers or transport workers but children.

It was on Thursday, 14 September 1911, that the unrest began. The Cowgate School was first to feel its effects when a large number of pupils walked out in the morning. The school had been built in 1889 as a half-timers school – where the pupils would spend half of their time in lessons and the other half at work. The adult world of work and industrial unrest was not, therefore, a world with which these children were unfamiliar. Indeed, at work many were expected to read the newspapers to their older workmates who could not read themselves. Word of the school strikes happening elsewhere probably reached the children in this way. The teachers' union, the Educational Institute of Scotland, blamed the press for encouraging 'a game of follow the leader'.

Was the walkout at the Cowgate School, then, merely a copycat action? As in all industrial disputes, the opinions of the 'management' and the strikers varied considerably. The teachers said that they were unaware of any grievance but children interviewed by the press repeated the mantra of less homework, more holidays and 'less of the strap'.

This strike proved short-lived, though, and the first children began to return around eleven o'clock in the morning. The Cowgate pupils had been out long enough, however, for news of their exploits to filter to other schools in the town. Children now began to walk out of the schools at Wallacetown,

The Cowgate School, the first school in Dundee to fall victim to student strikes

Victoria Road, Blackness, Balfour Street and Hill Street and to congregate in the city centre. Attempts were made to persuade other schools to come out – but a gang that turned up at the High School of Dundee could not persuade anybody there to join the demonstration.

By the evening, things were getting out of control, as 1500 schoolchildren accompanied by what the press referred to as 'a number of rowdies' now paraded through the streets. This was by far the biggest demonstration since the wave of school strikes began. It was not, as many of the others had been, good-natured and peaceful. The pupils were armed with sticks and stones. School buildings were attacked and numerous windows were smashed. A teacher coming from an evening class was recognised and attacked.

Dundee woke up the next morning to the aftermath. At Victoria Road School, there was said to be hardly a pane of glass left intact. Over 100 windows in all were said to have been smashed at the various school buildings visited by the demonstrators the previous night.

By the start of the school day, the protest itself was crumbling as many children, including some of the ringleaders, were subjected to parental pressure. Parents and grandparents all over the city were seen dragging wayward pupils to the classroom. In some cases, policemen were stationed at the school gates to encourage attendance.

The presence of a policeman did not prevent the strike from continuing at Brown Street School where around fifty boys refused to enter the classroom. Pickets composed of senior pupils were stationed at the gates and managed to persuade some others to come out, but before the day was over they had returned to the classroom. Only a few hardy souls at Glebelands remained out of the classroom for another day.

By the end of September, the school strikes nationally had fizzled out too. That left only their motivation and meaning to be debated in the press. A letter sent to *The Scotsman* by 'A School Inspector' was typical, saying the strikes 'show how quickly the spirit of conflict with law and authority will spread if unchecked and that it will soon reduce the social system to anarchy'. Some correspondents exonerated the pupils of blame only to damn their parents for having set the bad example of having gone on strike themselves. Many people, as in every age, just seemed to despair of the younger generation altogether.

Perhaps, though, some of those who shook their heads in disbelief had been schoolboy strikers themselves. The strikes were not, in fact, a new thing. A similar wave of school strikes had swept the country in 1889. These too had reached Dundee when the older children in a Lochee school, including many who were 'half-timers', walked out at dinner time complaining of long hours and too many lessons. They assembled in front of the school and shouted and cheered when the headmaster and other teachers tried to persuade them to return to lessons. Instead they toured other schools in the vicinity – but could not persuade anyone else to join them. Undeterred, they contended themselves with parading the streets shouting and singing popular songs.

The next day pupils from Butterburn School came out and they too tried to spread the action to other schools but this time with more success than the Lochee pupils. Children from Clepington, Balfour Street and Hawkhill schools, among others, joined the demonstration until a noisy crowd said to number thousands of children marched to the docks and along the Esplanade. Fewer lessons, shorter hours and less homework were the familiar demands of the strikers.

Like the children of 1911, the pupils of 1889 could not really expect the school authorities to submit to their demands. They could, on the other hand, confidently expect severe punishment from school and parents alike. They had, nonetheless, in an authoritarian age, enjoyed delivering a defiant gesture to all the authority figures who constrained them and, like those in 1911, they had, if only for one glorious afternoon, tasted freedom.

4
American Tales

In 1980, when the Palestinian flag was flown in the city to mark the fact that Dundee had become the twin town of the West Bank town of Nablus, there were some who said that this was an unprecedented intrusion by the local authority into the realm of international affairs. Almost exactly 200 years earlier, however, the Provost, Magistrates and Councillors of the town had intervened in another pressing international situation. In 1775 they issued a statement denouncing the American colonies' rebellion against the crown. George Washington, undefeated by the British forces, was hardly likely to crumble in the face of the combined might of the Dundee Corporation, but it was still an inauspicious beginning to the town's relationship with the nascent United States of America.

Things were to improve over the next century, though, particularly in the area of trade. The wagons that opened up the American West would often be covered with tarpaulin from Dundee and the ill wind of the Civil War brought heavy demand for Dundee's textiles from both sides. So important had trade with America become by 1873 that Colonel Frank Stewart Sandeman gave his new state-of-the-art jute mill in Dundonald Street the name Manhattan Works.

In that same year, Dundee investors led by Lochee-born Robert Fleming began to pump money into ventures from railroads to cattle ranching. This was the genesis of the merchant bank Robert Fleming and Company, which in 2000 was sold to the Chase Manhattan Bank for $7.7 billion. The son of a grocer, Fleming never forgot his humble roots and, among other gifts to the city, provided for the building of the houses around Fleming Gardens and Hindmarsh Street (Kate Hindmarsh became Mrs Fleming in 1881). Fleming's grandson Ian became famous for another type of bond – James Bond.

Undoubtedly, one of Dundee's biggest exports to the United States was people. Many sailed there seeking prosperity or simply a better life for their families. Many of them went on to make their mark on the country in various ways and affect things that we think of as quintessentially American. Among these were James Macdonald, who left Dundee when he was an infant and was to provide the voice for Walt Disney's Mickey Mouse for many years, and James V. MacKinnon, who was born in Corso Street, Dundee, in 1881 the son of a carpet weaver, but went on to become president of the Stetson Hat Company.

Emigration was partially responsible for the fact that the United States now has several Dundees of its own – in New York State, Florida, Minnesota, Michigan and Illinois. Dundee, Illinois, acquired its name when a native of Dundee, Scotland, named Alexander Gardiner, won a ballot held among the town's early settlers. The Florida town was named by a man called Menzie who was also a Scottish Dundonian. This town also shares a tradition of marmalade and confectionary production with its parent city. None of these Dundees, however, has joined Nablus on the list of Dundee's twin towns – that honour goes to Alexandria in the state of Virginia.

In the twentieth century, the years after the Second World War saw large American firms such as NCR, Timex and Veeder-Root set up in Dundee and provide a new type of employment for large numbers of its citizens over the ensuing decades. By the early years of the twenty-first century, however, it was clear that this particular area of American influence on Dundee had long passed its high-water mark.

Perhaps the biggest influence of the United States in Dundee was a cultural one. From the early 1920s until the late 1950s, there were always at least twenty cinemas in the city – rising to thirty in 1936. At the height of Hollywood's popularity in the 1930s and 1940s there were said to be 30,000 cinema seats in Dundee – one seat for every six people. It seems unlikely that any other city fell so completely under the spell of Tinseltown and so it is perhaps fitting that the following stories deal, in the main, with some of the more glamorous aspects of American life – money, fame and Hollywood stardom. For some Dundonians, it seems, the American Dream was a reality. Even dreams can have a downside, though, and sometimes after the movie ends, there are the grim realities of everyday life to be faced.

William Duncan – the Lochee Cowboy

Armed with nothing more than sticks and cheap toys, generations of children in Dundee played 'Cowboys and Indians'. Running across the wide open plains of the city's public parks, herding cattle at back green ranches and staging gunfights on cobbled streets, their games owed more to Hollywood than to the true story of the American West.

The Western as a genre of film had been established at the very beginnings of Hollywood when the events portrayed were still within living memory but sufficiently distant to be transformed into a fantasy where the lines between the good guys and the bad guys were clearly defined and the good guys always won. This was a story that children could understand and re-enact anywhere. Not many of them knew, however, that a pioneer among the screen cowboys they imitated – one of those responsible for their games and indeed the whole Hollywood image of the West – was, like them, a child of Dundee.

Few boys growing up in Lochee at the end of the nineteenth century could hope to achieve anything out of the ordinary. The suburb, which had only been officially part of Dundee since 1859, had grown up around the textile industry and employment was dominated by the Cox Brothers' Camperdown Works. It was certainly an unlikely birthplace for one of

Hollywood's first Western stars. William Duncan was born in Nicoll's Lane, Lochee, in December 1879 – the month of the Tay Bridge disaster[1]. His father, also William, was a stonemason and was originally from Newtyle. His mother Jane worked as a dressmaker. If young William did not follow in his father's footsteps and become a stonemason, it seemed certain that he would be a mill worker of some sort.

His destiny was to be completely altered in 1890, though, when he was ten years old. It was then that the family set sail for the United States, arriving in New York. Far from becoming a mason or a mill worker, William was ultimately to embark on a career that would lead to his name and appearance becoming familiar to millions in a way that could not have been imagined when he was born.

He attended the University of Pennsylvania but was much more successful in the sporting arena than the academic. This was the era that saw the rise of physical culture and body-building and Bill (as he was to be known for the rest of his life) embraced these enthusiastically. At the end of his second year he transferred to the Physical Culture Health Home founded by Bernarr Macfadden. Macfadden was known as the father of Physical Culture. He was the original sickly child who had overcome weakness through exercise and was a mentor to Charles Atlas. Bill also worked on Macfadden's *Physical Culture Magazine*, which had the motto 'Weakness [is] a Crime – Don't be a Criminal'.

To supplement his income, Bill dabbled with the world of professional wrestling for a few months. It was while doing this that another life-changing moment occurred. He came to the attention of the world-famous strongman Eugen Sandow. Sandow was the archetypal strongman with his leopard skin loincloth and handlebar moustache. In 1906, Bill joined Sandow's vaudeville act.

After performing for a while in vaudeville, he began to acquire a taste for more serious, dramatic theatre. He joined the Forepaugh Stock

---

[1] Duncan's Birth Certificate was signed by an interim registrar. The previous Lochee registrar, David Neish, had perished in the disaster along with his five-year-old daughter, Isabella.

William Duncan

Company in Philadelphia and later acted with companies in Rochester, New York, and Memphis, Tennessee, as well as embarking on acting tours. Eventually, he was spotted by a talent scout for the Selig Polyscope Company. Selig was one of the oldest film companies, having been founded in 1896 by Colonel William N. Selig of Chicago.

Duncan made his first films as early as 1911. These were mainly one-reel outdoor action movies where his supporting cast often included the most famous silent cowboy of them all – Tom Mix. They were often filmed in the Arizona Desert and so conditions could be harsh. Bill soon acquired a reputation for doing all of his own stunts and quickly became popular with audiences. He took time too, to learn all aspects of the fledgling film industry and began to write and direct his own pictures.

Duncan's career might have ended as soon as it began when he was almost shot in 1912. Filming on location at Colorado State Penitentiary and dressed as a convict, he lit his pipe in the prison yard during a break in filming. Thinking he was a real prisoner, a tower guard shouted a warning at him to put the pipe away, but Bill did not think the shouts were directed at him. He soon realised that they were, though, when the guard opened fire. Duncan had to fling himself to the ground to avoid the bullets. Location filming was still a fairly new idea in 1912 and the lines between fact and fiction had become almost fatally blurred on this occasion.

In 1915, Duncan joined the Vitagraph Company. Like Selig, Vitagraph had started as early as 1896 and had even captured film of the Boer War before becoming a producer of highly popular films and serials. It was these serials that were to become the mainstay of Bill's career in the years ahead. His athletic build and penchant for daredevil stunts meant that he was ideally suited to this type of action adventure and his writing and direction skills meant that action scenes could be staged just as he wanted. He always fixed it, he claimed, so that he was rescued in time. Cliffhanger endings, though, kept the audiences coming back week after week just to make sure he or the leading lady was unharmed.

Every serial star needed a heroine to rescue on a weekly basis and William Duncan was initially cast against Carol Holloway. Though the combination proved popular, it was Edith Johnson who was to be his enduring leading lady both on and off the screen.

Edith Johnson was born in Rochester, New York, in 1895. Rochester was the home of the Eastman Kodak photographic company and Edith initially achieved fame as the 'Kodak Girl' – her image appearing in numerous advertisements in newspapers and magazines. At one point she was known as 'the most photographed girl in the world'. Edith was definitely the outdoor type and she was proficient at a number of sports. She was ideally suited, then, for the kind of action picture that Bill made. She began

Edith Johnson, Duncan's leading lady both on- and off-stage

acting in movies in 1914 and was first cast alongside William Duncan in 1918. Together they proved an unstoppable team and became known as the king and queen of the serial. They were married in April 1921.

This period was the height of Duncan's success and serials such as *Fighting Fate*, *Smashing Barriers* and *The Steel Trail* thrilled audiences in their millions. Many Dundee youngsters at this time must have looked disbelievingly at their parents when they claimed that the man they watched on the screen or whose exploits they read about in the increasingly popular movie weeklies had been a childhood friend in Lochee.

The extent of Duncan's popularity is shown in the new contract

Vitagraph gave him in 1919. He was committed to direct and star in two serials each year for three years. For this, he was to be rewarded with an average weekly salary of $10,000 – an unimaginable amount of money to those childhood friends working in the jute mills and factories of Dundee. Vitagraph doubled the size of their Hollywood studios to meet the requirements of Duncan's productions.

Film production in those days was not without its hazards, though, and Duncan's insistence on doing his own stunts increased these. Writing and directing his own films meant that he had a greater degree of control than might have been the case otherwise but things could still go wrong. A scene in *The Silent Avenger* (1920) involved Bill driving a car across a burning bridge. When he had just completed the crossing the bridge was to blow up. That was the theory anyway. He left it until the last minute to start his crossing, which meant he had a matter of seconds to drive over before the dynamite destroyed the bridge. Halfway across, however, the car stalled. Blinded by smoke, Bill had to climb out and start the car with the starting handle. Somehow he managed to do this, jump back in the car and drive over the bridge. He made it to the other side with barely a second to spare before the explosion. He was shaken by the experience and described himself as smelling like a dressed turkey, but his first thought was that the scene was now much more exciting for the audience. On another occasion, after he was 'shot' in a film, Bill nearly drowned when using weights to stop his natural buoyancy after landing in the water. He struggled to release the slipknot on the weights but eventually managed to free himself.

Bill could be impatient with anyone who didn't share his professionalism. Some of the actors on his films were hard-bitten cowboy types who did not have the same concern for the finished product or the audiences. One day a cowboy named Pete didn't show up but instead sent his wife to tell Bill that he had an ulcerated tooth. Bill sent her home to get Pete who turned up with something more resembling a hangover rather than any dental problem. Bill then filmed Pete's death scene followed by the deaths of all the other actors. He then had the ability to insert their deaths into the film at any point if any of them did not turn up to work. There was said to be little drunkenness or absenteeism after that. It was not the last time that a Hollywood director got a death scene 'in the can' as an insurance policy, but Bill was probably the first to use this tactic.

Having achieved all that they wanted to in the film industry and being financially secure, Bill and Edith were able to retire from movies in 1924. Bill was forty-five and Edith thirty. Back home in Dundee, many of Bill's contemporaries would toil in the jute mills into their old age. Bill and Edith, though, were lucky enough to be able to tour about the United States and beyond. Apart from a spell when they had a vaudeville act together, Edith never worked again. Instead she concentrated on raising their family.

Bill grew restless, though, and returned to the movies in the talkie era in guest roles. Any old friends from Lochee who had imagined throughout the silent era that he had retained his Dundee accent would be disappointed when they heard him speak for the first time in forty-five years. In truth, like many children moving to a new country, Bill had lost his Scottish accent shortly after arriving in the United States back in 1890.

Bill's revived career in the 1930s saw him starring alongside *Flash Gordon* star Larry 'Buster' Crabbe in a couple of movies but his most famous talking role was in the Hopalong Cassidy movies. He appeared in several films as Buck Peters, the boss of the Bar 20 Ranch. Few young lads sitting in the Astoria Cinema in Logie Street, Dundee, cheering on William Boyd and George 'Gabby' Hayes, would have any idea that the man playing Buck Peters had at one time lived in the very street where they now sat. (Bill's family had lived in Logie Street for a time after leaving Nicoll's Lane.) By the time the films became popular on television years later, the actor's connection with Dundee had been almost completely forgotten.

William Duncan retired again in 1940 and this time his retirement was permanent. His last movie was, like so many of his previous ones, a Western – *Texas Rangers Ride Again*. Bill had made a great contribution to the development of this type of movie and had paved the way for the Western stars of the sound era such as Gary Cooper and John Wayne.

In his later years, Bill suffered illness and was confined to his home. Nevertheless he lived to the age of eighty-one – dying on 8 February 1961. He is buried in Inglewood Park Cemetery, Inglewood, California, the last resting place of stars such as Gypsy Rose Lee, Ella Fitzgerald and Sugar Ray Robinson, and a long way from Lochee. Those who knew him remember a kind and very likeable man with – for all his success – very simple tastes. Edith Johnson outlived her husband by seven years. She died in 1969 in Los Angeles from injuries sustained in a fall. She was seventy-five years old.

Few in Dundee have heard of William Duncan these days. Silent movies mean little to many of us in the digital age and few of his movies survive anyway. Film was seen as a short-lived medium and nobody involved could have imagined in their wildest dreams that people might be interested in seeing any of these films almost 100 years later. Few pay any attention to Nicoll's Lane either – which still exists in Lochee, sandwiched between a pub and Lochee West Church. It would be sad, though, to forget the fact that this was the birthplace of one of Hollywood's earliest stars. There is a patch of grass where the tenement in which William Duncan was born once stood. Perhaps one day this site could house a statue of William Duncan, the Lochee Cowboy, and, as a symbol of what a boy from an ordinary background can achieve, he would be once again speaking to us without words.

Hail to the Chief

It is difficult to imagine opening one of Dundee's newspapers today and finding a letter from the current President of the United States among the offerings from more regular contributors, but that is what readers of the *People's Journal* were able to do on 8 October 1949 when the paper published a letter from the then President Harry Truman. It is even harder to imagine that the catalyst that indirectly inspired President Truman to write to the paper was a cartoon strip by DC Thomson's most famous artist – Dudley D. Watkins.

The cartoon was a serialisation of Sir Walter Scott's narrative poem 'The

Lady of the Lake', part of the series of adaptations of famous books that Watkins did for the paper under the banner of 'Told in Pictures'. The adaptations consisted of drawings by Watkins with blocks of text underneath them. The last illustration in the edition of 6 August 1949 shows Roderick Dhu, the chief of Clan Alpine, standing in the bow of a boat as it comes in to land while the caption beneath refers to a hundred men of Clan Alpine raising their voices in the famous song 'Hail to the Chief'.

This comic strip was undoubtedly what inspired an article in the same issue on the origin of the tune of the same name that heralds the arrival of the US President at any formal occasion. The article reported that the tune of 'Hail to the Chief' was 'said to come from an old Gaelic air' and in adapted form had found its way into Sir Henry Rowley Bishop's opera the 'Knight of Snowdoun', which in turn was based on 'The Lady of the Lake'.

This article somehow came to the attention of a man named Ward Murphey Canaday. Known as the 'Father of the Jeep', Canaday had been head of the Willys Overland Company who had developed the vehicle and thus made a great contribution to America's war effort. He was also a friend of President Truman's. He sent Truman the clipping, which inspired the President to write to the *People's Journal*. Truman had always had a great love of music and history and combined with the association with the presidency it made an irresistible combination for him – 'Truman's Curiosity Up' as a headline in the *Cincinnati Enquirer* would later proclaim.

In his letter to the *Journal* Truman admitted that he had been unaware of the origin of the song and that knowing its origin would make him 'all the happier to stand at attention when it is played on my official arrival at various cities of the United States'. He concluded with a plea for any further information other than that contained in the original article.

The news that the President had written to the paper itself made headlines across America. Both the *Los Angeles Times* and *The New York Times* carried the story and Dundonians living in the United States soon began sending clippings from their local newspapers. Ward Canaday's secretary even sent a cutting from the *Toledo Blade*.

Many readers offered their theories on the origins of the tune and how it came to be associated with the President of the United States. One correspondent suggested it had happened at around the time of Walter Scott's centenary, while another claimed the glory for Clan Macgregor. None of the answers was really satisfactory, though.

Modern research has uncovered that the tune comes from one of several stage productions of 'The Lady of the Lake', which opened soon after the poem was published in 1810. A production opened at Philadelphia's New Theatre in 1812 using a version of 'Hail to the Chief' that had featured in a London production – not that written by Sir Henry Rowley Bishop but one composed by James Sanderson. 'Hail to the Chief' was first associated with a President on 22 February 1815, when it was played in memory of George Washington. In 1829 it was played for a living president, Andrew Jackson, and it was also played during the inauguration ceremony for Martin Van Buren in 1837. In the 1840s it began to be used to herald the President's arrival at official events.

The anthem was normally played as an instrumental. Walter Scott's original words related to Roderick Dhu and Clan Alpine and commences:

> Hail to the chief, who in triumph advances,
> Honored and bless'd be the evergreen pine!
> Long may the tree in his banner that glances,
> Flourish, the shelter and grace of our line.

There were lyrics written to Sanderson's music by Albert Gamse but these are not often heard. They begin:

> Hail to the Chief we have chosen for the nation,
> Hail to the Chief! We salute him, one and all.
> Hail to the Chief, as we pledge cooperation
> In proud fulfilment of a great, noble call.

In essence, though, the original *People's Journal* article was correct when it said that in America it was a 'song without words' – the title alone (the first four words of Scott's anthem) aptly fitting the arrival of a President.

In 1954, the year after Truman left office, the US Department of Defense established 'Hail to the Chief' as the official musical tribute to the President. Could it be that this came about as a result of the revived interest in the tune that arose after the President of the United States wrote a letter to a Dundee newspaper?

The Richest Woman in the World

On 16 December 2008, at Bonhams' salerooms on Madison Avenue, New York, a pearl necklace was sold for $600,000. Consisting of three strands, it contained 224 natural pearls and two diamond-studded Cartier clasps. The names of two previous reputed owners of the necklace were on everybody's lips that day – one was Catherine II, Empress of all the Russias, who is remembered by history as Catherine the Great, and the other was a woman born Christina Thomson in a two-roomed tenement house in Shepherd's Loan, Dundee.

Christina Stevenson Thomson was born in 1871, the third child of William Thomson, a rope and sail maker and his wife Elizabeth, a mill worker. The couple had married ten years earlier in Coldingham, Berwickshire where Elizabeth had worked in service, but both originally hailed from Dundee. They returned home the year after their marriage and lived at Dallfield Walk and then at the West Port before moving to the house in Shepherd's Loan around the time of Christina's birth. The family later moved to nearby Crofts Lane in Peddie Street.

Christina's father's work often took him away to sea and it may be that he was away when she was born as her birth was registered by her maternal grandmother, Marjory Stevenson, who lived in Wilkie's Lane. It is tempting to imagine the old woman adding the 'Stevenson' to the child's name, but whatever it said on the birth certificate, Christina Thomson was to be known for most of her long life by a name that did not feature there at all: Anna. This was a name she adopted primarily to avoid being called Teenie – the nickname that she had grown up with.

Anna Thomson and her two sisters were said to have had a particularly strict upbringing. In addition, they would have had to endure all the hardships that went hand in hand with working-class life in nineteenth-century Dundee. For Anna, though, there was always the distraction of music. Having shown promise at school, she became a competent piano player.

In 1880, the family emigrated to Detroit in the United States where Anna's father was employed by a ship's chandler. Anna continued to study music and when she left school she was able to supplement the income she received working in The Morton Baking Company by giving piano lessons. It was a life that seemed to have better prospects than those she had faced in Dundee, but it was still a world away from the life she was to lead in the years to come.

In 1896, Anna married Horace Dodge who was employed as a 'skilled machinist' at a company called Dominion Typograph in Windsor, Ontario, Canada. Despite being in a different country, Windsor is separated from Detroit only by the Detroit River and in many ways they form a single metropolitan area. It was not the most romantic of weddings, as it happened in Horace's lunch hour. The groom returned to work after the ceremony while the bride returned home on the ferry to Detroit.

Horace enjoyed tinkering with anything mechanical and when he noticed that the bicycle he rode to work each day was not working as efficiently as it should, he began to set his mind to the task of finding a solution to this problem. He came up with a new ball bearing that did not so easily clog up with dirt, making the bicycle run more smoothly. The idea must have been a good one as it attracted the financial backing of a businessman named Fred S. Evans.

Together with his brother John Dodge, Horace and Evans set up the Evans and Dodge Bicycle Company in 1897. This company did not last long, however, as it was taken over twice by larger firms. Horace emerged from this with a royalty payment for the use of his ball bearing and $7500 in cash. John received the same amount. The brothers then set up a firm of their own in 1900 named Dodge Brothers with which they would pursue their new interest – cars.

As early as 1902, the firm received an order for 3,000 transmissions for the Oldsmobile Corporation, who at the time produced around a third of the cars in America. The money they received was ploughed back into expanding the business.

These early years were among those that Anna Thomson Dodge would later look back on with fondness. She still packed Horace's lunch each day. She would look after the home and their two children – a daughter, Delphine, born 1899 and a son, Horace junior, who was born in 1900. Her piano playing days were over, though, as she had damaged a tendon in her hand when she fell one day while carrying a milk bottle. For the woman born in the Dundee tenement, life was about to change in unimaginable ways and with remarkable rapidity. Although her husband and brother-in-law had what by any standard was a highly successful business, they were about to risk it all by signing a contract with a man who was seen by many as a dreamer with no track record of business success. His name was Henry Ford.

The venture with Ford was a fantastic success and as Ford's car company grew, it brought the brothers' firm around ten million dollars per year. They eventually began to tire of being dependent on Ford though, and in 1913 decided to start manufacturing entire cars themselves. The first Dodge Brothers car rolled off the production line at the end of 1914. By the end of the decade they were making 145,000 cars per year and were the third bestselling car manufacturer in the country behind only Ford and General Motors.

John and Horace Dodge still owned shares in Ford's business and when he refused to pay out dividends to his stockholders, the brothers successfully sued him for around two million dollars. When Ford decided to buy them out, the brothers received another $12.5 million each. It was around this time that Horace Dodge is said to have told his wife that she could have 'any earthly thing' she wanted. Anna decided she wanted pearls and Horace purchased the pearl necklace, which was reputed to have belonged to Catherine the Great, from Cartier.

The necklace is an indication of the luxurious lifestyle that the couple lived by this point. They had built a mansion called Rose Terrace at Grosse Pointe, Detroit's affluent coastal area. Horace Dodge had commissioned a new 257-foot steam yacht to be named the *Delphine*. They also gave generously to charitable causes. In particular, and perhaps reflecting Anna's musical interests, the Dodges built Orchestra Hall, the home of the Detroit Symphony Orchestra.

As 1920 dawned it was difficult to see how there would be anything other than continued success for the Dodge brothers. By the end of the year, however, they would both be dead. In January, while attending a motor show, they had each taken ill with what was reported as pneumonia arising from influenza. Horace had recovered but John did not. Horace never really got over his brother's death and died in December the same year. The immediate cause of death was reported as haemorrhaging complicated by cirrhosis of the liver. The fact that both Dodge brothers had died in such quick succession led some conspiracy theorists to believe that there was foul play involved but it seems more likely that both their deaths originated in the Spanish Flu pandemic that swept the globe in this period.

The lifestyle that Anna Thomson Dodge was living by the time of her husband's death can be seen in the fact that in 1921 she filed a petition at the Probate Court for a year's living expenses – the sum of half a million dollars. Four years later, Anna and her sister-in-law Matilda sold the Dodge Brothers Motor Car Company to the investment group Dillon Read for the astonishing sum of $146 million. This was at the time the largest cheque ever drawn by an American Bank. Some newspapers then suggested that the former resident of Shepherd's Loan and Peddie Street was the richest woman in the world.

In the process of purchasing a Palm Beach mansion, Anna met her second husband, a former actor turned estate agent named Hugh Dillman. Born Hugh Dillman McGaughey in Ohio in 1885, Dillman had appeared on stage and also briefly in silent movies where his most notable role was in *An Amateur Widow*, a film that concludes with his character marrying a woman who has inherited a lot of money. It was a role that he was to play for real on 8 May 1926 when he married Anna Thomson Dodge at Rose Terrace. Anna gave her age as forty-nine but she was actually fifty-five years old by this point. Even the groom, it appears, was unaware of her real age.

Anna would later say of Dillman: 'Hugh taught me how to have fun with my money.' Their expenditure over the next few years was certainly lavish. The Rose Terrace mansion was demolished and replaced by an even grander model, the *Delphine* was completely refitted after catching fire on the couple's honeymoon, and extravagant parties were held at the Palm Beach mansion with features such as two entire orchestras, a champagne fountain and what became known as Anna's trademark – a carved ice swan filled with beluga caviar. Among those entertained by the Dillmans were the Duke and Duchess of Windsor – the former King Edward VIII and Mrs Simpson.

Despite all the glamour, Anna's later years were to involve a great deal of sadness. The marriage to Dillman did not last and the couple were divorced in 1947 after a lengthy separation. Her sister May, the last of her Dundee family, died the next year. Anna was also to outlive both her children. Delphine died in 1943, suffering from the effects of alcoholism. Anna had at one time given Delphine the Catherine the Great necklace but she had been too frightened to wear it and kept it in a bank vault. Horace junior died twenty years later. Both Anna's offspring had needed to be bailed out financially by their mother over the years and both had multiple marriages.

In her twilight years Anna became more reclusive, hidden away in her bedroom at Rose Terrace where she spent much of her time watching television, often keeping three TV sets going at the one time. She was said to be so devoted to this that guests would only be admitted during the commercial breaks. Just as she had taken years off her age at the time of her marriage to Dillman, now she added them. At the time of her death in 1970, she was reported to be 103 years old, but she was in fact ninety-eight.

Had her family not decided to emigrate, the woman known as Anna Thomson Dodge, who died in a mansion and lived as one of the richest women in the world, could have expected a life working in the jute mills and would have ended her days as she started them in a two-room tenement flat. As it was, as well as her millions, she left behind thousands of possessions and priceless works of art. The contents of her music room at Rose Terrace alone, which she left to the Detroit Institute of Arts, included Gainsborough paintings, a chair reputed to have belonged to Marie Antoinette and a jewel casket that had belonged to Maria Feodorovna, Empress of Russia. Also uncovered among her belongings after her death was a small religiously themed storybook, which, poignantly, still bore on the flyleaf the name and address of a little girl from Peddie Street, Dundee.

The Boy with Two Stomachs

At the end of March 1877 an article appeared in *The New York Times* that mentioned Dundee. Dundee did not often feature prominently in the pages of this publication – so what had happened there for the news to be reported in New York?

A boy with two stomachs, the article said, had recently been 'produced' in Dundee. It continued, 'His inventor has the effrontery to describe him as an improved style of boy.' The author thought this was 'an atrocious example of the very worst type of objectionable inventions'. The standard boy had more than enough in the way of stomach capacity – 'How much jam can be put into one boy has never yet been ascertained.'

The author went on to say that it mattered very little 'whether a Scotch boy has one or two stomachs' because the Scottish diet consisted solely of oatmeal and the occasional haggis. The real problem was that Scottish ideas had a tendency to spread and soon this would be a worldwide problem, leading to famine and other problems. For one thing, a boy with two stomachs would have twice as much colic. The article concluded, 'The simple truth is that the boy of Dundee is an irredeemably vicious invention.' The author called on the authorities to suppress the boy and punish his inventor.

This was surely an early April Fool's Day joke. Dundee's reputation as being a centre of excellence in science and medicine was a long way off in 1877 and genetic engineering was then the stuff of science fiction. Nobody could invent 'a new style of boy'. Any doubt as to the nature of the article could be safely cast aside with its description of the haggis: 'a bird so tough and fishy in flavour that it is never shot for the table south of the Scottish border'. The author had no doubt picked Dundee out at random or as someplace obscure to add to the whimsical nature of the piece. There surely could not be even the smallest grain of truth in this story.

Amazingly, there was. In January 1877, a story was published in the local press stating that a boy with two stomachs had indeed been born in Dundee. He was said to eat 'quite as much as two ordinary children of the same age'. This was picked up and copied unquestioningly by numerous regional newspapers across Britain and beyond. It was, after all, just an amusing oddity – useful for filling up any spare column inches. Perhaps somebody employed in the Dundee press had been having a joke, which threatened to get out of hand as the story began to be taken up by newspapers across the world.

Some specific information was given, which could have lent credence to the tale. The child's father was said to be named Thomas Hood. This would have rung alarm bells to anybody acquainted with Dundee's literary past. Thomas Hood was a well-known poet and humorist who had died in 1845. He had spent some time in Dundee and had friends and relatives in the area. The use of the name was perhaps the best indication yet that the entire story was a hoax. The *Courier* claimed that this Thomas Hood was unemployed and added, 'We are sure all our readers will sympathise with him on account of having to fill one stomach more than was expected.'

However, the Thomas Hood that the papers said was the father of a boy with two stomachs did indeed exist. He was in his early fifties and was currently out of work, having worked previously as mechanic in a factory. He lived in Peter Court in the Cowgate. His second wife, Barbara, had given birth to a son – also named Thomas – in early 1877. The trail from *The New York Times'* incredible story then led back to the sad story of a real boy in Dundee.

Thomas Hood junior was born on 12 January 1877. His mother had been healthy during her pregnancy and had experienced nothing untoward at that time. It was only after his birth that it was noticed that her son had a large growth taking up the whole of the right hand side of the abdomen as well as another smaller one in his groin. The larger growth must have given the appearance of being an extra 'stomach'.

The Victorians had a fascination for the unusual and for what they termed the freakish. Circus sideshows at the time featured people born with additional fingers or toes or those born with extra limbs, among the more outlandish attractions such as mermaids and human/animal hybrids. It is easy to imagine a 'boy with two stomachs' becoming the subject of fascination and gossip among the neighbours in the Cowgate and the story eventually finding its way to the ears of a local journalist. It may even have been the boy's parents who contacted the press. The *Courier* article stated that his father was willing to show the child to 'anyone who wishes to see it'. This followed on from a sentence that described the family's financial hardships. It seems likely that the near-destitute family would be charging some kind of admission fee.

Events then took a tragic turn. Less than two weeks after the birth of his son, Thomas Hood senior was paralysed by a stroke. He died on 24 January. His wife Barbara was then left in what one newspaper report called 'destitute circumstances'. As well as young Thomas, she had two other young children to bring up – her daughters Jessie and Agnes. She would undoubtedly have also had to contend with gossip and curiosity about young Thomas wherever she went. In addition, this poor, illiterate mill worker now found herself in the company of learned medical men eager to learn about her son's condition.

Thomas was attended by various doctors – none of whom, of course, diagnosed an extra stomach. Doctor McLagan saw him when he was three months old. McLagan later noted 'a general bulging of the right side of the abdomen, giving one the impression that the muscular walls of that side are deficient. It is certainly not a second stomach, and, so far as I can learn, no medical man ever said that it was so.'

Thomas was also taken to Edinburgh where he was seen by Professor Annandale. Annandale diagnosed a tumour of the abdominal wall. He wanted to make an exploratory incision to see if the tumour could be safely removed in an operation but Mrs Hood persistently refused to give the necessary permission.

Meanwhile young Thomas had passed his first birthday developing normally in all other respects with a healthy appetite and no pain from his 'extra stomach'. He was also said to be running about freely and the tumour did not affect his digestive system.

From the beginning of October 1878, though, his health began to decline and the tumours became inflamed. By the time Dr Anderson was called in, in mid-October, Thomas was described as looking emaciated. There was little the doctor could do. Poultices were applied to the tumours and attempts were made to keep the child's strength up, but in vain. Thomas Hood, 'the boy with two stomachs', died on 9 December 1878. Dr Anderson carried out a post-mortem, which concluded that the larger tumour – said at that point to be the size of a large coconut – would not have been able to be safely removed by an operation during the boy's lifetime.

So much had been written about this boy during his short life, much of it far-fetched. A New Zealand newspaper confidently said that he had been declared by 'the unanimous opinion of the Dundee doctors to be endowed by nature with two stomachs' and that he required 'the nutriment of two ordinary children'. The stomachs were said to be 'packed one over the other like the two kernels of a Philippine nut'. The *Belfast Telegraph* reported that the child's appetite was 'corresponding to its digestive powers'. A correspondent to a London newspaper was said to have joked that with prices almost certainly rising because of war in Europe, now was an unfortunate time to have a child with two stomachs.

Then, as now, though, stories drift away from the headlines and it is unlikely that any of those fascinated or appalled, or any of those who joked or satirised, gave a thought to or were even aware of the grieving mother left in Dundee.

Heir Apparent

Rose Ann's Story

In the early hours of 29 April 1904, Rose Ann McAvan and her husband Jimmy were keeping a vigil in the Dundee Royal Infirmary. Rose Ann knew that her mother – Margaret Morris – did not have long to live. Though the dying woman's voice did not have the power it once had, by leaning over the bed they could make out what she was saying. At one point, as Jimmy leaned over to hear her, Margaret told a story that she claimed never to have told anyone before – something that would challenge everything Jimmy and Rose Ann thought they knew about the Morris family.

The old woman's story concerned Rose Ann's brother Thomas Patrick, known as Tommy. He was not, as Rose Ann had always supposed, her real brother. He was the son of one Mary Ellen Devine and a John G. Wendel. On hearing this story, Rose Ann concluded that her mother's condition had made her delirious. The couple stayed by Margaret's bedside until she died at just after 3am.

When the McAvans were cleaning Margaret's room after her death, they found a small tin box filled with letters and other papers. Among these was a letter from John G. Wendel dated 1897. Rose Ann read the letter out loud (as her husband could not read). In the letter Wendel stated that he intended to visit sometime in May or June of that year and that he hoped that 'son Thomas P.' was behaving himself. Jimmy McAvan remembered on hearing this that

John G. Wendel was the exact name his mother-in-law had mentioned on her deathbed.

Twenty-seven years later, in 1931, another woman lay dying. This woman lived far away from Dundee in New York City. She was eighty-one years old and her name was Ella Virginia von Echtzel Wendel. She lived in an old house that had hardly been altered since it was built in 1854. Though the house was located in downtown Manhattan it did not have a telephone or electricity. An improvement in the bathroom facilities was the only sign of encroaching modernity that a visitor might have noticed – not that there were many visitors. Ella Wendel was the last of her family, as her five sisters and one brother had all predeceased her. She had no children and neither had any of her siblings, that is unless her brother John G. Wendel was indeed the father of Thomas Patrick Morris from Dundee. If the story was true, Thomas Patrick Morris would be Ella Wendel's nephew and thus her heir. An unexpected windfall could be heading his way and quite a substantial windfall, in fact. Ella Wendel's estate was valued in the region of thirty million dollars.

The Wendels were an eccentric family of German ancestry who had made their fortune in real estate. Following the death of their father John D. Wendel in 1859, John G. had ruled over his sisters with an iron hand. So determined was he to maintain the family fortune that he refused to sell (or indeed repair) any of their properties no matter how much their value increased. Famously, the yard in which Ella Wendel's dog exercised was valued at $1,410,000. Another property – a $550,000 garage at the corner of Broadway and Fiftieth Street – was left empty for years as Wendel simply did not want it leased for any other purpose. He also disapproved of tall buildings, so even in the heart of Manhattan none of the Wendel Properties went above six stories. It seems that John G. Wendel hated change of any kind. This could work to the advantage of some tenants who he saw as reliable. They would see their leases renewed and higher rival offers turned down.

Wendel also forbade any of his sisters to marry in case anyone else should be entitled to claim a share of the wealth. Only one of the sisters – Rebecca

– ever defied his wishes and married in middle age. This took real courage as two other sisters who rebelled at times – Augusta and Georgiana – had been committed to insane asylums. However, over time, Wendel's recipe for maintaining the family fortune was to be its undoing, as one by one the sisters died with no heirs. Wendel himself died in 1914, leaving only two childless sisters, Rebecca and Ella. Rebecca died in 1930, leaving Ella as the last of the Wendel line. When she passed away, the fortune would be split among distant relatives and charities, unless the rightful heir was indeed the thin, fifty-two-year-old, angina-suffering house painter from Dundee, Thomas Patrick Morris.

Not surprisingly there had been a rush of claimants to the Wendel fortune after Ella Wendel's death. Long lost 'relatives' – around 2000 of them in all – had emerged from the woodwork on a daily basis. Of these, only twenty-seven were seriously considered by the court, and of this remaining twenty-seven, it was Thomas Patrick Morris who claimed the closest relationship to the Wendels. If his claim was successful the Wendel fortune would be his alone.

On 26 July 1932 then, bearing, according to *The New York Times*, 'a striking facial resemblance to the surviving photographs of John Wendel', Thomas Patrick Morris took the witness seat at the special court set aside for such disputes, the Surrogate Court in Chambers Street, Manhattan. Under the guidance of his attorney Raymond L. Wise and the watchful eye of the presiding official Surrogate James A. Foley, Morris began to tell his story.

It started in 1885, he told the court, when he was five years old. It was then that John Wendel first visited the home of the couple that Morris now referred to as his foster parents at John Street Dundee. Morris recalled, 'He would pick me up and hug and kiss me and let me play on his knee. He told me to call him Papa Wendel, and I did.'

Morris left school at the age of fourteen and worked in a jute mill and in the shipyards. He then spent some time at sea. Wendel's visits, he claimed, continued almost every year and always in the summer, breaking off only when Morris left home to join the army.

In 1901, when Morris was twenty-one years old and back staying with his adoptive family, John Wendel visited again. The family was by then living in Dallfield Walk, just off the Hilltown. On this occasion, John G. Wendel and Thomas Patrick Morris went for a walk. While they were out, Wendel gave Morris a watch and chain and a book wrapped up in paper, telling him to read it but never to show it to anybody. When he arrived home Morris unwrapped the book. It was a copy of a book called *The Blockade of Phalsburg* but it was not the printed content of the book that engaged his interest. In the front flyleaf of the book was a letter:

March 1, 1901

My Dear Son,

I am writing this to clear up any doubt you may have in your mind as to your parentage. I, John G. Wendel of 442 Fifth Avenue N.Y. City and Mary Ellen Devine of Edinburgh, Scotland were married at Castle Garden, June 11, 1876, promising to marry her later on in the Church of her faith, Roman Catholic. My family being Methodist, I refused to carry it through. I was kept busy through the death of your grandfather, straightening out matters and in the latter part of May 1879, your mother and I quarrelled, and being with child fled to friends – a Mr and Mrs Morris living at 4 John Street, Dundee, Scotland. I followed and tried to make a reconciliation but allowed religious scruples to stand in the way.

You were born on 3 January 1880. Your mother still refusing to be reconciled, about two weeks after your birth disappeared leaving you in bed when our friend was out shopping. Fearing the scandal and that the news might drift back to my family in the States, I refused to report it. I arranged with our friends to register your birth as their own and care for you, living in hopes that your mother would return. My hopes were in vain. You were registered as Thomas Patrick Morris – the first two names the wish of your mother whom you dearly loved.

The foregoing statement is true,
So help me God,
Your Loving father,

John G. Wendel

At the back of the book was an even more remarkable document:

<u>WILL</u>

March 1, 1901

I, John G. Wendel of the City of New York and County of Kings and State of New York declare that owing to my sisters, especially Mary and Ella's objections and refusal to recognise my son by a secret marriage and their threats to publicly expose me and fearing the destruction of my will, I take this unique way to safeguard my son's interest, I hereby make publish and declare this to be my last Will, thereby revoking all former Wills made by me.

1. I direct that all my just debts are paid.

2. All of my estate real, personal and mixed of whatsoever kind and wheresoever situated, I give, devise and bequeath to my son, Thomas Patrick Morris Wendel.

3. I request Charles G. Koss family lawyer to be our son's advisor in the management of the estate.

In witness whereof, I have hereunto set my hand and seal this 1st day of March 1901.

Signed John G. Wendel, 442 Fifth Ave., New York

Witnessed by – Michael Lynch, 442 Fifth Ave., New York City
Charles Dietoch, Libby Hotel, New York City
Richard Lundy, 442 Fifth Ave., New York City

After the book was produced in evidence, Morris continued with his story, explaining how he came to New York in 1906 working in the engine room of a boat called the *Caledonia*. Some time after this, he met Wendel by chance in City Hall Park, New York. After this they began to see each other on a regular basis. In early March 1907, Wendel attempted to introduce Morris to his Aunt Ella but their visit to her house had been brief and unsuccessful. There had been an argument between the siblings over Thomas Patrick. 'Get you and your brat out of here!' had been the parting shot from Ella Wendel as Morris recalled it. After this, he said, he saw his father only once more in Clifton, Arizona, where Morris was working in a copper mine.

Morris was subjected to a ruthless cross-examination by John M. Harlan, the Counsel for the Wendel Estate. 'Would it surprise you,' he asked Morris, 'to know that John G. Wendel did not leave New York between 1879 and 1914, that during July 1901 he signed cheques here in New York and wrote letters to his employees from Quogue, Long Island – would it surprise you to know that?'

'Yes it would,' said Morris.

'If I tell you that Mr Wendel was in New York during the part of July you say you saw him in Scotland, does that change your recollection about the date?'

'That's the best of my recollection.'

'And if I tell you that on February 16, 1907, Miss Ella Wendel and her sisters set sail for Europe and were gone until July, does that change your testimony about the dates?'

'No, sir.'

Things looked bad for Morris's claim in the light of this. It is unlikely, though, that Wendel would have left a record of visits to a secret son and may have even gone out of his way to cover them up by postdating letters and cheques. As for the visit to the Wendel Mansion, Morris might have simply been mistaken about the date.

Several witnesses then came forward whose testimony added weight to Morris's case.

Helen Sanders was the great-niece of Michael Lynch who was one of the witnesses on the will. She stated that the signature in the book looked to her like that of her great uncle. In addition, she told the court how her uncle, who had become deeply religious in his later years, had once said to her, 'Helen, never be ashamed of being a Catholic. John G. Wendel was ashamed of his wife and child because they were Catholics. He lost his wife and son because they were Catholics.'

Charles Edgar was a stationer who had served John Wendel as a customer for more than twenty-five years. He recalled a conversation they had had around 1901. Edgar had made a remark to the effect that it was a good thing that Wendel was a bachelor with all the money he had. 'A bachelor! Huh!' came the reply. 'You ought to see my big boy.'

Some years later, Edgar had enquired after the 'big boy'.

'The big boy is alright,' Wendel had replied, 'but I can't bring that big boy to my house without being insulted by my sisters.'

Rose Camp and Thomas Mack were former employees of the Wendels who both testified as to Morris's resemblance to John G. Wendel.

Mrs Newbold Morris of Lennox, Massachusetts, was a leading socialite and the daughter of a close friend of Wendel's. She described the resemblance as 'very marked'.

Morris was pressed as to why he had waited so long before making his claim. John Wendel had died in 1914. Why had he not come forward then? He stated that he was unaware of the deaths of any of the other family members. It was only when he saw a story about the death of Ella Wendel among a bundle of old newspapers he was clearing out that he read of the death of John G. Wendel. This story also gave him the address of the Wendels' attorney to whom he could make his claim. He said that he pondered the situation and, after about a week, decided to go and see the attorney, Mr Koss.

'Why did you wait – why did you ponder, as you call it, for a full week before you went to see Mr. Koss?' asked Mr Harlan.

'Because,' Morris replied, 'I thought I might be an illegitimate son.'

William Lopez Diaz, a secretary who had been employed by the Wendel family since 1889, now gave evidence for the Wendel Estate. Numerous cancelled cheques and cheque stubs were produced, purporting to prove that Wendel had been in New York when Morris said that he had been in Dundee.

Morris's attorney Raymond L. Wise made the point to Mr Diaz that these cheques could have been made out for the payment of bills months before they became due.

Diaz replied, 'That could be true, but it goes against the grain to admit it.'

'You are a legatee under the will of Miss Ella Wendel, aren't you, Mr Diaz?' asked Wise.

'Yes.'

'And is that why it goes against the grain to admit it?'

'Yes.'

Diaz then admitted that Wendel's writing could vary but, under questioning from Mr Harlan, denied that the writing in the will or the letter in the book that Morris had presented was that of John G. Wendel.

At this point the presiding officer, Surrogate Foley, interjected, 'What about the signature? Is that Mr Wendel's signature?'

'It's familiar,' Diaz replied to much excitement from the courtroom. 'There's something about that signature that compels a second look.'

Pressed by Mr Harlan, however, he said that the signature was not that of John G. Wendel.

Surrogate Foley had decided that the case could not be properly assessed without hearing evidence elsewhere. A statement was taken from Morris's elder. brother Bernard, an Army pensioner, who at that point lived in Manchester, England. Bernard Morris described how Tommy (as they had always known him) had been brought up in the family and that they had always believed him to be their full brother. He did recall an argument between Tommy and his father where his father had said, after Tommy had run from the house, 'What can you expect? He is no son of mine.'

Bernard said that the family received packets of money from America about twice a year and that he also recalled the visits of a 'foreign-looking' man who 'displayed unusual affection' towards Tommy. The first he had heard of Tommy's true parentage had been after his mother's funeral when Rose Ann had told her story.

The scene then shifted to Dundee, to the offices of the American Consulate in Albert Square where the session was presided over by Vice Consul Julian K. Smedburg acting on behalf of Surrogate Foley. The first witness was James McAvan, the brother-in-law of Thomas Patrick Morris who recounted his version of the events surrounding the death of his mother-in-law in the Dundee Royal Infirmary in 1904 and the uncovering of the letter from John G. Wendel. He also told how his late father-in-law Peter Morris, a cobbler, had possessed a small wooden box, which had later come into the possession of McAvan's wife Rose Ann. Last Hogmanay, they had found in the brown paper lining of the box a Marriage Certificate between Mary Ellen Devine, Edinburgh, Scotland, and John G. Wendel. This had been sent to the lawyers in New York. The certificate read:

This certifies that John G. Wendel of New York City and Mary Ellen Devine of Edinburgh, Scotland were united by me in the bonds of Holy Matrimony at Castle Garden on 11th day of June in the year of Our Lord 1876. Signed, James F. Calhoun D.D., pastor of Castle Green N.Y. in the presence of William C. Swigert and Louise Schmidt.

The hearing then took evidence from the Right Reverend Monsignor John Turner of St Andrew's Roman Catholic Cathedral. Seventy-nine-year-old Monsignor Turner, a native of Banffshire, was a well-respected priest who had been at the Cathedral for many years and knew the Morris family. It was he who had conducted the McAvans' wedding. He identified the baptismal certificate of Thomas Patrick, which stated that he was the lawful son of Mr and Mrs Morris. Monsignor Turner said that he had visited Margaret Morris but she had never given a hint or mentioned that

Thomas Patrick was not her lawful son. He had also helped Thomas Patrick get a job on a ship when he was unemployed but said that no mention had ever been made to him of the name Wendel, a strange visitor from America, a book or a will.

The next witness would surely be more favourable to the Morris case. She was Mary McLean of Duke Street, Leith – Morris's elder sister. Mary McLean knew all about the kind of dispute that might have led John G. Wendel to become estranged from Mary Ellen Devine. Mary had left home at the age of fourteen in a dispute with her parents over a boyfriend who was a Protestant. She had subsequently married this boyfriend, George McLean, against her parents' wishes in a Church of Scotland ceremony at the City Churches in 1887. McLean was a ship's steward and the couple had later moved to Leith. Mary had been a widow since 1895. Her father had moved to Leith to live with her in the period before his death in 1912. During that time her father had not told her anything concerning her family history. Any enquiry would be greeted with a call to 'mind her own business'.

She did not recall either her father bringing papers or a box from Dundee after his wife's funeral but admitted that it was quite possible he had made another trip to Dundee unknown to her. In this case, she agreed not only would her father not have told her about anything he had brought back but he would also have resented any enquiry being made.

Morris's other sister Rose Ann McAvan reiterated the story of her mother's dying statement. She was also quizzed about the box belonging to her father in which the marriage certificate had been found. She had not, in the seventeen years the box was in her possession, looked into the box to see if there was anything that she could throw away. After her mother's death, her father had not asked for the box nor looked into it. Rose Ann simply kept the box as a keepsake but she did not consider it important in any way.

John M. Harlan, the counsel for the Wendel Estate, had travelled from New York to Dundee for the session. He asked Rose Ann McAvan about what she had described as 'periods of flushness' that her family had enjoyed between 1888 and 1901. During these times, she claimed, there was something extra in the house – plenty of food, extra dainties, extra clothes.

'What else was there?' Harlan asked her.

'My father went on the beer,' came the reply to much laughter in the temporary courtroom.

Rose Ann said that these 'periods of flushness' usually happened in May or June and denied that she was saying this because she had read in the newspapers that her brother had said that this was when Wendel usually visited. She recalled the visits herself, she said, because Wendel stood out among any other visitors to her father, as he was not Scottish.

If the Morris family did indeed enjoy 'periods of flushness' then they did not share much of the proceeds with their landlords. Evidence was brought forward of various rent arrears at properties rented by the Morris family. Only one of these, though, was prior to 1901 when Rose Ann said that the 'flushness' ended and the landlord agreed that being in arrears did not mean that the tenant did not have the ability to pay.

Back in New York, Thomas Patrick Morris once more took the stand. His counsel, Raymond L. Wise, led him through a series of birth, marriage and death certificates to refresh his memory of the various dates he had given at the earlier hearing and now Morris changed his mind. It was 1907 when he met Wendel in the City Hall Park. It was 1902 and not 1901 when Wendel presented him with the book with the will inside. Was this the first real sign of a crack in the edifice of Morris's version of events or just a correction in the detail of his memories of the events of more than a quarter of a century earlier?

Events took a surreal twist when a bust of John G. Wendel made by the sculptor Julian Bowes was brought into the courtroom. Morris was made to stand alongside the bust. Much hilarity followed when it transpired that the bust's bowler hat, spectacles and moustache were all detachable – so much so that Surrogate Foley had to bang his gavel for order.

After the comic appearance of the bust with the detachable accessories, a deadly serious and decisive piece of evidence was now to be presented. Elbridge W. Stein was an examiner of questioned documents. He had been asked by the counsel for the Wendel Estate to examine the 1876 Marriage Certificate between John G. Wendel and Mary Ellen Devine. The certificate was of a type included in a large family Bible. The head of the firm that published these, William K. Holman, also gave evidence. Fourteen large Bibles printed between the years 1873 and 1923 were presented; each one contained a marriage certificate.

Stein demonstrated that a microscopic examination of the certificates showed how the metal plate used to print them deteriorated over the years. Tiny flaws in the shape of the letters worsened over time and new flaws appeared. He showed that every flaw that was contained in a 1913 Marriage Certificate was present in the certificate presented in evidence for Morris and furthermore the Morris Certificate contained imperfections present in a 1923 certificate that were not present in the one printed in 1913. It was clear that the Wendel/Devine Marriage Certificate, which purported to be from 1876, was, in fact, printed between 1913 and 1923. It was a devastating blow to Morris's case and would bring the whole house of cards he had constructed tumbling down. Morris's attorney, Raymond L. Wise, knew when he was beaten and accepted that the date of the certificate had been established.

Surrogate Foley's conclusions were straight and to the point: 'that Morris was not the legitimate son of John G. Wendel; that no marriage ever took place between John G. Wendel and Mary Ellen Devine; that Thomas Patrick Morris was not the nephew of Ella Wendel and therefore not the next of kin.' Foley also criticised Morris for his 'indecent presentation of the claim' and said he would ask the Public Prosecutor to investigate.

Thomas Patrick Morris was arrested pending a trial for fraud. The would-be multi-millionaire could not afford bail, which was set at $10,000. He was indicted for fraud and conspiracy in front of Judge Freschi on 21 December 1932. Also indicted in their absence were his sister Rose

McAvan, her husband James and an unknown fourth collaborator given the name John Doe.

The McAvans could not be forced to go to the United States, as they were not fugitives. At home in Mid Kirk Style, Dundee, they stuck to their story. Not surprisingly, Mr McAvan told a reporter that he had no intention at present of going to America to answer any charge. The following June, Thomas Patrick Morris alone was sentenced to 'not more than three years imprisonment'.

A case like that of Thomas Patrick Morris would be unlikely to occur today due to the advances in forensic techniques – not least DNA testing – since 1932. It was, nevertheless, the forensic examination of the documents that eventually did bring the Morris case crashing down.

The greatest mysteries remain, though. How did a combination of what *Time* magazine called a 'dull-witted housepainter', his mill worker sister and her illiterate husband get to the stage where their case was seriously examined by a New York Court? Did they receive help from the mysterious John Doe? Was it he who wrote the letters and will and forged the marriage certificate? If so, was this someone with inside knowledge of John G. Wendel who could at least make an attempt of forging his signature, and who knew his addresses and who was likely to be a witness on the will? Or would careful reading of the newspapers provide all this information? Did John Doe even exist – perhaps Morris was not as 'dull-witted' as he appeared.

What about all the witnesses who came forward swearing that Morris resembled Wendel? Perhaps they did see some resemblance – or were they simply mistaken? Not so easily explained away are those who swore that Wendel told them he had a son, such as the stationer Charles Edgar or Annie Gordon, a nurse who claimed that Wendel had confided in her when he was very ill with pneumonia. Here, a letter produced in evidence may provide a clue. The letter was written by Morris to James Poole who worked in the Arizona Copper Company and contained the lines 'if I am successful in this case, no friend of mine will be in need. But here's the rub. I've got to find someone who saw us together in Arizona or elsewhere.' This letter could be interpreted as either just a friendly letter explaining Morris's current predicament or as offering a financial inducement to 'remember'. Perhaps some witnesses had hoped there might be such an inducement even without having received a letter or having had any contact with Morris.

Of course, it could be that these witnesses were telling the truth and Wendel did have a son. This would not mean that the son was necessarily Morris, but is there a possibility that Morris was Wendel's son, that the forged certificate was just an attempt to provide concrete evidence that backfired? One person could certainly answer that – Mary Ellen Devine, the supposed mother of Thomas Patrick Morris, 'whose name', Surrogate Foley said, 'floats like a wraith, almost a ghost through the whole story'. Rumours circulated about her at the time of the original hearing – she had died some years earlier; she was in Ireland; she was seventy-two years old and living in London. All attempts to find her at the time, or to find evidence of her since, have failed. The conclusion must be drawn that she never existed.

Even Thomas Patrick Morris gave up on her. Throughout his time in prison and after his release, he maintained that Wendel was his father. His pleas got more and more desperate. There was even a claim that he was in fact the product of an incestuous relationship between John G. Wendel and his sister Mary. (It is difficult to see how such a child, if it existed, would end up in the tenement home of a Dundee shoemaker and his wife.) In 1935, he insisted that new evidence was coming from Germany from the secret daughter of Georgiana Wendel, but Morris must have known that he was clutching at straws.

The Wendel millions did not come to Thomas Patrick Morris. There may be descendants of the Morrises and McAvans walking around Dundee today but they are unlikely to be multi-millionaires. The money was eventually distributed between distant relatives and the charities specified in Ella Wendel's will. 'This is either a monstrous hoax or else it is absolutely true,' Surrogate Foley had said at the beginning of the initial hearing. His verdict and the verdict of history are clear.

5
Heroes

The people who are regarded as heroes in any particular city are usually easy to spot. Admiral Nelson, for example, looks down on London from his column in Trafalgar Square while, from a high plinth, Daniel O'Connell guards the street that bears his name in Dublin. A wander around central Dundee, however, might leave a visitor puzzled in this regard. Besides the statues in Albert Square (more on those later), there is a statue of Admiral Adam Duncan, a statue of a dragon and likenesses of the DC Thomson comic characters Desperate Dan and Minnie the Minx.

Duncan is certainly the most conventional hero of these. The victor of an important naval battle, he had to wait for around 200 years to be commemorated in his birthplace. It could be argued that the dragon, who features in a centuries-old local legend, had an even longer wait. In any case, it is not the hero of that tale who is commemorated. Dundee has not immortalised Martin, the man who slew the dragon in the story, but instead the maiden-devouring villain of the piece. This is presumably because the dragon made for a more interesting artwork than the man. Similarly, it is not the reclusive press baron David Coupar Thomson himself who is shown striding through the High Street, but rather it is left to the fictitious but more instantly recognisable characters of Desperate Dan and Minnie the Minx to mark the contribution of DC Thomson and Company to the city over many years.

Proposals for other statues in Dundee, from the news vendor and local worthy Tommy Small to the former city MP Winston Churchill, have run into controversy. Dundonians, perhaps, find it easier to knock people off of their pedestals than place them onto them. The following stories look at some very different and largely unrecognised Dundee heroes.

For Valour

Fishing bodies out of the water was an occupational hazard for Dundee Harbour Police in the nineteenth century. The river was not then, as it is today, separated from the city by a hotchpotch of carriageways and the approaches to the Tay Road Bridge, but rather it swept up into the heart of the town, tamed only by the system of docks, harbours and landfill that had grown up over the centuries. The docks and the streets that led down to them teemed with life and activity. All roads seemed to lead to the water, the life-blood of a busy seaport that had built much of its prosperity on whaling ships and imported jute. The routes to the bottom of the water were fewer – the main ones being suicide and accidental (often alcohol assisted) drowning.

At around nine o'clock in the morning of Friday, 10 January 1868, a thirty-seven-year-old police constable by the name of Sutherland Bremner spotted a body floating in the River Tay to the east of the Craig Harbour. When the body was recovered, Constable Bremner, together with Sergeant William Gordon, arranged to have it transferred to the mortuary. It was not difficult to determine the identity of the deceased. He had few personal effects in his pockets – a fourpenny coin, a penny and knife – but it was obvious that this was the body of a soldier as there were medals pinned to the breast of his jacket. One of these medals had the name Pte Peter Grant inscribed on the suspension bar. The reverse of the medal had the date 16 November 1857. The other side had only two words: 'For Valour'. The dead man was wearing a Victoria Cross.

From the time the award was instituted in January 1856 to the present day, there has never been a single day that produced as many Victoria Crosses as 16 November 1857 when twenty-four of the medals were awarded. The place was Lucknow, India, at the time of what came to be known as the Indian Mutiny but which many now see as India's First War of Independence.

The reasons why a revolt took place among the Sepoys (the native Indian soldiers of the East India Company) were many and complex. In general terms, though, many Indians had come to feel that their religious beliefs and customs were increasingly under threat by the actions of the East India Company. The incident that was traditionally seen as starting the rebellion involved – of all things – a new musket cartridge. The cartridges were covered in tallow made from beef and pork fat, which had to be bitten open. This managed to deeply offend both Hindus and Muslims at the same time and unite them against the colonial power. The incident had, no doubt, merely served as a catalyst to bring pre-existing tensions to the surface. The rebellion, though not universally supported, quickly spread throughout large parts of India.

In Lucknow, the outnumbered forces of the East India Company took refuge in the fortified residency of the British Commissioner. There, they were besieged by the rebels for almost ninety days before what became known as the First Relief of Lucknow when British troops under Sir John Outram fought their way through to the residency. Unfortunately, given the number of wounded and non-combatants, evacuation of the residency proved impractical and Outram's troops had to remain with the survivors of the siege. A second Relief of Lucknow would be needed.

Private Peter Grant was among Sir Colin Campbell's force that arrived at Lucknow to relieve the residency for a second time. Blocking their path were several heavily defended and fortified obstacles, the first of which was the Secundra Bagh – a villa with a walled garden. On the morning of 16 November, Campbell's gunners managed to knock a small hole in the Secundra Bagh wall. Led by Colonel John Ewart, the men from the

93rd Highland Regiment including Peter Grant and the Sikhs of the 4th Punjabi Infantry advanced to the sound of the bagpipes. During the ensuing attack it is estimated that 2000 Sepoy rebels were killed. The ground was said to have run red with their blood.

Inside the main building of the Secundra Bagh, Colonel Ewart spotted, through an open doorway, an enemy standard leaning against a wall. He could see too that there were at least two armed rebels inside the room but he was determined to capture the flag. Ewart had one eye on the history books. A Sergeant Charles Ewart had famously captured the standard of the French 45th Regiment at the Battle of Waterloo and now Colonel John Ewart was keen do the same. He admitted as much in his memoirs:

A namesake of my own had captured a Colour at the battle of Waterloo. He was a sergeant in the Scots Greys, and was given a commission. Having made up my mind to get this one, I now prepared for a final effort; so going back a few yards, I took a short run; and guarding my head as best I could with my sword, dashed through the doorway. They luckily missed me with their tulwars [swords]; and after killing them both, I seized the Colour, which was heavy, and had a crimson case; having time to observe that my two antagonists were apparently native officers of some sort, being dressed, as far as I could make out, in blue, with gold sword-belts.

Once outside Ewart was again thinking of posterity: 'On emerging from the room, I considered what would be the best thing to do with the Colour; and the thought suddenly occurred to me that if I could take it to Sir Colin Campbell I should get the Victoria Cross.'

Ewart does not mention the incident that followed his capture of the colour and where Peter Grant earned *his* Victoria Cross – probably saving Ewart's life in the process. Keen to recapture the colour and some of their honour, some of the rebels attempted to follow Ewart. Grant picked up one of their own swords and single-handedly killed five of Ewart's pursuers.

If Ewart was not aware of Grant's bravery, then his comrades certainly were. In an unusual outbreak of democracy in the Victorian army, a clause in the Warrant that instituted the Victoria Cross provided for the award of the medals by ballot where a whole body of men performed an act of outstanding gallantry. Five Victoria Crosses were awarded to members of Grant's Regiment – one elected by the officers, one by the NCOs and three by the 'private soldiers of the regiment'. One from this last category went to Peter Grant.

Peter Grant was invested with his Victoria Cross by Major General Garrett at Umbeyla, Peshawar, India, on 6 December 1859 – the summit of a military career that had also seen service in the Crimean War earlier in that decade. As a holder of the Victoria Cross, he was now entitled to a £10 per year allowance.

Eight years later, Grant was back in Scotland, stationed in Aberdeen, but had travelled to Dundee while on leave. On Friday, 27 December 1867, he was seen leaving Wheatley's Public House in the Overgate. There was not another reported sighting of him until Constable Bremner spotted his body floating in the Tay.

Little is known of Grant's background. He was around forty-one years old and had never married. Both his parents had predeceased him. Some sources list him as being of Irish origin. He was buried in the Eastern Cemetery, Dundee, in common ground.

Victoria Crosses have, of course, become highly collectable items and while many remain as family heirlooms, some form part of collections in public or regimental museums and yet others have been sold to private collectors. While replicas have been made, it does not appear that Private Grant's original medal has ever been auctioned. Sometimes such a medal will turn up eventually when someone uncovers it and realises its true worth. It may be, though, that Grant's Victoria Cross was buried with him and that it too lies in a pauper's grave.

That a holder of the nation's highest award for gallantry should be placed in a lowly common grave in Dundee should surely be considered a scandal but when Grant's coffin was lowered he was not, in fact, the first holder of the Victoria Cross to be buried in such a grave in the Eastern Necropolis.

Thomas Beach was a native of Dundee who had joined the 92nd Regiment of Foot in April 1840 at the age of sixteen. Initially stationed at Fort George, he was later to be posted to the West Indies and the Greek Islands as well as Gibraltar. His father had also been in the army and it may have been that he was expected to follow a similar career. Certainly, he does not seem to have settled easily in to military life. His name was entered in the Regimental Defaulters Book some twenty-one times and he faced two courts-martial. This does not sound like the record of a man who would go on to win the Victoria Cross but his misdemeanours were largely confined to his younger days. In later years his behaviour improved and he earned two good-conduct badges.

Beach's regiment was not involved in the Crimean War, being stationed in Gibraltar in 1854 when the war against Russia broke out. However, several hundred soldiers were seconded to other units. Among those who volunteered was Private Beach who was attached to the 55th (Border) Regiment. Beach saw action in three of the most famous incidents of the conflict – the Battle of Alma, the Battle of Inkerman and the Siege of Sevastopol.

It was at the Battle of Inkerman on 5 November 1854 that Beach earned his Victoria Cross. Just as Private Grant had done, Beach demonstrated his heroism in coming to the aid of an officer. He was on piquet duty, positioned some way forward of the main lines to warn of any enemy advance. Here he came upon several Russians who were robbing Lieutenant-Colonel George Carpenter of the 41st (Welsh) Regiment, as he lay wounded on the ground. Despite the odds being so heavily stacked against him, Beach decided to attack the Russians and killed two of them. He stayed with the wounded man until some of his comrades from the 41st arrived. Carpenter's honour may have been saved but unfortunately his life was not as he later died of his wounds. He is buried at Inkerman.

The Victoria Cross was not instituted until January 1856 but was made retrospective to recognise the bravery of those involved in the Crimean War. The first investiture of the Victoria Cross was made by Queen Victoria herself in Hyde Park, London, on Friday, 26 June 1857. Thomas Beach was not among the sixty-two recipients on that occasion. At the end of March, he had rejoined his own regiment in Gibraltar and received his medal there.

Beach left the army in June 1863 and returned to Dundee. He followed in his father's footsteps once more and got a job as a railway labourer. After spending most of his life in the army, he must have been disorientated to some extent. Re-adjustment to civilian life after a long time in the armed forces is difficult for many people even in the twenty-first century with all the support services that are in place. It is estimated, for example, that there are currently over 1000 ex-Service homeless in London alone on any given night. It can readily be imagined how much worse this situation was in Thomas Beach's time.

It is impossible to know what drove Beach to seek solace in alcohol but the sudden loss of the whole military framework of his life must surely have been a factor. He died in the Dundee Royal Infirmary from the effects of his alcoholism in the early hours of 24 August 1864, less than a year after his discharge from the army. At the time of his death, his usual residence was noted as being Edinburgh. Like Peter Grant, Beach was in his forties and unmarried.

Thomas Beach's Victoria Cross now forms part of a medal collection at The Sheesh Mahal or the 'Palace of Mirrors' in Punjab. The collection was assembled by Sir Bhupinder Singh, Maharaja of Patiala in the 1920s. Also in the collection is the Victoria Cross of Lance Corporal John Dunley who won his medal at the Secundra Bagh in Lucknow at the same time as Peter Grant. Attached to this medal is a musket ball that was removed from Dunley's knee.

There is a brass plaque commemorating Lieutenant-Colonel George Carpenter in the Royal Garrison Church, Portsmouth. There is a memorial to Colonel John Ewart in St Giles Cathedral, Edinburgh. Until 2003,

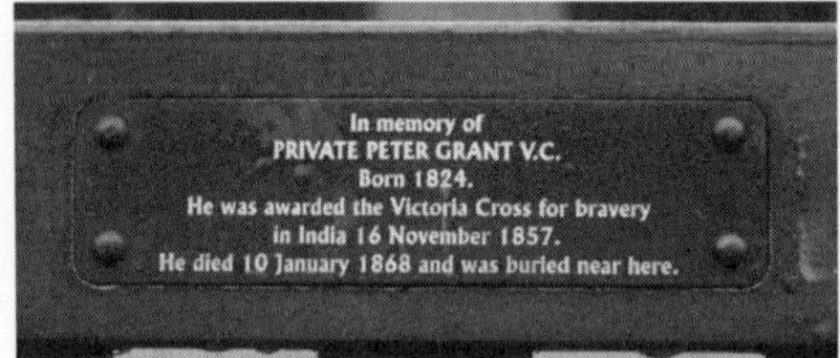

Top: Bench commemorating Private Peter Grant *Lower left*: Private Peter Grant's plaque
Lower right: Private Thomas Beach's plaque

however, there was no memorial to either of the men who risked their lives protecting them. Following the mention of the two men on an Internet message board, the City of Dundee branch of the Royal British Legion of Scotland decided to raise funds to erect a permanent memorial to them. It was not possible to place a memorial on the common ground in the Eastern Cemetery where they are buried. The common ground was in effect a number of mass graves and it is not always possible to tell where an individual is located. It was decided therefore that a bench with a plaque to the two men should be placed nearby. The money raised, however, was sufficient for two benches, which were placed on the edge of the poor ground, looking over the Tay.

Over 100 people, including representatives of the successor regiments of those to which Grant and Beach belonged, attended a service of dedication. Deputy Lord Provost Charles Farquhar, who attended the service, summed up the situation aptly: 'They got the highest honour that could be bestowed on any soldier and it's the least we can do to say thanks and to pay our respects. Unmarked graves are not befitting to them.'

A Hero of the Skies

On 23 February 1942, high over the North Sea, the four-man crew of the Beaufort had set course for Leuchars. The difficult part was over, their offensive patrol of the Norwegian coast was completed and they were heading back to their base. They could just about begin to relax. Suddenly the peace was shattered – one of the engines was spewing fire and smoke and the plane was diving towards the sea at great speed. Despite the state of confusion, the wireless operator somehow managed to send a distress signal as the plane made its rapid descent and then it was over. The Beaufort had ditched into the North Sea.

Squadron Leader W.H. Cliff found himself tipped half way out of the cockpit of the downed plane through the hatch that the navigator, who was known as Mac, had opened. Mac had managed to get the dinghy out and, after a moment of panic when they thought it was not going to work, had got it inflated and all four of them somehow managed to scramble aboard.

They then had one more chance to get a message out regarding their plight. The aircraft had been carrying two pigeons for release in emergencies and the container had survived the crash. Coastal Command aircraft had been carrying pigeons since the outbreak of the war and this was later extended to all bombers. In all, the RAF used around 80,000 pigeons during the war. For one thing, they were not so easily intercepted as radio messages. As the damaged container was dragged aboard the dinghy, one of the pigeons made a bid for freedom. It perched on the fuselage of the downed aircraft. The crew tried to manoeuvre the dinghy nearer to re-capture the bird but it stayed out of their grasp and, after circling a couple of times, flew off.

The bird had gone with no message attached to its leg and the crew reckoned that their chance of rescue had been cut in half. Nobody was pinning any hopes on their distress signal having been picked up. They made sure that a tight hold was kept of the remaining pigeon as Mac wrote a message on a piece of paper and put it in the little container on the bird's leg. It was thrown into the air and they watched it disappear into the distance. They could only hope that this bird would make it home.

Later that day the Beaufort had been missed at base and the operation to find out what had happened to the crew had begun. The distress signal had, in fact, been picked up but it was too weak to give any more than the vaguest indication of the plane's position. A wide area would have to be covered by the searchers. The crew would soon be facing a night at sea.

Just after dawn the next morning in Long Lane, Broughty Ferry, a dirty, wet and bedraggled-looking bird flew in to the loft where James Ross, a master plumber and member of the National Pigeon Service, kept his pigeons. The pigeon was exhausted and oil-stained but Ross recognised it was one of his own. He looked in vain for a message but there was nothing in the container on its leg. There was a good reason for this. This was not the pigeon that had been sent with the message. That pigeon would never be seen again. This was the bird that had escaped when the plane had newly ditched into the water. Ross immediately contacted the operations room at Leuchars. He had no message to pass on but he was able to give the pigeon's registration number – NEH.40.NS.1. The station controller checked this number against the records they held and found out that this was one of the pigeons kept in the downed plane for emergency release. With no message attached, the worry had to be that this pigeon might be the only survivor of the crash.

Nevertheless, the bird might be able to provide a significant clue as to where the plane had come down. It was known roughly when the accident had taken place because of the faint distress signal. Sergeant Davidson of the RAF Pigeon Service made a calculation using the flying speed of the pigeon and the fact that the bird would not fly at night. Mr Ross had stated that he believed the pigeon had just managed to reach the coast before nightfall. Using all this information it was possible to significantly cut the size of area to be searched. The new information was radioed to all the aircraft searching for the downed crew and within twenty minutes they were spotted by the crew of a Hudson of Royal Netherlands Naval Air Service – in the area that Sergeant Davidson's calculations had indicated.

An extra dinghy containing supplies was dropped and around two hours later an RAF rescue launch picked the crew up. They had spent around twenty-two hours in the water. They were given hot food and drinks and were able at last to get some rest. Their rescue was in no small part due to the efforts of pigeon number NEH.40.NS.1. This was the first rescue during World War Two to be attributed to a pigeon. The bird had travelled 129 miles in all, 120 of them before she reached the coast.

'She's a tough little bird,' Mr Ross proudly told the press. 'She was number one in the National Pigeon Service 1940 breed and although she's been on a few training flights, this was what the RAF would call her first operational trip. She crossed about 100 miles of sea in a dirty and wet condition. I have a lot of faith in her because she was one of three survivors out of seventeen which the RAF put through a number of rigorous tests.' Like the rescued crew, the pigeon was rewarded that night with a clean up and special feed, but this was not to be the last of her rewards.

On 5 March 1942, Winkie, as the pigeon was known, was guest of honour at a dinner attended by the crew. She had become known as Winkie as she had appeared to be winking since the rescue – as if admitting she knew the full significance of her actions. In fact it was said that the slow movements of her eyelids were the after affects of fatigue. She was presented with a plaque depicting a pigeon flying over the sea together with an inscription of thanks.

Winkie's biggest honour came on 2 December 1943 when she received the Dickin Medal. The Dickin Medal is regarded as the animal equivalent of the Victoria Cross. It was named after Maria Dickin, the pioneering founder of the People's Dispensary for Sick Animals. Working among the poor of London's East End, Dickin noticed the extreme suffering of the animals whose owners could barely afford to look after themselves and thought that some provision should be made for them. She founded the PDSA in 1917. In the quarter of a century since its foundation, the charity had gone from strength to strength.

Dickin thought that the contribution of animals to the war effort should be recognised too and the Dickin Medal was instituted in 1943 with the support of the War Office. Winkie received her medal from Maria Dickin herself and was the first pigeon to be awarded the medal. The citation read: 'For delivering a message under exceptionally difficult conditions and so contributing to the rescue of an Air Crew while serving with the RAF in February 1942.' Of course she did not actually deliver a written message, but her very presence, in the event, spoke more clearly than any scribbled note written in such circumstances ever would have done. More than thirty pigeons in all would be awarded this medal during the Second World War.

Winkie had already been immortalised in fiction. A children's picture book *Watching for Winkie* by Theresa Kalab was published in the United States in November 1942. It tells the tale of a pigeon called Winkie stationed at Dundee. Her owner in the story is a boy named Tommy Macintosh whose father is a pilot in the RAF. Winkie is, as in real life, assigned to a bomber on offensive patrol off Norway. The bomber is damaged by German fire and comes down in the North Sea. Winkie makes it back to dry land in record time and the crew are rescued. It turns out that the crew includes Lieutenant Macintosh – Tommy's father.

Winkie is also remembered in the only national memorial to wartime carrier pigeons in Beach House Park, Worthing. The memorial consists of two boulders on a mound. One inscription reads: 'In memory of the

Winkie the war hero

warrior birds who gave their lives on active service 1939–45 and for the use and pleasure of living birds.' The other boulder contains a quote from the Book of Ecclesiastes: 'A bird of the air shall carry the voice and that which hath wings shall tell the matter.' Winkie's story is told on a separate plaque. An impressive memorial to all animals in war was unveiled at Brook Gate, Park Lane, London, in 2004.

As well as being remembered on a war memorial, a human hero may be lucky enough to be the subject of a statue after death, but an animal hero is more likely to have to suffer the indignities of the taxidermist's art. Winkie was stuffed and is presently located in the McManus Galleries. She has left Dundee a few times since her death, for exhibitions and fairs. In 2008 she was part of *The Animals' War* exhibition at the Imperial War

Museum in London. After such excursions, however, just as in life, Winkie, Dundee's heroic pigeon, always returns home.

The Word on the Street

Couttie's Wynd, which runs between the Nethergate and Whitehall Crescent, is the proverbial dark alley that you would not want to walk down alone at night. A dingy graffiti-ridden lane, home to nothing but wheelie bins and the occasional sheltering smoker, it is certainly not the most welcoming street in Dundee. It is hard to believe that this was once a thriving thoroughfare and one of the principal routes to the river. It is probably one of the oldest streets in Dundee with a history going back to the foundation of the burgh. In older documents it is referred to as Spalding's Wynd but took its present name from a butcher who lived there in the sixteenth century. Prior to the construction of Whitehall Crescent, the wynd led down to Fish Street at its junction with Yeaman Shore.

In the 1860s, a young man used to stand at the foot of Couttie's Wynd preaching to anyone who would listen. He was not the most smooth talking of preachers. His language and manner were rough and ready compared to many of the town's more cultured ministers of religion. No one could doubt the young man's sincerity, however, or the passionate nature of his beliefs, but he had not always been so fervent a believer.

Like all the best Christian stories, the story of this young preacher, Robert Annan, is one of reform and redemption. The son of a stonemason, Annan was born in the Hilltown in 1834. An unruly and restless child, he was said to be difficult for his parents to cope with from a young age. By his teens, he was no stranger to alcohol and violence. In 1856, he was sent to prison for four months for the theft of a silver watch and some other articles from a man he had met near Downfield village. This was the final straw for Annan's father, who gave him some money and sent him off to the United States to make a fresh start. Robert Annan, though, was not ready for a new beginning and soon slipped back into his old habits. On one occasion he fell asleep sprawled across a railway line but somehow managed to survive the experience unscathed.

Like the biblical prodigal son, Annan squandered the money his father had given him. Destitute, he crossed into Canada where he enlisted in the 100th (Prince of Wales's Royal Canadian) Regiment of Foot. He would at least be fed and housed in the army and his passage back over the Atlantic was secured when the Regiment decamped to Aldershot in England. He deserted soon after this, however, and made his way to London. His situation was soon desperate again and he enlisted in the navy under his mother's maiden name.

On 24 September 1859, Annan's ship the *Edgar* arrived in Gibraltar – an unfortunate destination from his point of view as it was where his old army regiment was stationed. He then deserted from his ship, but there was nowhere to run and he eventually gave himself up to the authorities. His family had to come to his financial aid once more and secure his freedom.

Back in Dundee, Robert Annan moved in to the family home in a terrace of houses that his father had built in Wellington Street. He worked as a mason – presumably for his father. Any resolution to make a fresh start, however, was soon drowned in alcohol as he returned to his old ways, but salvation, it seems, was at hand.

The early 1860s was a time of religious revival in Dundee. Many revival meetings were held in places such as the Kinnaird Hall and Barrack Park. It was an experience after one such meeting at the Kinnaird Hall that left Robert Annan with the religious fervour that was to drive him for the rest of his life. Having made up his mind to attend a follow-up enquiry meeting, he found the door closed on him just as he was about to enter. The symbolism of this moment struck him deeply and after an emotional visit to his local minister, the Reverend John Macpherson, he spent the remainder of that night and most of the next day considering the error of his ways. Lying face down in a hayloft, he wrestled with thoughts of redemption and even suicide. His family were said to have been unable to persuade him to eat or drink for the next three days.

There is no doubt that the Robert Annan who emerged from this extended bout of soul-searching was a changed man. With the zeal of the convert, he was off the next day to hand out tracts at the door of a meeting in Bell Street, held by a prominent sceptic named Barker. He became an enthusiastic member of Hilltown Free Church and spent his spare time and money preaching.

The year 1862 saw big changes in Annan's personal life. In June, his father died after a long illness. In November, he married twenty-four-year-old Jane Hutchison in a ceremony conducted by his friend, the Reverend

Robert Annan

John Macpherson. By this time, he had become involved in the North East Coast Mission and spent the next couple of years in a hard apprenticeship. Stationed in Stonehaven for several months, he was taunted and sometimes even physically assaulted. He endured similar hardships working in Aberdeen and among the navvies near Banchory. A year or two previously he would have responded to such trials with his fists, but now he offered a smile or a prayer.

Annan returned to Dundee to work in 1864. He spent almost every spare moment preaching but he was afforded little honour in his hometown either. Using a chair as a makeshift pulpit, he would endeavour to get his message over to an often less than welcoming audience. Mud, stones, flour and soot all rained down on him at times and here too he was often verbally and sometimes physically assaulted. He would also be moved on by the police for causing an obstruction – often at the behest of local publicans who felt that his message was detrimental to their trade. Nevertheless, every Sunday morning and evening would find him at the end of Couttie's Wynd, welcoming anyone who wanted to listen to him.

From this vantage point at the foot of the Wynd, Annan could see the docks and the river beyond. He had always been at home in the water. As a youth he was nicknamed 'the Water Dog' and had saved the life of his younger brother Ebenezer when he got out of his depth. In later years he had saved several other people from drowning. In 1866 he was given the Dundee Humane Society's silver medal for his efforts and an award of £2. He spent £1 of this money becoming a member of the society and paying his subscription in advance for the next eight years. He was to see the dawn of only one of these years. The year of 1867 began with Robert Annan standing, shouting in the snow – a voice crying in the wilderness unheeded or abused by midnight revellers. Seven months later he was dead.

One week before his death, Annan was floating on a raft on the Tay when a feeling of great serenity and spiritual calm came over him. It was later said that he had had a premonition that his time on earth was done. The following Sunday he is reported to have told his morning meeting at

Couttie's Wynd of the experience and added, 'I may never have another opportunity of speaking to you. I may be in Heaven before next Sabbath and methinks I may look down from Glory on Couttie's Wynd.'

Perhaps this talk of a premonition can be dismissed as deriving from a sentimental re-writing of events in later years, but Annan's final public actions were well documented at the time. On the morning of Wednesday, 31 July, he hung two placards on the wall of his house. One of them ended with the question: 'Where will you spend Eternity?' He also wrote the word 'Death' on his gate and 'Eternity' on the pavement outside his house in chalk before proceeding to his work as a foreman at the wood merchants William Kirkland and Son at the docks.

Some time around midday a young boy named John Graham fell into the water at Craig Harbour. Annan was one of the first on the scene. He threw off some of his clothing but only had time to remove one of his boots in his hurry to dive in to try to save the boy who was rapidly being carried away by the current. Onlookers saw Annan reach Graham and get hold of him but although he came close to Craig Pier he too was soon being swept away. Annan was seen to be submerged several times but he always managed to keep the boy's head above the water. A boat set out to pick them up but it was too late for Annan. In one final effort he was seen to push the boy away from him so as not to take him down with him as he disappeared beneath the waves. It was thought that the strong swimmer had suffered from cramp.

A man named Daniel Anderson dived into the water and managed to pick up John Graham and get him onto the boat. The boy soon made a rapid recovery but, although only four or five yards from the pier, Robert Annan was lost. A search commenced immediately but it was not until around half past eight that evening that his body was recovered.

Robert Annan's funeral took place the following Saturday. The bells of the Old Steeple were tolled in what was, at the time, a unique tribute to someone who was not a civic dignitary or person of high social standing. Hundreds walked behind the hearse and thousands lined the streets from

Wellington Street to the Eastern Cemetery where Annan was buried. The Reverend John Macpherson conducted the ceremony. The next day Macpherson preached a memorial sermon at the Hilltown Free Church – or rather in a neighbouring field as around 3000 people had turned up.

Money poured into a memorial fund for Annan and two years later an obelisk was erected in the Eastern Cemetery. The inscription read:

Sacred to the memory of Robert Annan, a hero in humble life, born at Dundee on 5th October 1834, who, after embracing the cross of Christ, devoted his leisure hours to the salvation of the degraded and outcast. Instrumental in saving, at different times, eleven persons from drowning, he was awarded the medal of the Dundee Humane Society for his exertions on behalf of humanity, and perished while in the act of saving the twelfth at the Craig Harbour Dundee on the 31st July 1867. The bells of the town were tolled as his remains, accompanied by a large number of sympathising friends, were borne to this spot, and buried amidst the tears of thousands who had come to witness the ceremony. In admiration of his heroic death, this monument has been erected by contributions by all ranks and professions and in gratitude for his noble sacrifice, there was also placed under the management of trustees a sum sufficient to enable his widow to bring up their children in a manner consonant with his wishes while living.

Impressive as this monument was, it was a simpler memorial that was to do most to keep Annan's name alive after his death. The word 'Eternity', which he had written in chalk outside his house on the day of his death, had still been visible at the time of his funeral. The word was later cut into the stone to stand as a memorial to Robert Annan. Many memorial services were to be conducted at this 'Eternity Stone' down the years. It also served a more evangelistic purpose as an article in the *Herald of Mercy* magazine pointed out: 'There it lies before the eyes of every passer-by, a reminder that time will not last forever.' The article went on to say that 'by and by the traffic of countless feet will wear that stone away; every day the word will become fainter and fainter, till no trace is left.' This reckoned without Dundee's predilection for demolition a century after Robert Annan's death.

Annan's Terrace was demolished in the early 1970s and the site is now occupied by Our Lady's Primary School. The Eternity Stone was removed for safekeeping. It was hoped to place it in the Hilltown Free Church but this too was demolished. The stone was later moved to St Peter's Free Church, Perth Road. It is difficult to resist the feeling, however, that there should be a memorial to Robert Annan where he was – out on the street among the people of Dundee. The Eternity Stone could easily be duplicated and where better to place it than at the foot of Couttie's Wynd where Dundee's Christian hero Robert Annan preached more than a century ago?

Francisco Drummond

In early 2010, it was reported that the Argentine vessel the *ARA Drummond* had entered disputed waters around the Falkland Islands. The *Drummond* was said to have promptly changed course when radioed by the British Destroyer *HMS York*. The story sounded like a non-event from the start and this impression was strengthened when the Ministry of Defence issued a statement declaring that the incident had in fact happened in international waters and that 'after a friendly dialogue by radio' the ships had 'each continued with their own exercises'.

This incident had, nonetheless, revived memories of the 1982 conflict between Britain and Argentina over the sovereignty of the Falkland Islands – particularly since the *Drummond* had seen active service in that conflict. What nobody appeared to question, though, either in 1982 or 2010 was how an Argentinean ship came to have such a Scottish-sounding name. The answer is that it was named after a man from Dundee.

Francis Drummond was born in Dundee in 1798. His father – also named Francis – was the captain of a merchant ship. It is likely, then, that young Francis grew up listening to tales of life at sea. In addition, Francis lived in the busy seaport of Dundee during what many consider to be the greatest era of naval warfare. He would have been immersed in talk of the great naval battles from a young age. The year before he was born, local hero Admiral Adam Duncan had won a historic victory over the Dutch at the Battle of Camperdown. Duncan's name would no doubt have been on everybody's lips again at the time of his death in 1804 when Francis was six years old, and the following year Francis would surely have heard talk of Nelson's victory at the Battle of Trafalgar in which several Dundonians took part.

Just over a year after the Battle of Trafalgar, in November 1806, Francis's father's ship, the *Lavinia*, was on a voyage from Riga to London with a cargo of hemp. Relatively close to her home port, around a mile and a half east of Crail in Fife, the ship ran into trouble. The sea was said to be 'running very high and covering the vessel at every moment'. The crew took to the rigging for safety and remained there overnight. They all survived. At around six o'clock in the morning, they watched helplessly as Captain Drummond, who had remained on deck, was washed overboard and drowned. A newspaper report stated that Drummond had left 'a widow and a numerous family of young children to deplore his loss' – among them eight-year-old Francis.

The sea had claimed his father's life but it was clearly in young Francis Drummond's blood. At an early age he joined the Royal Navy, yet it was not as a member of the British forces that he would be remembered. His future was to be shaped by events unfolding in far away Brazil. With the Napoleonic Wars at an end, the Royal Navy had more officers and men than it needed and many were unemployed – some were on half pay and some on no pay at all. Brazil, meanwhile, had declared independence from Portugal and the new state required a navy, quickly. Among those recruited for the fledgling service by Felisberto Brandt, the Brazilian Chargé d'Affaires in London, was Francis Drummond.

The man chosen to head the Brazilian Navy was another Scotsman,

Thomas Cochrane, veteran of the Napoleonic Wars and more recently commander of the Chilean naval forces against Spain. In March 1823, he arrived and took command of the new Brazilian fleet. Within a couple of weeks Cochrane had blockaded the Portuguese in the port of Salvador de Bahia, eventually forcing them to evacuate with a combination of the effects of the siege and the cleverly leaked talk of the 'fireships' that he was about to turn against them. Cochrane then proceeded, despite the inferior nature of the force at his command, to hound the Portuguese as they fled. Most of his ships eventually gave up this chase but one was said to have doggedly followed the Portuguese for three months all the way home to the mouth of the Tagus at Lisbon. This was the *Niteroi* – the ship upon which Francis Drummond served as an officer.

Meanwhile, Admiral Cochrane had turned his attentions to the province of Maranhão, which was still in the hands of the Portuguese. He sailed into the port with one ship and somehow managed to convince the Portuguese that this was merely the flagship of a larger force. Once again, Cochrane's audacious move worked and he was able to introduce a form of democratic rule to the province – but it was not to last. By April 1825, Maranhão was collapsing into anarchy and Cochrane sent shore parties to restore order. He called upon Francis Drummond, by then a sublieutenant on the frigate *Piranga*, to lead one of these parties. Drummond must have acquitted himself well as Cochrane's records show that he was awarded an additional month's pay for 'extra services' on this occasion.

It would have been thought, then, that Francis Drummond would by this stage have been considered one of the heroes of the Brazilian Navy and be in many ways above reproach, but this was not the case. He had already faced a court martial for insubordination in 1824 and by 1825 was due to face another one. More than anything, this was because of the almost absurdly legalistic way in which the Brazilian Navy applied its rules. Things that would never have reached a court martial in the British services were pursued to the ultimate conclusion in Brazil.

Drummond did not wish to undergo another trial and somehow managed to escape from the prison ship on which he was being held. He then made for Buenos Aires where he offered his services to the navy of the United Provinces of the River Plate – the forerunner of the Argentine Navy. Indeed, one account claims that this had been his intention all along and that he had actually been imprisoned due to word of his plans reaching his superiors.

Whatever the truth of this, Drummond was soon to make a good impression on his new commander – the Irishman from County Mayo who was to become known as the Father of the Argentine Navy, Commodore William Brown. Brown made Drummond captain of the schooner *Maldonado*, but the Commodore was not the only member of the Brown family who was impressed with Francis Drummond. Brown's teenage daughter Eliza fell in love with Drummond and the couple became engaged. It was a love story, however, that was to have a tragic ending.

Drummond found himself facing his erstwhile employers at the Battle of Juncal in February 1827, part of the ongoing battle for supremacy in the River Plate that had commenced in 1825. Although the Brazilian and Argentine forces were well matched, the Argentine victory was decisive. Three Brazilian ships were burnt and a further twelve were captured, while not one Argentine ship was lost. Drummond had found himself the victor in a fierce struggle against his former comrade – the Englishman George Broom, the commander of the *Bertioga*. The war may have been between the navies of two emerging independent South American countries, but it was to a large extent manned by personnel from the old world and the British Isles in particular. Drummond was awarded a medal and two months' extra salary for his efforts at Juncal.

Buoyed by the success at Juncal, the Argentineans decided to take the battle to the enemy. Commodore Brown selected his best men and ships for this mission, among them Francis Drummond as commander of the *Independencia*. This time, however, things were not to go so smoothly. The *Independencia* and another ship, the *Republica Argentina*, ran aground not far outside of Buenos Aires. Although the other Argentinean ships managed to protect and re-supply the stranded ships for a while, they were ultimately at the mercy of the Brazilian gunboats.

The crew of the *Independencia*, led by Drummond, fought on bravely and refused to abandon ship. Drummond himself suffered a serious head wound, losing an ear. The ship was continually pounded and the number of dead and injured began to rise but still they did not give in, returning fire with everything they had. They reputedly even used the links of the anchor chain as ammunition when the cannonballs ran out.

The Brazilian bombardment of the *Independencia* eventually claimed forty-three lives, among them that of Francis Drummond himself. His pelvis was shattered by a twenty-four-pound shot. With his dying words he talked of his home and ordered that his watch be taken to his mother and his ring be given to his fiancée, Eliza Brown. According to her father, his final words were, 'Tell the Admiral that I have done my duty and die like a man.' Francis Drummond was buried in the protestant cemetery in Buenos Aires. His entry in the cemetery records reads: 'Captain Francis Drummond, 30, seaman, 9 April 1827'.

In December of that year, Eliza Brown drowned in the River Plate. It was said that she had never recovered from the death of Drummond and that she had committed suicide. Some accounts have her calmly walking into the water wearing her wedding dress. It is likely that this detail is a later romantic addition but the possibility remains that her death was deliberate and brought about by grief. Her gravestone reads:

> Victim of the treacherous wave
> This marble o'er thy lowly grave
> Thy mournful parents raise
> Who whilst they weep thy helpless fate
> And early virtues contemplate
> God's dispensations praised.

The exact whereabouts of Francis Drummond's own final resting place remain a mystery as the cemetery in which he was buried has twice moved location. Some like to think that he was reburied with Eliza but, again, this may only be a romantic notion. His original gravestone is held in Argentina's National Maritime Museum. Drummond is remembered elsewhere in Argentina, however, with streets and even an entire district bearing his name, as well as the naval vessels that have been named after him over the years. For all his enduring fame, though, this hero of Argentina remains virtually unknown in his hometown of Dundee.

6

Villains?

In a lonely grave in Dundee's Eastern Necropolis lie the remains of a woman born Ellen Elliot in Walworth, London, in 1856. Dundee was to provide her last resting place, yet she lived in the city for less than a month. Her life was ended at the hands of the man who brought her to Dundee – her husband, William Henry Bury. To some, her death is notable as she was the victim of Bury, the last man to be hanged in Dundee. To others, she is also the last victim of the world's most notorious serial killer, Jack the Ripper.

Much has been written about the possibility of Bury being the man behind the killings in London's east end in 1888, but then much has been written about the possibility of all sorts of people being the Ripper. Of all the candidates for this dubious distinction, though, there are several points in William Bury's favour. He lived in Bow near Whitechapel at the time of the murders. He was certainly capable of such murders, as the killing of Ellen and the subsequent mutilation of her body show. James Berry, the hangman who executed Bury, was convinced that he had hanged the Ripper. One thing is certain: after William Henry Bury moved to Dundee in January 1889, there were no more Jack the Ripper murders in London, but a murder with many similarities to the Ripper crimes did take place in Dundee.

Whether or not Jack the Ripper ever set foot in Dundee, the city has produced many villains of its own over the years, although, as some of the stories on the following pages will show, a few of these could more properly be called victims of the times in which they lived.

The Shadow of the Hangman

Dundee seems always to have had an uneasy relationship with capital punishment. Indeed, there seems always to have been a degree of sympathy in the town for anybody condemned to death no matter how heinous their crime.

There had been, however, many executions in Dundee over the centuries. It is not known how many were executed in the town, for example, for the crime of witchcraft. In 1569, an account of the progress of James Stewart, Earl of Moray, states that 'he causit burn ane other company of witches in Dundee'. A century later the infamous burning of Grizzel Jaffrey for the same crime entered into Dundee folklore.

In the late sixteenth century, Dundee employed its own executioner, Michael Mores, albeit that he combined this role with various other duties including expelling vagabonds and slaughtering stray pigs. In later years, hangings took place outwith Dundee, usually at the place of trial. In 1788, for example, James Falconer and Peter Bruce were hanged at Edinburgh for the theft of over 400 pounds from the offices of the Dundee Banking Company. The dawn of the nineteenth century, however, brought public hanging back to Dundee. These are the stories of the men who met their deaths in this way.

John Wat or Wast 1801

Windmill Brae would have been a familiar landmark to generations of Dundonians. Originally known as Corbie Hill, it was quarried out of existence in the nineteenth century and eventually replaced by South Lindsay Street. That street too has now vanished. While North Lindsay

Street remains today, all trace of its southern counterpart was obliterated when the first Overgate Shopping Centre was built in the 1960s.

Just over 200 years ago, a man named John Wat or Wast burst open the door of a house in this area and stole some small pieces of cloth. Wat, a weaver by trade, was said to be on the verge of starvation. The background circumstances of the perpetrator, however, played little part in the judicial system of this time. At the conclusion of Wat's trial in Perth in April 1801, where he was also charged with a similar robbery in Meadow Street, the sentence handed down was one of death by hanging.

There had not been a hanging in Dundee for around 100 years. The *Scots Magazine* reported that in the future it was intended that all criminals sentenced to die should be executed in the places where they committed the crimes for which their life was to be forfeited. The magazine called this a 'wise and salutary measure' – no doubt believing that a local execution would have an increased deterrent effect.

The town would require a new scaffold for the event and this was constructed for the sum of £31 14s 2d. The resulting structure was what the *Piper o' Dundee* called 'an ugly, clumsy and unwieldy conglomerate of wood and iron'. This would nonetheless have been viewed at the time as a wise investment for the town.

The scaffold was erected at the east window of Guild Hall in the Town House on Friday, 12 June 1801. Wat was accompanied by three clergymen – Reverends McVicar, Innes and Paterson and was said to have 'behaved in a manner becoming his unhappy situation'. He was hanged at three o'clock before a large crowd.

Among the expenses that the town incurred for the execution was a fee of £1 7s 6d for porters to carry the body to the burial ground and one of £7 16s 0d for the executioner who also received £2 19s 6d for 'eating and drinking'. The largest expense, besides the cost of erection of the scaffold, however, was one of £22 13s 6d for 'the Entertainment at Morren's'.

Alexander Morren's hotel was situated across from the Town House at 46 High Street. An early guide to the town gives it the following recommendation: 'In Inns we are completely accommodated. Neither Gordon's nor Morren's would do dishonour to any town in Europe.' This was the place in which the great and the good of Dundee gathered and ate and drank on expenses to mark the execution of a poverty-stricken man who had resorted to petty crime.

David Balfour 1826

At around twenty minutes before nine on the morning of Wednesday, 21 December 1825, a man named David Balfour walked into Dundee's Town House, where the town's jail was then situated. Balfour calmly requested that the turnkey, Charles Watson, should lock him up as he had committed an atrocious crime – the murder of his wife. Six months later, David Balfour would be dead, hanged outside the building in which he then stood.

David Balfour's sad tale begins at Ecclesjohn in the Parish of Dun near Montrose, where he was born in 1786. The following year, the house and estate of Ecclesjohn were renamed Langley Park. Balfour's father worked as a coachman on this estate. When he was ten years old Balfour came to Dundee where he was apprenticed to Robert Lithgow, the master of the Brig *Helen*. The sea was to provide Balfour with his livelihood for the rest of his life. After completing his apprenticeship he was pressed in to the navy where he served for eleven years.

David Balfour married Margaret Clark in Dundee on 24 July 1805 while both were still in their teens. They set up home together in the Seagate, but Balfour was often away at sea, both in the navy and later when he sailed on merchant ships. His absences undoubtedly sowed the seeds of the couple's problems. To supplement her income, Margaret Balfour had taken in a lodger named Alexander Hogg. When he returned home, David Balfour noticed a change in his wife's attitude towards him and became suspicious as to the nature of her relationship with Hogg. It was at this point, as the *Dundee Advertiser* put it, that 'peace and happiness fled from the house'.

Balfour attempted to get his wife to leave Dundee with him but instead she opted to move into her parents' house – as did Alexander Hogg. Distraught, Balfour moved to Aberdeen where he was based for three years. Despite their differences, Margaret Balfour visited her husband from time to time during this period. Eventually she was persuaded that they could make a new life together and the re-united couple moved to Greenock.

The fresh start did not last long, however, as Balfour became suspicious once more, this time of his wife's relationship with their landlord, Torquil Macleod, a widower with a young son. Arriving home unexpectedly from a voyage, he watched as she left Macleod's house at two o'clock in the morning. Despite this evidence against his wife, Balfour was willing to make another attempt to save their marriage, but this time, he reasoned, they would have to leave Greenock behind and return to Dundee.

Margaret Balfour returned to her father's house in the Murraygate but brought with her Torquil Macleod's son, leaving the couple's own son David behind in Greenock. Living with Macleod's son in the house was too much for David Balfour to bear and he ensured that the boy was returned to his father. Margaret told Balfour around this time that this would 'cost him dear'.

In early December 1825, Balfour was working on the Newcastle and Berwick Packet, sailing between Dundee and Liverpool, when his ship the *Duthie* ran aground at Blackpool. He did not get back to Dundee until 18 December and when he went to his father-in-law's house in the Murraygate his wife would not let him stay. After wandering the streets all day he returned to the house and, despite his wife's coldness towards him and his brother-in-law's attempts to throw him out, he stayed overnight.

The next morning he rose early and again wandered the streets all day returning home around six o'clock when he found his wife sitting with a visitor, Margaret Ireland. Ireland later claimed that Balfour told her that night that he would be in jail the next morning. Balfour walked her back to her house in the Hilltown and then returned to the Murraygate around ten o'clock. He tried to make peace with his wife and persuade her to show him some affection but she barricaded herself in the bedroom.

At around seven o'clock in the morning of 21 December, Balfour met a former shipmate, Thomas Houston, at the docks and they shared a drink. The two men had sailed together for around three years and Houston had always remembered Balfour talking very fondly of his wife. Now, however, he said that she was 'not what she should be' and that he intended to lay hands on her. A few hours, he said, should settle it.

After leaving his friend, Balfour went into a butcher shop and asked for a knife to 'kill a lamb'. The butcher's son, William Small, told him that it was not the season for lambs but Balfour said it was to kill an animal he had brought with him on board a vessel. Small gave him the knife and within the hour Margaret Balfour was dead.

David Balfour was tried at Perth and sentenced to be hanged in Dundee on 2 June 1826. There was much public sympathy for his plight and the jury made a recommendation to mercy. Lord Pitmully, however, in his summing up said, 'Jealousy, revenge, anger from insult or other provocation, and every other passion to which human nature is subject are aberrations of the mind, but not such as to justify so heinous a crime as that with which the panel is charged.'

A petition for mercy was rejected by the Home Secretary Robert Peel and the sentence was to be carried out as planned. Balfour was calm throughout the proceedings and joined in the singing of a hymn. He made a short speech to the largely sympathetic crowd in which he entrusted himself to the mercy of God and regretted the disgrace that he had brought upon the town.

The unease with which Dundee watched David Balfour go to his death was demonstrated in strange waves of panic that spread through the crowd immediately before his execution. Some viewed these as a supernatural sign that Balfour should not be hanged, but at quarter to three the execution went ahead. His suffering was not prolonged but his body was left dangling for fifty minutes. After being cut down it was delivered over to Dr Munro, Professor of Anatomy at the University of Edinburgh, for dissection[1].

Mark Devlin 1835

The traditional caricature of an executioner shows him wearing a mask but this was certainly not the norm in nineteenth-century Scotland. There was only one execution by a masked hangman in Dundee and that was the execution of Mark Devlin in 1835.

Devlin was an Irishman of twenty-six years of age who had fallen in with a bad crowd. He had been arrested together with two other men, James Leys and David Walker, for the crime of reset, following a robbery in the Hawkhill area. At the subsequent trial, Leys was transported for seven years and Walker for fourteen but Devlin was never to face the charge. While he was in custody, a more serious crime came to light. He was accused of raping a girl named Ann McLachlan at the back of the Law. Rape was then a hanging offence.

It is an indication of Dundee's antipathy towards capital punishment in general that when Devlin was found guilty in May 1835, there was widespread sympathy for him despite the nature of his crime. This is evidenced in the fact that the hangman who undertook the job elected to wear a mask. When the rumour spread that a hobby-horse proprietor James Livingstone had carried out the task, he had a letter published in the local press stating that he was in Forfar on the day of the execution together with a signed statement from the Forfar Magistrates.

Mark Devlin spent his last night in a prison cell at the Town House. At around one o'clock in the morning he was awakened by the noise of joiners constructing the scaffold on which he was to hang, but he somehow managed to get back to sleep again.

[1] Munro was said to be an uninspiring teacher, being the third generation of his family to hold what had virtually become a hereditary post. Many students instead turned to private schools such as that run by Dr Robert Knox, whose access to bodies for dissection was limited until the intervention of Messrs Burke and Hare in 1827. When Burke was hanged in 1829, his body was delivered to Munro.

A large crowd began to gather outside from the early morning and shops in the town centre remained closed. The crowd spilled into the newly opened Reform Street and every other possible vantage point. At around ten past two in the afternoon, Devlin was led onto the scaffold in the company of Father McPherson, Dundee's only Catholic priest, and Father McKay from Perth. After the priests had attended to him Devlin addressed the crowd: 'Brethren, this is a disgraceful death in the eyes of the public but I hope the Lord will have mercy on me. I trust in his mercy and the merits of Jesus Christ and I hope that he will have mercy on my soul this day. I ask his pardon and the pardon of all and I forgive all – I forgive all my enemies from the bottom of my heart and I hope that you will pray that God may be merciful to my soul this day.'

Death was almost instantaneous. The crowd was said to have remained still, gazing at his body as it dangled on the rope for around half an hour before being cut down. Mark Devlin's was the last hanging to take place in Dundee's High Street and the last for the crime of rape in Scotland.

Arthur Woods 1839

Look for a street named Thorter Row on a map of Dundee today and you will find it located in a relatively recent development at City Quay. There was once another, much older Thorter Row, though. This street ran between the High Street and the Overgate and was known by that name from the fifteenth century until it was wiped off the map by the demolitions of the 1960s. Tradition has it that it was here that General Monck's massacre of the town's inhabitants in 1651 was stopped by the sight of a child suckling its murdered mother.

At half past one in the morning on Sunday, 5 August 1838, Duncan Macnab, night watchman, was passing the entrance of a passageway leading off Thorter Row into a courtyard known as Monk's Court. Macnab could hear noise coming from one of the houses in the courtyard as if there was a fight going on. No doubt going on his previous experience of the area, he

Scene of the Thorter Row murder

concluded that the commotion was due to the activities of drunks and, as no one else seemed to be complaining, he would not investigate further. Twenty minutes later, though, his beat brought him back to Thorter Row. This time he did venture into the courtyard. By the light of his lantern, he saw a man lying on his back beside a short flight of steps that led up to a house. Macnab grabbed the man by his coat collar, thinking that he was a drunk, but found to his horror that the man appeared to be dead.

William Annal, a tailor, was returning home from a night in Wright's Tavern when he met Macnab. Together they checked the body for any sign of life but found none. Annal was left in charge of the body while Macnab went to get help at the police office.

When Police Sergeant James Low arrived on the scene, he brought with him a barrow to wheel away the corpse. Low recognised the body as that of a man named John Woods. Woods's father and stepmother occupied the house outside which he was found. Low climbed the seven or eight steps to the house where he interviewed Arthur Woods, a man of around sixty, and his young wife Henrietta. He asked the couple where John Woods was. Arthur Woods said that he did not know where his son was, adding, 'He is not here and he shan't be here.' Woods's wife said that he had been at the door earlier but that his father would not let him in. She did not know where he had gone but thought that she had heard him fall over the stairs. Woods was heard to mumble a denial of having anything to do with his son's death.

The evidence said otherwise, though. A mark was found on John Woods' neck, which pointed to him having been strangled. A length of rope was found in the Woods's pantry that matched these marks. A witness, Mrs Scott, who had been awake waiting for the return of her lodger (a 'tailor boy', probably William Annal), claimed to have seen Mr and Mrs Woods carrying the body down the stairs and placing it in the position in which it was found.

Arthur and Henrietta Woods were both charged with murder. Their trial was delayed until the next year due to Mrs Woods's pregnancy. She later gave birth to her child in prison. The jury found Arthur Woods guilty but decided that the case against Henrietta Woods was not proven. Arthur Woods was condemned to be hanged in Dundee on 18 March 1839.

There was much sympathy in Dundee for Woods – a man who had seen his fortunes rise and fall again. Born in Ireland around 1779, he came to Scotland about 1808, working as a hawker, and at first settled in Glasgow. In 1811, in Edinburgh, he married Agnes Drew, a native of Perth. The couple moved to Perth but later came to live in Dundee where their ill-fated son, John Drew Woods, was born in 1813.

Things were looking up for Arthur Woods during this period. He managed to gain employment at an auctioneer's where, according to a pamphlet published at the time of his death, 'He recommended himself so much to the favour of his employers by his good humour, bland man-ners, activity, honesty and sobriety that his business largely increased and his was in a fair way of realizing a genteel competency.' This good life was not to last, however, and an unwise investment brought his world crashing down around him. He turned to drink in his despair and his wife left him. She later died in an accident. Eventually he returned to Ireland with his son and daughter.

In 1824, Woods returned to Dundee and to a lower standard of living than he had enjoyed in the town previously, working as a hawker and later a street porter and straw mattress maker. He had left his son John with his grandmother in Ireland but he too returned to Dundee in 1831, the same year that Arthur Woods married his second wife, Henrietta Young. John Woods at first helped his father with the mattress making, but he was often drunk and did not see eye to eye with his stepmother. This dislike of the son seems to have spread to the father. The week before the murder the two had come to blows in the house at Monk's Court. Henrietta Woods on that occasion was witnessed attacking her stepson with a poker.

Petitions were organised on behalf of Arthur Woods but all appeals to the Home Secretary, Lord John Russell, failed. The execution was to take place at the new prison at Bell Street. Around 10,000 people had gathered to see the hanging. Woods made an address to the crowd and protested his innocence of the crime of which he had been convicted. He also denied that his wife had had anything to do with the incident and that she was not the cause of any quarrelling in the family. Many in Dundee were impressed by his testimony at the time but it seems unlikely that an inno-cent man was hanged that day. Arthur Woods's speech in the face of death seems designed to protect the reputation of his young wife. It is a testament to his devotion to her – a devotion that probably cost John Drew Woods his life.

Thomas Leith 1847

On the morning of Wednesday, 21 April 1847, a woman named Ann Leith made some porridge for herself and her children. She did not have enough oatmeal for everybody but used barley meal to supplement her children's breakfast. She herself ate only the barley meal. Around two hours later she was seized with violent pains and began vomiting. Despite receiving medical attention, including the application of a stomach pump, by early afternoon she was dead. The children too had been taken ill but later recovered. The conclusion had to be that the barley meal had been poisoned.

It was not the first incident of alleged poisoning in the family. Around a month before, Ann Leith's husband Thomas, a tailor, had begun vomiting after drinking some tea that his wife had brought to his shop in the West Port. A doctor confirmed that arsenic had been added to the tea. Thomas Leith refused to eat anything his wife cooked for him in the future.

The couple was not, therefore, on good terms at the time of Mrs Leith's death and Leith had often talked about separating from his wife but she did not agree to this. Suspicion for his wife's murder immediately fell on Thomas Leith and he was arrested. A large crowd followed as he was taken to the police station.

At Leith's trial in Edinburgh he maintained his innocence but the jury returned a verdict of guilty albeit with a recommendation to mercy. The foreman of the jury said that they had made this recommendation partially because they disapproved of the death penalty and that a considerable number of them would have opted for a verdict of 'not proven' if they thought that such a punishment would be carried out.

Leith was given a brief respite when the execution was postponed for two weeks but ultimately all his appeals failed. There was considerable disquiet in Dundee at the sentence. On the eve of the execution, posters began to appear signed by 'a working Man' appealing to other working men not to go to the execution of Thomas Leith: 'It is time that scenes so degrading to the dignity of human nature should cease and that a decisive testimony should be borne by the community, that capital punishments for whatever crime, be abolished and something more efficient for the good of the public, as well as of the offender substituted.' The poster went on to suggest that working men should bear this testimony by not going to the execution and 'show that public opinion in this town is against capital punishments'.

Nevertheless, around 15,000 people did turn up to witness the execution in Bell Street on the morning of Tuesday, 6 October 1847. Before he died, Leith placed his hand on his heart and pronounced himself not guilty of the murder of his wife. It was said that many who had gone to the execution believing him to be guilty came away believing him to be innocent. Thomas Leith was the last man to be publicly executed in Dundee; a change in the law in 1868 meant that future executions would be held behind the prison walls. There would only be one more hanging in Dundee in any case – that of William Henry Bury in 1889.

Stage-struck

The show did not go on at London's Adelphi Theatre in the Strand that winter night in 1897. Herbert Budd, acting assistant manager of the theatre, walked onto the stage and made an announcement: 'Ladies and gentlemen, I am deeply grieved and pained to announce to you a serious, nay terrible, accident which will render the performance of *Secret Service* this evening quite impossible. I will also ask you to pass out into the street as quietly as possible. It is hardly necessary for me to add that your money will be returned on application at the pay boxes.' The exact nature of 'the terrible accident' was not announced but the rumour soon spread – William Terriss, the star of the show, had been stabbed and was badly injured. When confirmation finally came, the news was even worse. Terriss was dead.

Known as Breezy Bill, William Terriss had been one of the leading lights of the West End stage. He was a popular star and a dashing hero in an era when the term 'melodrama' was not an insult. He may have been unable to produce the thoughtful performances of his contemporary Henry Irving but audiences loved him. In an industry notorious for backbiting it seems too that he was genuinely loved by his fellow actors, but now his life had been ended by a tragedy more shocking than any of his exploits on stage.

Star of the stage, William Terriss

The scene was already set and the villain waiting in the wings when Terriss's cab arrived at the corner of Maiden Lane behind the Strand at around seven o'clock in the evening of Thursday, 16 December 1897. Terriss was accompanied by his friend John Henry Graves. The two men got out of the cab and walked the short distance to the private entrance of the Adelphi – the door that had been installed so that Queen Victoria could pay low-key visits to the theatre. Terriss retrieved his keys from his pocket and bent over to unlock the door. Suddenly, a figure emerged from the shadows and moved swiftly across the road. Terriss was hit twice in quick succession on the back. Graves thought at first that his companion was merely the recipient of a friendly pat on the back, albeit roughly delivered. When Terriss instinctively turned round, however, he received a further blow to the chest. There was no doubt then as to the violent nature of the attack.

'My God!' he cried out. 'I am stabbed!'

Graves managed to hold the assailant for a few minutes before delivering him into the custody of Constable John Bragg. Bragg had appeared on the scene swiftly, responding to the cries of 'Police!' and 'Murder!' that had begun to ring out in the vicinity. Graves told the policeman that the man had stabbed William Terriss. The two men accompanied the prisoner to Bow Street police station. Some mumbled words about 'blackmail' were the only explanation he gave as to his motive. At the station, the man took a bloodied knife from under his cape, saying, 'That is what I stabbed him with, he had due warning, and if he is dead he knows what he had to expect from me; he prevented me from getting assistance from the Actor's Benevolent Fund today, and I have stopped him.'

Back at the Adelphi, Terriss had staggered into the doorway where he slumped to the floor at the foot of the stairs that led to the dressing rooms. Medical assistance had arrived from Charing Cross Hospital but nothing could be done. The final stab wound had been to his heart. William Terriss died at around eight o'clock. His leading lady in the current production, Jessie Millward, was at his side.

Take a walk down Castle Street in Dundee today heading towards the River Tay and you will be walking in the footsteps of a man named Richard Archer. Look up to your right and you will see a bust of William Shakespeare nestling in a high alcove. The façade that houses Shakespeare is all that remains today of the Theatre Royal building. It was here that young Richard Archer became a frequent playgoer – lured, perhaps, by the lights and the glamour as he trudged home from work as a dock labourer in the 1870s. He certainly became ensnared enough by the theatrical world to want to take to the stage himself. He gained work at the Theatre Royal as a supernumerary or 'super' (the theatre equivalent of a movie 'extra'). Archer's first faltering steps onto the Dundee stage were also the first steps on a path that would take him to London's West End and not to fame, but to infamy when he plunged his knife into the heart of William Terriss.

Richard Archer was born in May 1859 at the farm of Balmydown on the outskirts of Dundee where his parents were employed. His emerging eccentricities as a child were put down to an incident that occurred when he was with his mother who had been working in the fields on a particularly hot day. The child suffered sunstroke and had to be taken to the doctor. 'He was blue in the face, and his eyes were very bad,' his mother recalled. It was after this that he developed a squint in his eyes.

Growing up in Hillbank Street and later Crescent Street, Dundee, Richard Archer was a dour, bad tempered child prone to fits of anger. He did not play much, his mother said, and his lack of social skills was not compensated for by any academic brilliance. He was a slow learner who had difficulty grasping ideas. None of this, however, led to any diminution of his self-esteem and he was always prone to vanity.

After leaving school at fourteen, Archer worked in the shipyards as a labourer and a plater, being first employed at Borr and Ireland's, and then at Gourley's where he was said to be a 'very steady, attentive and obliging workman', albeit with an eccentric manner. It was around this time that a love of the theatre took hold of him. Robert Beveridge, a theatre attendant, later recalled that Archer 'seemed to be stage-struck at that time, so far as I could see – he became quite professional in his way at the theatre altogether before he left for London; he was not like other professionals; he seemed to think himself above everybody.'

Richard Archer seems to have first appeared at the Adelphi as a 'super' around 1880. He was employed on a regular, if casual, basis there, appearing in minor (probably mainly non-speaking) roles over the next few years. His name rarely featured in the theatre's programme. Nor does Archer seem to have troubled the reviewers. 'We would also like to give praise to the impersonation of Lanty by Mr Archer,' for his performance in *Arrah-na-Pogue* in July 1885, was probably among the best he received.

A new figure then entered Richard Archer's life. In 1885, William Terriss moved along the Strand from a successful run at the Lyceum to the Adelphi to star in *Harbour Lights* and subsequent melodramas. It seems that Archer's animosity towards Terriss dated from this point. Charles St John Denton was also in the cast of *Harbour Lights*. He later told how Archer 'used even then to express animosity against Terriss, and it was common chaff to say, "No doubt you ought to occupy his position."' Those who indulged in this banter were not aware of the seeds that were being planted in Richard Archer's mind.

Archer continued to work at the Adelphi for the next few years, changing his name towards the end of the 1880s to the grander sounding Richard Archer Prince. There was no equivalent upgrading, however, in status of the roles he was given to play – the relatively minor role of Tim O'Grady in *The Union Jack* probably being the largest assigned to him. He seems to have been dropped from the pool of 'supers' around this time, although he told his mother that he had left to join a touring company for more money.

In June of 1889, Prince did join the touring company of manager J. F. Elliston. He was to remain in Elliston's employment off and on, with only what the manager referred to as 'very brief intervals' until 1893. While touring in a version of *The Union Jack*, Prince returned to Dundee, staying at the family home at 7 Rosebank Road. He would be back in Dundee often during the next six years – a period when his lofty theatrical ambitions were consistently thwarted and his mental state seemed to go into rapid decline. One of Prince's performances at this time caused him to be singled out by the reviewer in *The Era*, but not for a compliment: 'Mr Richard

Prince as Tom Chuckle would do well to remember that *The Union Jack* is not exactly burlesque.'

Prince's state of mind was becoming apparent to everyone. A neighbour, Andrew Moffatt, recalled hearing him through the adjoining wall reciting and singing, 'I have known him sing from seven p.m. till one a.m., and to the best of my ability I always considered that the man who would do that was not of sound mind.' Moffatt also recalled Prince's appearance at this time: 'He was dressed like a madman, too; I have noticed him with a collar six or seven inches; no other man would have worn it in Dundee but himself.' As well as the large collar, Prince would wear a felt hat, and a long coat – sometimes with a sash – and with his cuffs tied up with string or ribbons. He told his brother Harry, 'They don't know the way to dress in Dundee and London.' A darker side to Richard Prince's peculiarities then began to emerge. Just after New Year in 1895, he threatened his brother Harry with a knife and poker. On another occasion, he threw his mother out of the house and she had to flee to her neighbours for help. Nevertheless, these 'fits of passion' would eventually subside, and he would become calm.

Prince re-joined Elliston's company for a short tour of the play *Alone in London* at the beginning of 1895 but this time his humiliation was complete as Elliston engaged him only as a baggage man. He obviously thought such work to be beneath him, as Elliston recalled, 'I had complaints that he refused to handle bags and said his position ought to be better and he ought to have parts.'

Dismissed from Elliston's company, Prince found himself back in the employment of Gourley's Iron Works in Dundee – the very place where he had worked before he left for London all those years ago. There his fellow workers tormented him. They called him by his old nickname of 'Tripe' and mocked his theatrical pretensions. His vanity made him the natural butt of their derision and sometimes this would drive him to rage.

Nor did Prince gain any respite at home from the thoughts that plagued him. He accused his mother of trying to poison him and his brother Harry of being in league with her. He would pour tea that had been made for him down the sink, claiming it had been contaminated, and then make a fresh pot for himself. He accused a friend of his niece's of having been sent to spy on him. He even claimed, on occasion, to be the second Jesus Christ and that his mother was the Virgin Mary.

His visits to the Dundee theatre also gave cause for concern. When he had first arrived back in Dundee, he would attend Her Majesty's Theatre in the Seagate where he would present an envelope which described him as 'Mr Richard A. Prince from the Adelphi Theatre London' and expect to be admitted for nothing. Once inside, he would applaud at inappropriate moments and attempt to conduct conversations with the actors on the stage.

In March 1896, Prince took up a job at Wallace's Foundry. His new foreman Alexander Husband said that he 'performed his work to my satisfaction, and was always steady at it'. Ominously, though, Prince also spoke about William Terriss at that point. Husband later told how Prince claimed that Terriss 'blackmailed' him.

Around this time Prince made another visit to the Dundee theatre. Refused a free ticket, he paid for a seat in the stalls to watch *For the Crown* but ended up being thrown out after threatening one of the actors and producing a revolver. A theatre official was quoted in the press as saying, 'He has been a perpetual nuisance and we were not sorry when he left again for London.' Many in Dundee must have shared this sentiment when Prince left. On Friday, 23 July 1897, Harry Archer went to the station to see his brother off. Richard Archer Prince would never set foot in his hometown again.

Prince's destination was not London but Attercliffe near Sheffield where he was to join the touring company of one Arthur Carlton in what was advertised as a 'revival of the Great Adelphi success – *The Union Jack*'. Prince was probably hired because he knew the play well, having toured with it for so long in Elliston's company. Touring did not, this time, seem to have caused any improvement in his mental state as it had done in the past. The accusations of 'blackmailing' and poisoning had begun with the commencement of rehearsals. *The Union Jack* tour had made its way to North Shields by 18 October. It was here that Richard Prince left Carlton's company in what he claimed was a dispute over him smoking a clay pipe rather than a cigar. In truth, Carlton was probably glad to be rid of him under any pretext.

Ralph Croyden, another manager in the vicinity, however, was facing impending engagements and still in need of an actor to take on a couple of relatively minor roles. He met Prince at the Amphitheatre, Newcastle, on Saturday 23 October. The actor's experience obtained at the Adelphi and on the *Union Jack* tours made him sound ideal but by that point he was incapable of performing in a play. At the rehearsal he did not know any of the words and he struck ridiculously dramatic poses. His eyes rolled wildly in his head and he tugged at his hair or pressed his temples. He said that his brain was gone – he later claimed to have been poisoned – and asked for the theatre to be closed until the following day. Not surprisingly, Croyden dispensed with his services.

The next morning, Prince turned up at Ralph Croydens' lodgings asking for payment, which the manager understandably refused. Croyden told him that he should never have left the Adelphi, to which Prince replied that he would have been there still if it had not been for one man – and now he named William Terriss, calling him a 'dirty dog'. Croyden remonstrated that Mr Terriss was a well-regarded and successful actor to which Prince responded that, 'Fools often succeed where men of genius fail.' When the Croydens threw him out declaring him a madman he is reputed to have replied that the world would ring with his madness before long. Shortly afterwards Prince boarded a boat to London.

On Thursday, 28 October 1897, Prince, carrying only a brown paper parcel, took lodgings with Mrs Charlotte Darby at 16 Eaton Court, Eaton Lane, Buckingham Palace Road, at the rate of four shillings per week – a sum he was almost immediately struggling to pay. His landlady later confirmed that his diet at this time consisted mainly of bread and milk. She also noticed that his clothes began to disappear. Prince himself admitted that he sold them to live. Clearly, his financial situation was dire and there were few places for him to turn.

On arriving in London he had re-established contact with his sister Maggie who had lived there for several years. Now her smart Chelsea home began to receive visits from her shabby, desperate and mentally unhinged brother. At first she seems to have had some sympathy for him and gave him some money, but regular visits from someone in Prince's state of mind demanding money were bound to try her patience.

At the beginning of November, Prince turned up at the Adelphi. He gave the doorkeeper, Henry Spratt, a note to take up to William Terriss. A reply was forthcoming. This would be sent along with Prince's application for assistance to the Actors' Benevolent fund. Just over six weeks before the murder, William Terriss wrote of Prince:

> I have known the bearer, Mr Richard Archer Prince, as a hardworking actor for many years.
>
> William Terriss

It was a generous gesture from one of the highest-ranking actors in the land to one of the lowest. Adelphi stalwarts J. D. Beveridge, Henry Neville and Laurence Cantley also supplied references. These were sent off, together with Prince's own letter detailing his sorry circumstances, to the Benevolent Fund. The committee were moved enough to give Prince £1 the next day, but this certainly was not the last they would hear from him over the next few weeks. He did his best, nevertheless, to look for work. He approached his old fellow 'super' R. St John Denton, who was now a theatrical agent, at his office near the Adelphi. He would call at Denton's office nearly every day. The agent managed to secure a job for him, but Prince could not take it on account of not having a suitable coat. He was also rejected from a job in a pantomime chorus because of 'the cast in his eye'.

He contemplated returning home to Dundee but another job was always just round the corner – a part in *Julius Caesar*; a tour of South Africa; a part in a chorus. In the meantime he relied on the Benevolent Fund. One of his letters to them included 'a letter from my little sister' showing that Maggie was still helping him to some extent at this point.

In all, the Benevolent Fund made four payments to Prince of £1, £1 10/- and 10/- but by the beginning of December his financial situation was becoming desperate. It was around this time that he paid his final visit to his sister's house. It seems by this point Maggie had simply had enough of her brother and washed her hands of him.

Prince was now struggling to pay his rent. He asked Mrs Darby if he could postpone payment and she agreed that he could pay two weeks together on Thursday, 16 December. He said he was expecting a letter from his sister, presumably containing money. The letter, it seems, would never arrive. When 16 December came round Prince had no alternative but to tell Mrs Darby the truth. At around 3.45pm, Mrs Darby later remembered, he told her, 'I am sorry I have not got any money for you, what shall I do?' Mrs Darby replied, 'I don't know, Mr Prince, I am very sorry for you.'

Prince gathered his few meagre possessions and walked to the headquarters of the Actors' Benevolent Fund at Adam Street where he spoke to the clerk Archibald King Holland. Holland told him that the Committee would not be considering his case that day. Prince said nothing but turned and walked away. He went for one last time to the offices of R. St John Denton's in Maiden Lane at about 5pm and asked if there was any work. 'Nothing,' came the reply. Prince again quietly walked away. Broken, desperate and delusional with no prospects and no hope, Richard Archer Prince returned to Maiden Lane and waited for the man he blamed for all his misfortunes.

William Terris's funeral service was held at the Chapel Royal of the Savoy, proceeding to Brampton cemetery. It was estimated that around 50,000 people lined the route of the procession, which started from Bedford Park and contained over 100 carriages. All the leading lights of the late Victorian theatre were present and the floral tributes (which required two additional hearses of their own) included one from the Prince of Wales. It is difficult to imagine any greater expression of public grief for an actor in the era before film. The word 'assassination' was used frequently in the press in a way that it would not be used in respect of a popular entertainer until the murder of John Lennon in 1980.

It does not seem, though, that Breezy Bill was content to rest in peace. Terriss's ghost is said to haunt the Adelphi and, for some strange reason, Covent Garden Underground Station (which was not built until after his death). A memorial plaque in Maiden Lane marks the spot where he was slain.

Richard Archer Prince was found guilty of murder but was declared to be insane. He was transferred from Holloway Prison to Broadmoor where, despite rumours of his release, he spent the rest of his days, dying in 1937. He finally achieved the fame he sought, not on the West End Stage, but in Madame Tussaud's Chamber of Horrors where a 'portrait model' was put on display alongside the 'actual confession written by Richard Archer Prince'.

In terms of late Victorian Dundee, the story of Richard Archer Prince is the dark flipside of that of the poet William McGonagall. Whereas McGonagall's vanity and delusions as to the extent of his own talent at least provided amusement for the sneering onlookers the same traits in Prince ultimately led to tragedy. From the vantage point of the twenty-first century, the kind of freakshow mentality that haunted both men's lives may be seen as belonging firmly to the past. Yet, can we really be sure that among the stream of deluded and talentless individuals, hungry for fame, that are paraded across our television screens for our amusement in talent and reality shows there does not, somewhere, lurk another Richard Archer Prince?

Sister Act

The story of Richard Archer Prince's sister Maggie is in many ways as remarkable as that of her brother. Maggie Archer was not one to be constrained by either the social or geographical position that fate had handed her. At the age of nineteen, in November 1875 and against her mother's wishes, she had married an Edinburgh medical student, Josiah King, whose stepfather was a Free Church Minister in Dundee. The couple left for the United States soon after their marriage, but King turned out to be a drunken and abusive husband – even having to be restrained by the ship's captain on the outward journey to America. After spending some time in New York and Philadelphia, they returned to Scotland and lived in Glasgow at the home of one of Maggie's friends, but here King 'conducted himself so shamelessly' that they had to leave. Destitute in Glasgow, Maggie fled to her parents' house in Dundee. Josiah followed her and attacked her with a poker. The police were called and he was removed. This was the last Maggie Archer was to see of her husband for six years.

Maggie decided to start afresh in London. She also decided on a new career – she would follow her brother onto the stage. It was quite a transformation. It seems that her marriage had, if nothing else, left her a wealthy woman. Maggie had begun the 1870s working as a linen weaver, living with her parents in their one-roomed tenement flat in Crescent Street, Dundee. In 1877, when the newspapers reported a theft at her London home in St John's Wood, she was described as 'an actress' and the items stolen included a sealskin jacket and an opera cloak. The culprit was a servant of hers. Nobody back in Crescent Street ever had to worry about their servants stealing their sealskin jackets or opera capes.

Maggie's improved circumstances could only enhance her brother Richard's delusions as to what was possible and his sense of his own importance when he too moved to London. On the other hand, it is possible that it was one of Maggie's contacts that got him a foothold on the Adelphi stage.

In 1880, Maggie's husband Josiah King was married again. He had described himself as a widower on the marriage certificate but Maggie was still alive and well. Together with her mother, Maggie confronted Josiah in August 1882 at his house in Edinburgh, but he made no denial and indeed introduced his new wife. A few months later, King appeared at Edinburgh Police Court charged with bigamy. At the end of January 1883, Maggie was granted a divorce. (She would soon have been a widow in any case, as Josiah died of pneumonia at the end of May 1883.)

Returning to London, Maggie began work on what was to be the most ambitious project of what could be charitably called her theatrical career. She hired the Gaiety Theatre at Aldwych at the eastern end of the Strand for a matinee performance of a four-act play written by and starring herself called *My Life*. The plot concerns a young lady whose husband has married her bigamously. She decides to take up acting and stages a play about it at the Frivolity Theatre. It is not difficult to see where she got her inspiration.

It was an unmitigated disaster. At the beginning, the audience merely tittered at some of the clunking dialogue and poor acting, but by the end of act four, according to one critic, 'the house roared with laughter, several of the actors on the stage joining in the merriment'. One of the dizzying number of twists at the end of the play involved the marriage not, in fact, being bigamous as the clergyman who performed the original ceremony had committed some misdemeanor and so had been (in the words of the play) 'unfrocked by his bishop so his body belonged to the Queen'.

The critics were less than kind – 'a hopeless failure' said the *Bristol Mercury*. Miss Archer 'proved unhappily to be as deficient in the art of dramatic construction as she is wanting in the acquirements that are indispensable in a leading actress,' said the *Daily News*. 'The characters are unsympathetic, the dialogue wordy and repetitive, the plot obscure, the tragic situations comical and the comical portions funereal,' said the correspondent in *Reynolds's Newspaper*, while *The Era* concluded: 'Miss Archer has plenty of confidence but no acting ability.' It appeared that Richard Archer was not the only member of the family who was deluded about the extent of his theatrical ability. Other than pantomime appearances (an advertisement states unashamedly that her *Dick Whittington* was the 'greatest success ever known in Weymouth'), Maggie's stage career seems to have floundered.

In the early 1890s, Maggie Archer entered into an affair with the actor W. L. Abingdon, who had briefly been at the Adelphi with her brother. Seymour Hicks in his book *Between Ourselves* alludes to Maggie at that time as being a 'lady of uneasy virtue' and a frequenter of the 'notorious Empire Promenade'. This refers to the promenade at the Empire Theatre Leicester Square – an infamous haunt of high-class prostitutes and their wealthy clients. Hicks could hardly be seen as a neutral witness – he was William Terriss's son-in-law – but Prince himself rambled after his arrest about Terriss sending men 'dressed as swells to my sister's house in London to disgrace me and keep me out of an engagement'. Even Abingdon told his wife that Maggie was a 'fast lady'.

During Abingdon's later divorce hearing, letters were produced from Maggie Archer, including one sent from the Hotel de Paris Monte Carlo. Edward Arthur, an electrical engineer, also gave evidence of misconduct between the couple and the divorce was granted. Maggie's affair with Abingdon, however, was not to last. Abingdon moved to the United States where he married the actress Bijou Fernandez, but that marriage too ended in divorce. On 19 May 1918, the man who had made a career out of playing villains, made his final, tragic exit. He had cut his own throat.

Maggie's involvement with W. L. Abingdon, according to Seymour Hicks, may have sown the seeds for the murder of Terriss by Richard Archer Prince. Abingdon (identified by Hicks only as 'Mr A') was in the habit of entertaining his 'lady friend' – Maggie Archer – in his dressing room after the show and sometimes her brother would be invited. When Abingdon learned of the extent of Prince's theatrical ambitions he came up with a plan. Hicks continued that Abingdon 'had the part of the hero, the part Terriss was playing, typed for [Prince] to learn, and indeed went so far as to have what, to him, was a comic rehearsal called, and with the assistance of the extra people in the piece, had a hilarious hour watching the miserable weakling make a complete Jackass of himself'. The other 'supers' egged Prince on and, in Hicks's words, 'encouraged him for their amusement to talk more grandiloquently than ever of what he would do, should his great day ever arrive'. The effect of this on someone in Prince's state of mind can readily be guessed.

At six o'clock in the evening of Terriss's murder, according to Prince himself, he met Maggie in the street where she told him she would rather see him dead in the gutter than give him another farthing. This must have been a final, bitter blow to him. He later told Inspector William Croxton at Bow Street, 'Had she given me ten shillings this would never have happened, it is all through her.' He also accused her of being in league with Terriss.

After being visited by Inspector Croxton following her brother's arrest, Maggie Archer quietly vanished from London. It seems that she was not keen on the public scrutiny that a trial would bring. Writing in 1914, George R. Sims, co-author of Adelphi melodramas including *The Silver Falls*, intriguingly noted that she went on to be 'one of many mentioned in connection with a much-execrated European monarch who died a few years ago'.

She had certainly travelled a long way from the tenements and mills of Dundee. Her ultimate fate, though, was much less glamorous. Sims wrote: 'Unrecognised by her married name, she was found by a doctor, dead, in a house in London recently, a faithful little dog and a half-empty bottle of brandy by her side and without a human being near or within sound.'

7

Weel Kent?

At the end of the nineteenth century, a Yorkshire doctor, John L. Kirk, began to notice that things that had been features of his everyday life were fast disappearing and he began to collect anything and everything. His collection expanded at a great rate and eventually formed the basis of York's Castle Museum, which contains thousands of objects and recreated rooms and shops and even an entire Victorian Street.

Most people, though, are too busy getting on with their lives to pay attention to such change and things that were once commonplace vanish without being noticed. Nothing on the following pages would have been thought worthy of comment in Dundee in days gone by, but all are features of Dundee life that have slipped unnoticed into history.

The Smallest Shop in the World

One family literally stood and watched the changing face of Dundee city centre for almost three quarters of a century. They saw steam trams and horse driven carriages replaced by trams and buses; they witnessed the celebrations ending two world wars; they saw the eighteenth-century town house torn down and replaced by the City Square; they watched troops marching off to war and returning; they saw everybody from suffragettes to teddy boys go by and they did all this from a space three feet wide by three feet deep. Their name was Lamb and they ran the smallest shop in Dundee – some said in the world – the Hub newsagent in the High Street.

The story of the Hub begins with an unfortunate accident. The site of the shop was originally a steep and narrow wooden staircase leading to the billiard rooms above. A man was killed after falling down this staircase and it was condemned. Most people walking past the condemned staircase saw just that – a condemned staircase. A cabinetmaker by the name of Robert Lamb, on the other hand, saw an opportunity. He offered to rent the space and use it for the sale of newspapers, magazines and cigarettes. Lamb's instinct that there was money to be made in this way proved to be correct. The space was just big enough for one person to fit inside but that was all that was needed. The customer stood outside in the street.

The name of the newsagent's was reputedly the suggestion of a friend of Robert Lamb's, Alf Craik, who suggested that Lamb adopt the name 'Hub' after the centre point of a wheel. The shop was so centrally located in Dundee that all roads appeared to lead to it. Its central location meant that the Lambs often acted as an unofficial tourist information centre, giving directions to visitors and acting as a handy meeting place.

Robert Lamb died aged seventy-four in 1929 but the Hub had by then passed into the hands of his sons Robert and Alexander. An idea of how successful the business was by this time can be gained by the cost of the space when the Lambs decided to purchase it in 1925. They paid £1400 – an astonishing amount at the time – for the premises. The Lambs were also able to open a (full size) stationers and sports outfitters shop in the Overgate. Clearly the business was taking in a lot of money. Nevertheless, they were unperturbed about the thought of robbery. As Robert Lamb told the local press in 1960: 'There's no back door and there are too many spectators.'

International fame beckoned when a visitor from Detroit entered a photograph of the Hub into a newspaper competition to find the smallest shop in the world and won a prize. Whether or not the Hub was actually

The Hub

the smallest shop in the world is open to question – it was certainly the smallest business premises that Dundee has ever seen. It was not a shop, though, in the sense that the customer was able to actually enter the premises. The size of the Hub made it the source of several local jokes – such as the story of the man who took a job as a floorwalker in the Hub or the hotel that was hired for the Hub staff dance.

Alexander Lamb died in 1945 and his share of the Hub went to his wife Robina. The business, nevertheless, continued to thrive. In 1955, the Dundee-born journalist Wilfred Taylor wrote of the Hub, 'Its owner plies a sensationally brisk trade and is almost concealed by piles of newspapers and magazines.'

The Hub carried on until 1960. By this time Robert Lamb was seventy-four years old. He had first worked in the Hub as assistant to his father in 1908. In an interview with the *Courier*, he recalled those early days: 'We started at six in the morning and it was sometimes midnight before we got finished,' he said. He also recalled selling loose Woodbine Cigarettes, in the days before packets, at the price of five for 1d. Newspapers sold for ½d each. Lamb's son told the *Courier* that it was only the fact that his father had recently recovered from a serious illness that prevented him from carrying on.

The Hub was to be sold on but not as a going concern. In fact, virtually all trace of the popular landmark was to vanish from Dundee, although the canopy that had adorned the newsagent's in later years – or one very like it – was to turn up at the Matchbox in Dura Street.

Stand in Dundee High Street today, opposite where the Hub used to be, and you will see no evidence that it was ever there. It was bought by the neighbouring shop, H. Samuel the jewellers, and simply became part of their premises. At the time of the sale in July 1960, neither the Lambs nor H. Samuel would reveal the price paid for the premises. They did, however, tell the local press that it might very well be the most expensive square yard in Britain.

More than half a century on, the price can at last be revealed. H. Samuel bought the square yard from the Lambs for the astonishing price of £5500. To put this into context, in the same month a large detached house in Broughty Ferry sold for just over £3000. In July 1960, Dundee's smallest ever shop could certainly claim to be the city's most expensive square yard, if not the most expensive square yard in Britain.

The Other One O'clock Gun

Six days a week, at precisely 13.00 hours, a gun is fired from Edinburgh

Castle. At the same moment that the gun is fired, the Time Ball (a large white ball suspended above the Nelson Monument on Calton Hill) drops. Together, the gun and ball provide an audible and visible time signal for shipping in the Port of Leith and further out into the Forth. Interrupted only by the two World Wars, this has continued since the gun was first fired on 7 June 1861.

The idea of a time signal for shipping was one that other towns were soon keen to take up. In 1863, time guns were installed at Newcastle, North Shields and Sunderland. In 1867, a similar system was set up in Birkenhead. Possession of a time gun soon seemed to become a badge of honour for any town with a port. By 1876, the *Glasgow Herald* was bemoaning the lack of a gun in Glasgow or Greenock and asking why, when so many other towns had time guns, 'this gunless state of things [was] allowed to continue on the Clyde'.

There had, in fact, been short-lived time guns in both Glasgow and Greenock in 1863–4, installed by the Universal Private Telegraph Company, and for a similar period a gun had been fired at Dundee Harbour. By the early 1870s, however, it was felt that Dundee too should have its own permanent time signal. With its busy docks and the proximity to the Tay Estuary, the town was an ideal candidate for a time gun. As in Edinburgh, there was also a convenient military barracks housed in a castle on a high vantage point in the town. Dudhope Castle, once the home of 'Bonnie Dundee' himself, John Graham of Claverhouse, had been used as a barracks since 1796 and the council currently leased its grounds as a public park.

In August 1872, a platform for the gun enclosed by a wooden fence was erected in front of the officers' quarters at the castle. The gun that was installed, a twelve pounder with 2lb charge, dated from 1813 and was said to have been used on board a ship in the latter stages of the Napoleonic Wars. The world-renowned firm of clockmakers James Ritchie and Son of Edinburgh ensured the accuracy of the gun by means of what was described as a 'firing current' transmitted from the Royal Observatory on Calton Hill via the Edinburgh General Post Office to Dundee.

The gun was inaugurated on 3 September 1872 by Provost James Yeaman. A large crowd had gathered and a great cheer went up when it went off at precisely one o'clock. There followed a reception at the Town House attended by various dignitaries and speeches were made praising Yeaman's personal role in seeing the project to fruition.

At a council meeting the next month, an objection was raised as to the amount, £27, which had been spent on champagne among other things at this event. It was not the first or last time that Dundee council spending would be questioned in this manner but on this occasion Yeaman himself offered to foot the bill to avoid controversy. He was overruled. The Council accounts show that the cost of 'fitting up' the time gun itself came in at £22 17s 0d.

There were concerns, too, about the gun itself. Like its Edinburgh counterpart, it was to be discharged each day at one o'clock but would sometimes be fired too early and sometimes too late. In the event of the signal not being received from Edinburgh, it would not be fired at all. One exasperated correspondent wrote to the *Courier*, 'If the gun cannot give us the proper time daily there is no use in having it stationed here at all.' Another described the gun as 'a complete failure' as it could not be heard even on the High Street.

The amount of charge used was increased in order to remedy the problem of the gun not being heard. This appeared to be successful, although the first time the increased charge was used the gun was fired four minutes late. It could now be heard throughout the town in places as far apart as Lochee and Broughty Ferry as well as in the surrounding countryside and some parts of Fife. A correspondent in *The Scotsman* in 1910 claimed to have heard the Dundee gun 'more than once' on the northern slope of West Lomond in the heart of Fife.

The gun survived the removal of the military from Dudhope Castle in 1881 and the purchase of the grounds by the council in the 1890s. By January 1906, however, it was under threat. It was announced that an inspection had shown it was not fit for service and that it would have to be replaced by a more modern gun, probably a twenty-four pounder.

In June 1914 the gun nearly aided the destruction of Dudhope Castle itself. A bomb had been left in the doorway of the castle. It was suspected to be the work of suffragettes whose campaign was then at its height and who had strong support in Dundee. The bomb's fuse had been lit but it had subsequently blown out and no damage was done. Had the bomb gone off it might have ignited the time gun's store of gunpowder, which was kept in the basement of the castle.

The start of the First World War in August that year may have put the threat from suffragettes in abeyance but it was ultimately to end the daily firing of the gun. In February 1916, at a meeting of the council's Law and Finance Committee, Treasurer Soutar said that a great number of soldiers who were suffering from what might be termed as 'cannon shock' were now in the city and he had been informed that the firing of the time gun had a very bad effect on their nerves.

There had been complaints for many years about the gun's effect on patients at the nearby infirmary. In 1896, it was proposed that the gun be discontinued or removed to another location 'as the firing of it disturbs patients at the infirmary'. In 1910, hospital staff had urged that the gun be 'removed from the neighbourhood, to relieve patients from what can only be described as an addition to their sufferings'. It was noted that the reverberation was 'so great as to shake the windows and doors' and the complaint concluded that 'from the point of view of medical treatment, the noise of a loud explosion upon a sick person at a critical stage of illness has a detrimental effect upon his or her chances of recovery'.

The gun had not been stopped on those earlier occasions but this latest complaint could be seen as a test of patriotism. Councillor Soutar moved that the gun be stopped for the duration of the war – perhaps betraying the council's real motivation when he mentioned its £133 per year running costs. The motion was unanimously carried and the gun was silenced.

When the war ended, however, the firing of the gun did not resume, despite the fact that many people missed the old tradition and wished it to return. In 1924, council convener J. G. Fraser said that the gun should be reinstated. 'We should not have to depend on private firms; have our lives regulated by bummers [the local name for factory sirens],' he said.

The gun was, in fact, reinstated that year for the beginning and ending of the two minutes' silence on Armistice Day on 11 November. It was not an easy rebirth, though, as when it was inspected the day before, the gun was found to have had a spike or nail hammered into it, rendering it inoperable. It was thought that ship's rockets would have to be used instead to delineate the silence but the impediment was removed in time and the old time gun was heard in Dundee once more.

The gun would continue to be used to mark both Armistice Day and New Year until 1936. The marking of Armistice Day in Dundee in the inter-war years was a major event. In 1935, for example, it was reported that more than 12,000 people had congregated in the City Square for the remembrance ceremony. The gun was a simple way of reminding people, wherever they were, when the two minutes' silence began and ended. It was reported that year that in the Sheriff Court, Sheriff Malcolm simply held up his hand at the sound of the gun and stopped proceedings in the middle of a trial and a witness in the middle of a sentence. All over Dundee, people used the gun as a guide to mark the silence. The next year the gun's reliability was called into question again and its fate was sealed.

There had been problems with the gun before – in 1933, it had caused several panes of glass to shatter at a nearby welfare centre – but the events of 1936 were by far the most embarrassing. The gun was fired to mark the start of the silence that was observed by more than 10,000 people in the City Square, by people at the war memorial on top of the Law, by people in Lochee and Broughty Ferry and elsewhere in the city. When it came to be fired again to mark the end of the silence, the fuse misfired. The fuse had to then be cleared and set up again before the gun could be fired. Dundee alone observed a four-minute silence that year.

After this the gun fell silent once more, this time permanently. In 2007, there was a call by Councillor Neil Powrie for a time gun to be reinstated

Dundee's One O'clock Gun

in Dundee, although he told the *Evening Telegraph* that he did not believe that Dudhope Castle was the most suitable location, favouring somewhere near Discovery Point. Many people agreed that a reinstated gun would be an attraction that had a real link to the city's past.

Certainly, Edinburgh's gun has acted as a tourist attraction for 150 years. Calls for it to be abandoned at the end of the First World War similar to those made in Dundee were resisted. Correspondents to *The Scotsman* at the time expressed concern for shell-shock victims and those in the war hospital at the Castle, but the gun was continued and has become a much-loved feature of city life. Calls for it to be discontinued are few and far between in more recent years.

The Dundee time gun, even if restored to Dudhope Castle, would now, at least, face no complaints from patients in the Royal Infirmary – which has been converted into housing – and, unlike other pieces of Dundee's history that have been irretrievably lost, could be restored with relatively little difficulty.

Doc Stewart

Ask anybody in Dundee for directions to the Downfield Hotel and, if you are not met by a blank look, you will almost certainly be asked the question, "Do you mean Doc Stewart's?" The establishment has been known by this name for over 100 years yet few know who Doc Stewart himself was. Many will guess (correctly) that this was the name of a previous landlord but there will be few people alive who remember when James 'Doc' Stewart was behind the bar. Indeed anyone still alive who legally purchased a drink from Doc Stewart himself will be in line for – or already be the owner of – a telegram from the Queen.

James Stewart was born not in Dundee but in Glamis in 1860 where his father was a shepherd. His mother died when he was only nine years old. Stewart seems to have had a head for business from an early age and he managed to establish himself as a grocer first in Dundee and then in the nearby village of Downfield.

He came to the Downfield Tavern, as it was then known, through marriage. In 1893 Stewart married Jessie Warner whose family had been the licensees for several years. Together they had three children – James, Charles and Constance. Stewart was clearly very successful and by the turn of the century the family were living in a seven-room house and had a maidservant. This was a far cry from the living conditions of most of his customers and from his own humble origins.

Nobody today, though, would recognise the pub as 'Jim Stewart's' – so how did the nickname Doc come about? One theory is that, in the days when visiting a public house was not as acceptable as it is now and was considered something to be looked down upon, children would be told that their father had gone to the doctor's or the chemist's or some other such euphemism. It seems that Doctor Stewart had so many 'patients' that the name stuck.

In 1918 and 1919, a worldwide influenza epidemic erupted. The pandemic went on to kill more people than the First World War that had been raging for the previous four years. Between twenty and forty million people died and among them was Doc Stewart's sixty-one-year-old wife, Jessie, who died at the end of 1918. Stewart himself soldiered on for almost another two decades. He died in 1935 at the age of seventy-five, following complications after an operation.

None of Stewart's family seem to have had any enthusiasm for following in their father's footsteps. Less than two weeks after his death, an advertisement offering by private bargain 'the old established business carried on by the late Mr James Stewart at Downfield Tavern' appeared in the press. Indeed, Stewart's son Charles took an altogether different path in life, becoming a Church of Scotland Minister. He died in Annan in 1994 at the grand old age of ninety-seven.

The High Land

In the 1960s and 1970s, as nineteenth-century tenements were demolished, construction of new housing became a priority for local authorities throughout Scotland. Pressures of space and economy meant that the solid constructions of the immediate post-war period soon gave way to cheaper alternatives, and well-planned streets of houses with gardens were replaced with ill-thought-out architectural experiments culminating in 'streets in the sky' – known in Dundee as 'multis'. The 'multis' turned out to have a much shorter lifespan than the buildings that they replaced and only a couple of decades after they were built they began to disappear from the city's skyline.

The 'multis' were not Dundee's first experiment with high-rise living, however. In 1870, a nine-storey tenement was built at Larch Street in the Scouringburn area, which, at the time, was mainly inhabited by Irish jute workers. This tenement was also known as 'the High Land' or 'Robertson's Land' – the landlord being one Alexander Robertson. Robertson was the son of a linen manufacturer who had realised the income to be made from property ownership and was now trying to maximise his profits in a unique way.

Dundee's first high-rise, the High Land

Robertson was an odd and often awkward character as an article in the *Piper o' Dundee* pointed out in 1888. Written by someone identifying himself only as 'A Dundonian', the article noted that there were at one time four Robertsons who were elders at St David's Church in Dundee. While this particular Robertson was acknowledged to be 'an earnest worker for the Sabbath School', the author went on to say, 'Eccentricity gradually weaned him from any sympathetic connection with his brethren, and some of the other elders doubtless gave the cold shoulder to his peculiar suggestions; but, true it is – although I believe his intentions were good – he was the cause of much disputation.' In a move that some of his detractors believed demonstrated his contrary nature, Robertson ultimately converted to Roman Catholicism, though, in truth, this was not an action that anyone would have undertaken lightly or for any motive of social advancement in nineteenth-century Dundee.

'Robertson's Land' took in the postal addresses 2 to 22 Walton Street, 1 to 3 Urquhart Street and 3 to 13 Larch Street. It was eight stories high on the Larch Street side and nine storeys high at Walton Street due to the incline upon which it was built. The frontage to Larch Street was 126 feet, and to Urquhart Street 44 feet. The building was 102 feet in height from the ground to the top of the highest chimney. It contained 187 rooms, mainly divided into one- and two-room flats, which were let on a weekly basis. There was a water supply and toilet on every floor. The tenement contained two shops and at one point had an aerated water factory in its basement. It enclosed a single large courtyard and like its twentieth-century successors, its higher floors afforded wide-ranging views on a clear day.

Had it been a success, this building might have been the spark for the construction of such multi-storey blocks all over Dundee a century earlier than it actually happened. The year after it was built, however, the 1871 Improvement Act, which saw the removal of some of the city's narrow mediaeval streets, also prohibited construction of buildings over four storeys.

In addition, the higher flats proved to be difficult to let due to the climb involved each time the tenant returned home. The occupation of the higher flats also had consequences for those further down the building. Tenants on the second floor, called on to explain their failure to clean the stairs, objected to having to clean the dirt left by tenants of the seven floors above them. There were safety concerns too – the higher flats were well beyond the reach of any of the fire brigade's ladders. In 1873, a labourer named Hugh Mullaney unsuccessfully sued Robertson for £300 damages after his young son, Patrick, had fallen to his death from a sixth-storey window. In any case, the top three floors of the building were not officially used from the 1890s.

Life, for most of Robertson's tenants, was a hand-to-mouth struggle. Some poverty-stricken residents resorted to crime while others sought solace in alcohol. It is not surprising, therefore, that shebeens were common in the area. In 1874, for example, a woman named Ann McGuire was convicted of selling alcohol from her house in the building. A year later, ground-floor resident Mary Rennie was convicted of running a brothel from her flat.

Alexander Robertson's physical and mental health began to go into decline not long after the tenement was built and he was to spend more than twenty years in what was then known as Dundee District Lunatic Asylum at Westgreen, Liff, before his death in 1911. Several unsuccessful attempts to sell the building at Larch Street were made during this period. As early as 1890, an advertisement, while highlighting the annual rental income of £526 8s and 3d, admitted that 'there was and is a considerable portion unoccupied'. After Robertson's death, the building was in effect repossessed by those who had lent him money and subsequently sold for £2000 – although the original asking price had been considerably more.

Thirty years later, the building had undergone considerable decline. The cinematographer Wolfgang Suschitzky, whose later work would include films such as *Ring of Bright Water*, *Living Free* and *Get Carter*, visited the area in 1944 to make his first film, a documentary about young offenders called *Children of the City*. Suschitzky said that Dundee had the worst slums that he had ever seen – in particular he recalled 'a ten [sic] storey high tenement building'. When the building was sold again five years later it fetched only £500 – a quarter of its value in 1911.

Robertson's Land was eventually condemned but unofficial occupation continued. In 1965, it was subjected to a Compulsory Purchase Order and demolished. Ironically, by this time the construction of multi-storey buildings was continuing apace across Dundee. The planners might have done well to listen to the assessment of the anonymous writer in the *Piper o' Dundee* back in 1888. He wrote of Alexander Robertson's folly: 'He built a Tower of Babel and expected to let it; but the Emerald Islanders preferred to have their huts little nearer the earth and so this series of extraordinary tenements remains a monument to false economy.' Time would prove that the descendants of the 'Emerald Islanders' and other Dundonians were no different.

In Search of the Beefcan Close

> As I gaed up the Overgate,
> I met a bonnie wee lass,
> And she winked at me wi the tail o her ee,
> As I gaed walking past.
>
> Ricky doo dum day, doo dum day,
> Ricky dicky doo dum day.
>
> I asked her what her name was,
> She said, 'Jemima Ross.
> And I live wi' a wifie in a lodging hoose,
> At the back o the Beefcan Close.'
>
> Ricky doo dum day, doo dum day,
> Ricky dicky doo dum day.

Having been immortalised in this old folk song, the Beefcan Close is, perhaps, one of the most famous long-demolished addresses in Dundee. It is strange, then, that there is so much disagreement as to where it was located. The song itself, at first glance, seems to point to it being somewhere in the Overgate and many people maintain that the Beefcan Close was indeed situated there between a shoe shop and a butcher's. Others insist that it was located off William Street (later re-named William Lane), which ran between Victoria Road and King Street. Which, if either, is correct and how did the close acquire its unusual name?

The location usually given for the Overgate version of the Beefcan Close is between Birrell's shoe shop at 107 Overgate and the shop at one time occupied by Munro's butchers at number 105. The name, it is said, derives from the time when the butcher's shop was occupied by the British and Argentine Meat Company and the empty 'beef cans' were stacked up in the entrance of the adjoining close.

Those who favour the William Lane location give a different explanation. There, the name is said to originate from a time when poor country dwellers, drawn into the town seeking work in the jute industry, had no cooking utensils or dishes and used empty beef cans in their place.

The song itself gives little in the way of clues to the location. It tells the story of a young man out for a good time in Dundee. He meets a young woman named Jemima Ross who invites him back to her room in the Beefcan Close. Our hero, somewhat the worse for drink, believes himself to have spent the night 'in the airms o' Jemima Ross' but awakens to find himself lying on his back 'in the middle o' the Beefcan Close'. Luckily he has had the wherewithal to hide his money in 'the tail o' his sark'.

Lyrically, the song seems to derive from another ballad called 'The Overgate' which has an identical first verse. The tune and 'Ricky Doo Dum Day' chorus are borrowed from a song entitled 'The Keach in the Creel' or 'The Wee Toon Clerk', which was popular in nineteenth-century Scotland. As with all folk songs, though, there are nearly as many versions as there are singers. Some of these seem to place the events of the 'Beefcan Close' firmly in the Overgate but most agree that this is merely where the main characters in the song meet. Other versions, however, mention 'Todburn Lane, at the bottom o' the Beef Can Close'. This ties in with the other location as Todburn Lane was situated at the King Street end of William Lane.

A photograph of the Beefcan Close exists, showing some of the impoverished residents, mainly children, gathered around two rickety wooden staircases but this provides no real clue as to the location. Indeed, it merely adds another complication. An article in the *Evening Telegraph* in 1982, states the 'official view' of the then Chief Officer of the city's Museums and Art Galleries, James D. Boyd, that the Beefcan Close was located at 1 North George Street, a view supported, the newspaper said, by a reader (unfortunately anonymous) who identified the photograph when it was published in 1960.

Clearly, further investigation is required to establish the location of the original Beefcan Close. Any evidence of the named characters in the song – landlady 'Mistress Bruce' or Jemima Ross herself – living at one of the locations mentioned would certainly prove conclusive but their names rhyme a little too conveniently with 'hoose' and 'close' (in some versions she is Jemima Rose) for this line of enquiry to be taken seriously.

One thing which can be investigated though, is the company which is supposed to have deposited the beef cans in the close in the Overgate. The Dundee Directory lists the River Plate Fresh Meat Company, the predecessor of the British and Argentine Meat Company, at 105 Overgate only from 1906–7. Prior to that, the shop was occupied by John Jones and Son, linoleum merchants. It is safe to conclude, therefore, that the case for the Overgate being the location of the original Beefcan Close dates only from the early twentieth century. Were there to be any earlier evidence for William Lane then the case would surely be proved for that location – but does such evidence exist?

In fact, the evidence does exist in the form of an article in the *People's Journal* in February 1889. The article was part of a series looking at the 'Dens and Hovels of Dundee' and the title alone gives an idea of conditions in the Beefcan Close at that time. The article confirms the story that the close was so-named because the people living there at one time were said to have used beefcans in place of cooking utensils and dishes.

At the entrance of the close were two short flights of steps, which the writer of the article said were 'very much worn and dirty' and the close itself he described as 'filthy in the extreme'. The houses were entered by primitive wooden stairs, which he described as 'very much the worse for wear'. This description and a sketch that accompanies the article would appear to identify the location as the Beefcan Close depicted in the existing photograph.

The houses in the Beefcan Close at this time had no running water and damp walls yet the tenants paid rents of between 1/6 and 2/6 per week. Behind the tenement was a building used as a stable, which the writer concluded was 'far superior as a place of habitation than the building in front of it'.

The *Journal* article continued, 'The passages leading to the houses in the west corner of the building are dark and one has to grope his way through the prevailing gloom to the wretched homes of the poor people.' It seems that the author of the article had a very similar experience to the young man in the 'Beefcan Close' song:

> As I gaed up the close that nicht,
> The stairs was lang and dark,
> So I took my money fae mi inside pooch
> And tied it to the tail o' mi sark

It seems clear, then, that the original Beefcan Close was indeed located off the street then known as William Street, which ran between King Street and Victoria Road. Deemed unworthy of an official name, it gained its nickname from the extreme poverty of its inhabitants. Indeed, the neighbouring property to the south was also known by a nickname – 'the Tarry Twine Close'. By the time the empty beef cans began to pile up in the close in the Overgate, the phrase 'Beefcan Close' had become part of the local vocabulary and was no doubt adopted as its name too.

8
Written In Stone

Dargie Kirk at Invergowrie just outside Dundee has long been credited with being the oldest Christian place of worship north of the Tay. Only a ruin remains today and that certainly does not relate to the first structure on the site. Opinions vary as to the date of the founding of the church but it was traditionally seen as having been founded around the year 700 AD by a saint named Boniface or Kiritanus Albanus who arrived in the area at the invitation of Nectan, King of the Picts, and is said to have founded a church at 'flumen Gobriat in Pictavia' at the Gowrie river in Pictland.

According to legend, the Devil, spying the construction from across the Tay in Fife, was not pleased with the saint's intervention. His anger overtook him and he began to throw large rocks at the structure. The first two fell some way short of their target and landed in the river. These large boulders became known as the 'Goors [or gows] o' Gowrie' and were the subject of a famous prophecy by Thomas Learmonth (known as Thomas the Rhymer) in the thirteenth century: 'When the Goors of Gowrie come to land / The Day of Judgement's near at hand.'

The prospect of the stones ever being on dry land was so unlikely that it must have brought comfort to some with reason to be worried about the proximity of Judgement Day, but things changed in the 1840s, as an article in the *Courier* pointed out, 'these stones, since the Dundee and

The modern ruins of Dargie Kirk

Perth railway cut through the beautiful bay, will in a short time, by the rapidity with which sand is now depositing, be actually "come to land"'. The process has since been completed without the Rhymer's dire warning being fulfilled.

The Devil's next stone, which overshot the mark somewhat, is still visible today albeit now ensconced within the grounds of the Swallow Hotel. It is known as the 'Devil's Stone' or the 'Paddock Stone' and like the 'Goors of Gowrie' is thought actually to be an 'erratic' stone, transported to its present position on an ice-age glacier.

Some versions of the legend give the Devil one last stone to throw. This one landed on Menzies Hill, site of the present day housing scheme of the same name. This was by far the largest of the stones, measuring about seven feet in height above the ground, some four feet across and a foot thick. Part of the stone was broken off, evidently the result of a lightning strike. Around this stone was a thick clump of trees that became known as the 'Dark Stane Roundie'. This stone differed from the others, as the evidence seemed to point to it having been placed there deliberately by human endeavour at some point in the distant past.

The 'Dark Stane Roundie' was at one point a favourite haunt of children collecting birds' eggs and later of gangs who would go there to play cards. The latter activity seems to have been the pretext for its utter destruction in the late 1880s when the proprietor of the land had the trees cut down and the stone broken up to be used on the local roads. A correspondent to the *Courier* in 1889 wrote, 'Of this well known clump, I regret to say, there is hardly any vestige left. Everything is gone, stone and all, except some six or eight trees.' Signing himself Viator (meaning wayfarer or traveller), he added, 'Our local world is all the poorer by the destruction of such favourite spots,' before sarcastically ending his letter, 'All hail the march of improvement!' He would not be the last Dundonian to express such sentiments.

Back at Dargie Kirk, there were many stones placed over the years with greater care than those launched by the Devil. They were the stones placed to mark the resting places of those buried in the kirkyard. Among them was a table-top stone that contained the inscription:

> Erected in memory of Iames Cock, weaver in Locheye,
> our father, who dyed Oct. 15, 1741, aged 65 and of Isobel
> Doig, their mother, dyed March 31, 1733, aged 48

The stone was intricately decorated with symbols of the weaving trade. It was removed from Dargie kirkyard in 1914 to Liff Parish Church where it remains to this day. The name Cock was later changed to Cox and Locheye became Lochee where the descendants of James Cock the weaver later employed 5000 people. They, in turn, left behind a monument of their own – a chimney 282 feet in height and containing a million bricks, with the appearance of an Italian campanile or bell tower and known to generations of Dundonians as Cox's Stack.

Cox's Stack was not built to be a memorial to an industrial age but the widespread desire to retain it as one appears to reflect a need in human beings for a visible connection to the past. From the earliest times, people have sought to leave monuments behind them to commemorate their lives or what was important to them. There also seems to be a need to understand and explain the monuments and relics left by those who have gone before. The following stories concern all these instincts.

The Stone

It was said to be Jacob's pillow, brought to Scotland by the descendants of Scota, the daughter of an Egyptian Pharaoh. It was said to have been the Lia Fáil on which the High Kings of Ireland were crowned at Tara. It was said to have formed St Columba's seat or altar. It was the Stone of Destiny upon which Scotland's kings were crowned for hundreds of years before it was taken to London by Edward I of England. It was the symbol of Scotland's integration into a British State as it sat in Westminster Abbey under the coronation chair. It is currently the symbol of a resurgent sense of Scottish national identity as it sits in Edinburgh Castle while bemused foreign tourists pass by trying to understand why this country has a lump of sandstone among its national honours.

Such was the symbolic power of this particular piece of stone – the Stone of Scone – that its theft from Westminster Abbey on Christmas Day 1950 made headlines around the world. 'Theft' may have been the word used in the newspapers at the time but it remains a contentious one. Those who took the stone would maintain that the real theft had taken place in 1296 when the stone had been taken south in the first place.

Nevertheless, the Dean of Westminster, Alan Campbell Don, denounced the taking of the stone, questioning what motive there could possibly be for such a 'senseless crime'. In a radio broadcast, Don bemoaned the 'sacrilegious hands' that had touched the stone and vowed to 'go to the ends of the earth to recover it'. Ironically, the Dean was himself a Scotsman, having been born in Broughty Ferry in 1885. His father was Robert Bogle

Don of the well-known Dundee flax merchants Don Brothers, Buist and Co. The Dean had nevertheless lived in England for most of his life, having first left Scotland to go to school at Rugby. In 1921, however, he returned home to serve as Provost of St Paul's Cathedral in Dundee for ten years.

It turned out that the stone had been taken by four students with Scottish nationalist sympathies – Ian Hamilton, Gavin Vernon, Kay Matheson and Alan Stuart. In the course of its removal from the abbey, it was found to be in two parts. When both sections were taken over the border, the stone was back in Scotland for the first time in more than 650 years – that is, if the stone taken to England by Edward originally was really the genuine one. It has often been said that the English had been duped by the monks who had custody of the stone at that time and were given a worthless block of stone instead. The real stone, it was said, had been concealed and remained in Scotland.

Some time after its arrival in Scotland, the stone had been taken for repair to a Glasgow councillor and stonemason, Robert (Bertie) Gray, who inserted metal bolts to hold it together. Shortly after this, in April 1951, 631 years after the Scots had asserted their independence in the Declaration of Arbroath, the stone, draped in the Saltire, was found at Arbroath Abbey at the grave of King William the Lion. A note was left that expressed the hope 'that arrangements for the proper disposition of the stone may now be made after consultation with the General Assembly of the Church of Scotland who, as successors of the Abbots of Scone, are its natural guardians.' After spending the night in Forfar police station, however, the stone was soon back in Westminster Abbey and the decision was taken that it should remain there.

The escapade appeared to be over. The Dean had got his stone back. The students had made their point but were not, it was decided, to be prosecuted. King George VI, who knew his health was in decline, could be assured that any future coronation would include the stone as previous ones had done for hundreds of years. The Stone of Scone was back in Westminster Abbey. Or was it?

Bertie Gray had made more than one copy of the stone – including one made years before its actual removal from Westminster Abbey, in connection with another alleged plot. It was only a matter of time before the rumour emerged that the wrong stone had been returned.

In 1963, a group calling themselves 'The Scottish Guardians of the Stone' claimed that they had had the real stone since 1950 and had kept it near Dullater in Dunbartonshire. It would now be moved, they said, as its hiding place was threatened with redevelopment. Bertie Gray, interviewed in the *Glasgow Herald* at the time, claimed that replica stones could be made without difficulty and that a mix-up could have occurred quite easily. Gray had a mischievous sense of humour and liked to fool people. The question was whether he was just being mischievous now or if he had in fact fooled the authorities in April 1951.

On 9 June 1972 – St Columba's Day – a stone was put on display in Dundee that was claimed to be the stone taken from Westminster Abbey in 1950. The venue was St Columba's Church in Lochee Road (at its junction with Cobden Street) and the guardian of this particular stone was the Reverend John MacKay Nimmo. Nimmo was a Scottish nationalist of long standing and a friend of Bertie Gray. He had been asked to look after the stone by the nationalist 1320 Club and its president, the poet Hugh MacDiarmid. The club released a statement at the time as to the stone's authenticity: 'We are not ones to play practical jokes on ministers, and would not palm them off with some substitute.'

Bertie Gray also gave credence to the Dundee stone. At a service for the reception of the stone, when the Reverend Nimmo's wife asked for the truth of the matter, Gray is reputed to have asked if she really thought he would take part in a service for a fake. A spokesman for Westminster Abbey said at the time, however, that they were sure that the stone they had was the original.

The government, nevertheless, was sufficiently worried by the prospect that the real Stone of Destiny was actually in Dundee to launch an investigation into the authenticity of the stone held in Westminster Abbey.

William Kerr, chief constable of Dunbartonshire, who had been the detective inspector in charge of the hunt for the stone in 1951, concluded that it was the real stone that had been returned. A radiographic examination of the stone by the Home Office police scientific development branch confirmed that it had been broken and repaired by the insertion of metal bolts – just as the stone taken in 1950 had been. It was, of course, only the Westminster Stone that was examined in the course of this enquiry.

The Dundee stone, meanwhile, sat in an iron cage in St Columba's for the next seventeen years beside a plaque which read:

LIA FÁIL

The Stone of Destiny has been set here. An appropriate place for a symbol so venerable and significant in Scottish history. It has been given into the keeping of the Minister and Kirk Session of St (Columcille) Columba's Parish Church, Dundee, by the 1320 Club in association with Baillie (Municipal Officer and Magistrate) Robert Gray, of Glasgow, who helped to place the (fake) Stone in Arbroath Abbey on 12th April, 1951.

In 1989, St Columba's was found to be unsafe due to rot and closed at very short notice. The building would later be demolished. A care home bearing the saint's name now stands on the site. The stone, meanwhile, was passed into the care of a group that no modern story of ancient relics and conspiracy would be complete without – the Knights Templar.

The original Templars were founded in the twelfth century with the mandate of protecting Christian pilgrims en route to the Holy Land. Many different organisations today claim to be their legitimate successors. This particular group of Scottish Templars was the Saint Maolruadh Preceptory of the Sovereign and Military Order of the Temple of Jerusalem and had as its chaplain the Reverend John MacKay Nimmo.

The Dundee stone is next said to have gone on display at the People's Palace in Glasgow where it was to be exhibited as the genuine Stone of

Destiny. Tests carried out at this time appear to have shown that the stone was not the one from Westminster Abbey as it had not been fully split in two, yet questions remained. Would the Templars really have given their precious stone to the museum to tamper with? And just how many of Bertie Gray's fake stones were (or are) in circulation?

In an interview with the *Courier* in 2008, Arbroath historian Morris Scott suggested that Gray had made five or six replicas. He also recalled helping to move a stone in Arbroath that was seemingly the one bound for St Coulmba's but was not the one unveiled there. Bertie Gray's son and daughter claimed that he made two replicas that he broke and joined together again with metal bolts so that they were indistinguishable from the Westminster Stone.

The Templars bought the Parish Church in Dull, Perthshire, in 1989 and the Dundee Stone was housed there – in the same county as Scone, the ancient home of the stone – for the next few years. The church was later sold and the stone once more vanished from public view.

There appears to be little doubt that the Knights Templar sincerely believe their stone to be the one that was removed from Westminster Abbey in 1950. The return of the stone from Westminster in 1996 does not appear to have caused them to waiver in this assertion. Their stone still awaits a fully independent Scotland. On the other hand, the authorities north and south of the border are equally adamant that the stone now in Edinburgh Castle was the Westminster Stone. A conspiracy theorist might add, though, that even if they knew this stone to be fake they would not admit this and thus raise questions as to the validity of the present monarch's coronation.

Conspiracies and half-truths, secrets and fakery, all run through the story of the stone like lines through marble – yet there are only really two possibilities remaining in respect of the Dundee Stone. Either one of Bertie Gray's fake stones sat protected by an iron cage in St Columba's for seventeen years or the ancient Stone of Destiny on which the Kings of Scotland were once crowned spent that period in Dundee. Unless, of course, Edward

I of England really was fooled by the monks and the real stone has lain hidden somewhere in Scotland for more than 700 years.

Now He Sits in the Albert Square

> Rabbie Burns was born in Ayr,
> Now he sits in the Albert Square;
> If you want to see him there,
> Take the bus and pey your fare.

This piece of doggerel, well known to school children down the years, is so bad as to be worthy of Dundee's other favourite poet, William McGonagall. It is not unique to Dundee, though – the Glasgow version simply substitutes 'Geordie's Square' for Albert Square. In a similar way Dundee's statue of Robert Burns is not, as it is often thought, unique. This version of Rabbie Burns not only sits in Albert Square, Dundee, but in three other cities around the world.

The statue was originally commissioned for New York as a companion to the one of Sir Walter Scott (a replica of the one that sits in the centre of the Scott Monument in Edinburgh), which already adorned Central Park. The sculptor chosen was Sir John Steell who was responsible for the statue of Scott and whose famous statue of Wellington (The Iron Duke, in bronze, by Steell) had occupied a plinth at the east end of Edinburgh's Princes Street since 1852. Weighing around three tons, Steell's statue of Burns was taken from his foundry in Grove Street, Edinburgh, by road to Glasgow, from where it was shipped to New York in August 1880, becoming the first statue of Burns to be erected outside Scotland.

Before Rabbie was sent on his journey, however, Steell had issued a number of select invitations to a viewing at Grove Street. Seeing the comings and goings at the foundry, many local residents and workers had correctly guessed that the statue they had read about in the newspapers was now complete. A crowd soon gathered, hoping to catch a glimpse of it. When Steell heard this he said that everybody who wanted to see the statue should be allowed to do so. Word soon spread throughout the city and by the end of the evening around 2000 people had admired Steell's creation.

The earlier visitors to Steell's studio had included Dundee Bailie Drummond and builder James Sturrock. They were sufficiently impressed with the design to call a meeting back in Dundee to see if a replica could be purchased for the city. The money was to be raised through a combination of special events and public subscriptions. A broadside ballad of the time took up the cause:

> That the money will be gathered for that you need not fear,
> Already it is coming in frae friends both far and near,
> The bonny lassies at the mills they will gea what they can,
> And so they might, for Rabby loed the darlings every one.
>
> So let every man in Dundee put his shoulder to the wheel,
> And push the movement onward, and he'el the pleasure feel
> Of saying to his children each year as it returns,
> Here stands the statue o' our bard, immortal Robert Burns.

Not forgetting the chorus:

> So agitate ower a' the toun, and e'er January twice returns,
> We'll hae a statue o' the bard, our ain dear Bobby Burns

Even before it was erected the statue clearly inspired some truly awful poetry – and local poet William McGonagall had not yet had his say.

The unveiling of the Dundee statue took place on Saturday, 16 October 1880. It was a great occasion. The streets were said to be lined for two miles as a procession of almost 6000 people marched from the Magdalen Green to Albert Square. The procession began at just after three o'clock led by 200 Artillery Volunteers with their band and six large guns. The Provost's carriage followed flanked by outriders in scarlet jackets. Provost William Brownlee wore his full ceremonial robes and was accompanied by Frank Henderson MP who was to perform the unveiling ceremony. Then came the members of Dundee's various trades and societies. Many of the marchers wore uniforms or fancy dress – representing scenes from Burns's life and works. They were accompanied by around twenty brass bands, several pipe bands, flute bands and more than 100 horses. It was said that the procession took half an hour to pass any given point. When the first of the marchers reached Albert Square at around four o'clock, a salvo of guns fired by the artillery heralded their arrival and the bells of the old steeple rang out. It was nearly five o'clock before all were assembled.

Frank Henderson made a moving speech in which he said, 'The memory of no other Scotchman – I can truly say the memory of no other man – could have evolved a sentiment of love and reverence so deep and so universal as is manifest here today. We are here to unveil to you and to generations of Dundonians as yet unborn, a visible, tangible expression of the unseen but real power of that sentiment in our hearts today – to show to our children, and to our children's children, to all who now or hereafter may claim Scotland as their 'auld respected mither', that we in Dundee are not behind in doing homage to one of her most illustrious and most loving, although one of her poorest sons.'

The statue was unveiled to cheers from the vast crowd. It sat on top of a pedestal of Peterhead granite that weighed around twenty tons. The facial features of Steell's design were heavily influenced by Naysmith's famous portrait of 1787 – the year in which Burns made his only trip to Dundee. The posture was inspired by the story of the composition of 'Mary in Heaven', showing the poet seated, leaning against a tree stump with quill in hand. The first lines of this poem are on the scroll at Burns's feet.

A special booklet and a commemorative medal were issued to mark the

Dundee's statue of Robert Burns

occasion of the unveiling and souvenir prints and photographs of the statue were sold. Nor could Poet McGonagall, it seems, resist making his own act of commemoration:

> This Statue, I must confess, is magnificent to see,
> And I hope will long be appreciated by the people of Dundee;
> It has been beautifully made by Sir John Steell,
> And I hope the pangs of hunger he will never feel.
>
> This statue is most elegant in its design,
> And I hope will defy all weathers for a very long time;

And I hope strangers from afar with admiration will stare
On this beautiful statue of thee, Immortal Bard of Ayr.

Fellow-citizens, this Statue seems most beautiful to the eye,
Which would cause Kings and Queens for such a one to sigh,
And make them feel envious while passing by
In fear of not getting such a beautiful Statue after they die.

Neither was the New York statue to be spared McGonagall's attentions. On a trip there in 1887 he recorded that,

As for Central Park, it is lovely to be seen—
Especially in the summer season when its shrubberies are green
And the Burns Statue is there to be seen,
Surrounded by trees on the beautiful sward so green.

In July 1884, Steell's statue of Burns was unveiled for a third time – this time in Thames Embankment Gardens in London. There had been no great fund-raising effort needed on this occasion, as retired Glasgow merchant John Gordon Crawford, who had lived in London for many years, had met the costs. The ceremony was well attended but was not so elaborate as the one that had taken place in Dundee four years earlier and there was a steady downpour of rain throughout the proceedings. Lord Rosebery performed the unveiling – revealing a slightly modified version of Steell's original design with the head at a different angle. The Caledonian Asylum Band played 'God Save the Queen' and 'Auld Lang Syne' and there were three cheers for the sculptor Sir John Steell.

As they strolled away from the unveiling ceremony, a conversation took place among three leading Burns enthusiasts, David MacKay, David Sneddon and Colin Rae Brown, which led to the formation of a worldwide federation of Burns Clubs – still thriving today as the Robert Burns World Federation.

The next city to receive a copy of the statue was the furthest away from Burns's birthplace, but was, in fact, the city that had the closest personal connection to the poet. In 1847, Burns' nephew the Reverend Thomas Burns had been one of a group of Scottish settlers who had helped to found the city of Dunedin in New Zealand. Such was the influence of the Scots that Dunedin became known as the 'Edinburgh of the South'. The statue was situated in an area known as the Octagon in the heart of the city. The unveiling was performed by Thomas Burns's granddaughter – the poet's great grand-niece – on 24 May 1887 and a speech was given by Sir George Gray, Governor of New Zealand. It is estimated that around 8000 people attended the ceremony.

Back in Dundee, the statue was, at last, inspiring a better quality of poetry. In 1888, Dundee had sought the title of 'city' and had been granted it – officially achieving city status on 26 January 1889. The poet James Young Geddes, in his long poem 'The Glory has Departed', bemoaned how the citizens of the once 'Radical Toun' were now scrambling for the trappings that went with city status. In one section he turned his attentions to Rabbie:

Here you, Burns, star-gazing opposite Lambs,
Turn your neck this way;
Never mind the lingering star for a while;
Never mind your Mary in heaven, she is comfortable enough;
It is we who are vexed, we who are troubled.
Here is a theme for your satire;
Here are the people that raise statues to you;
Here are the people that sing 'A man's a man for a' that';
Here are the people that shout 'The rank is but the guinea stamp'—
See how they are crane-ing their necks for honours,
See how avaricious they are for gew-gaws, how their souls are athirst for
    trumpery title,
No, you won't look?
You won't listen?

Well, perhaps after all you are better employed.
Methinks if you were alive you would leap from your pedestal and flee
  the city.

In 1910 Burns did come alive, at least in the mind of local poet Joseph Lee in his poem 'The Whitewashin' o' Robbie Burns'. It seemed that the bard was pleased with mankind's progress:

> But yet that day of which I spake
> Draws nearer—
> Thou may see it break! It comes! It comes!

It wasn't coming just yet, for a' that. Within a few years, Lee would become well known locally as the 'Black Watch poet' as he chronicled the worst conflict the world had yet seen.

Rabbie then went back to sleep, it seems, but no doubt keeping a weather eye on the headquarters of DC Thomson – Dundee's foremost exponents of the printed word – which grew up opposite him.

Being an accepted feature of the Dundee landscape for over a century, the statue can be taken for granted, but it deserves better from the 'generations of Dundonians as yet unborn' that Frank Henderson MP referred to at the unveiling. Perhaps the recent refurbishment of Albert Square and 250th anniversary of Burns's birth will serve as inspiration for the inhabitants of what Burns himself called 'a pleasant town' to look again at this statue and appreciate it, and at the same time remember the others 'the world o'er' in the same image.

The Other Residents of Albert Square

Besides Rabbie Burns, Albert Square contains several other interesting memorials . . .

Queen Victoria

Dundonians reacted to Queen Victoria's coronation in 1838 by rioting and burning down a theatre, so it can perhaps be viewed as relief that they chose to mark her Diamond Jubilee with the erection of a statue. It was appropriately to be situated in the square that had been named after her late consort, Prince Albert. Some early photographs, however, appear to show the statue in a different position – in front of the High School – but this was in fact a replica that had been placed there to test public opinion.

Public opinion must have been generally favourable as the statue that was eventually unveiled was largely unchanged. Costing £3000, it was the work of the English sculptor Harry Bates and was cast in bronze. Weighing over six tons, it sits on a granite pedestal which houses four intricate panels depicting scenes from Victoria's reign. The Queen is seated and holds in her hand an orb with a sailing ship on top of it – perhaps to symbolise the British Empire's dominant position in the world at the time. If so, there is perhaps added symbolism in the fact that the ship had disappeared by the late twentieth century.

The statue was unveiled on 28 August 1899 by the Duke of Connaught who opened the Victoria Hospital for Incurables (later the Royal Victoria Hospital) on the same day. The unveiling would later be referred to by Dundee street orator and wit, W. S. Finlay, who often spoke in Albert Square, as, 'when the Duke hauled the sark off his granny'. Missing from those who attended was the sculptor, Harry Bates, who had died in January of that year at the age of forty-eight.

Queen Victoria had visited Dundee twice during her long reign. On the first occasion in 1844, Prince Albert had been at her side when they arrived at Dundee's docks. A commemorative Royal Arch was erected there four years later and stood until 1964 when it was demolished to make way for the Tay Road Bridge.

Victoria's second visit was as a widow on Friday, 20 June 1879, when she crossed the original Tay rail bridge. The day before the visit, she had learned

The statue of Queen Victoria in Albert Square

of the death of the French Prince Imperial who had been living in exile in England but had recently gone to fight in the Zulu War. Her diary records:

We reached the Tay Bridge station at six. Immense crowds everywhere, flags waving in every direction and the whole population out; but one's heart was too sad for anything. The Provost, splendidly attired, presented an address. Ladies presented beautiful bouquets to Beatrice and me. The last time I was in Dundee was in September 1844, just after Affie's birth, when we landed there on our way to Blair, and Vicky, then not four years old, the only child with us, was carried through the crowd by old Renwick. We embarked there also on our way back. We stopped here about five minutes, and then began going over the marvellous Tay Bridge, which is rather more than a mile and a half long. It was begun in 1871. There were great difficulties in laying the foundation, and some lives were lost. It was finished in 1878. Mr Bouch, who was presented at Dundee, was the engineer. It took us, I should say, about eight minutes going over. The view was very fine.

On 24 June, a notice appeared in *The Times*: 'The Queen has been graciously pleased to confer the honour of knighthood upon Mr Thomas Bouch, C.E., chief engineer and projector of the Tay Bridge.'

Just over six months later, the bridge collapsed, taking with it a train and all its passengers.

George Kinloch – the Radical Laird

On 16 August 1819 at St Peter's Field in Manchester, between sixty and eighty thousand people gathered to peacefully demonstrate in favour of reform in a Britain where only a tiny minority had the vote and where the vast majority lived in poverty. The authorities, undoubtedly panicking at the size of the crowd, sent in the local yeomanry with devastating consequences. The exact figures are not known but around eighteen people died and more than 700 were seriously injured. Mockingly recalling the Battle of Waterloo four years previously, the event became known as the Peterloo Massacre.

In early November that year notices began to appear in Dundee, which read:

MEETING

OF THE

INHABITANTS

OF DUNDEE, &c.

On WEDNESDAY, the 10th current at Twelve o'clock noon

A MEETING of the INHABITANTS of DUNDEE and NEIGHBOURHOOD will be held in the MAGDALEN YARD to take into consideration the present STATE of the COUNTRY with a view to suggest the means most likely to lead to a REFORM of ABUSES and an alleviation of the distress with which the working classes in particular are at present nearly overwhelmed.

Also to express their sentiments on the late *unprovoked, cruel and cowardly attack made on the people at Manchester,* while peacefully assembled for a constitutional purpose.

A COLLECTION will be made at the entries to the place of meeting in aid of the fund for obtaining justice for the Manchester sufferers.

The man delivering the main speech at this demonstration was not a poverty-stricken rabble-rouser but one of the city's Harbour Trustees, a landowner and Justice of the Peace. His name was George Kinloch. Kinloch had visited France as a young man and some of the egalitarian philosophy of the revolutionary period seems to have remained with him throughout his life. Towards the end of his life he still maintained that the republican form of government was the 'best ever devised by man'.

Kinloch had addressed a similar meeting at Magdalen Green in 1817 but this time the authorities were on edge and the atmosphere had changed substantially in the wake of the Peterloo Massacre. A large number of special constables had been sworn in and kept in readiness for any trouble but they, together with the military, mindful of what had happened at Manchester, kept away from the scene of the demonstration in the hope that it would pass off peacefully.

Around 10,000 people turned up to hear Kinloch speak that day, some carrying flags and banners with slogans ranging from 'the Voice of the People is Irresistible' to the more threatening 'Bread or Blood!' Twenty-one resolutions were passed denouncing what had happened at Manchester and promoting reform of Parliament. Calling for voting reform, Kinloch said:

> I cannot understand why one man should have a vote and another should not have one. Is not the life, the family, the property of the poor man as dear to him as the life, the family and the property of the rich man is to him? Do we not all contribute more or less, according to our means, to the needs of the State? Are we not all liable to be called upon at any moment to risk our lives for its defence? Why then should one man have a vote and another not, I confess I cannot comprehend.

These were revolutionary ideas in 1819 but Kinloch maintained that he wanted 'reform to prevent a revolution'. Those in power saw things differently, however, and a warrant was issued for Kinloch's arrest on a charge of sedition. There was little doubt that the authorities were irritated by what they saw as a betrayal by one of their own class. Kinloch almost certainly faced transportation to a penal colony. He opted instead to flee to France, saying that he found it 'preferable to visit the hospitable shores of France at my own expense, rather than subject my country to the expense of transporting me to Botany Bay'.

Kinloch was eventually pardoned and allowed to return from exile in 1823 after his case was reviewed by the new Home Secretary Robert Peel. Peel had replaced Lord Sidmouth, who was always unlikely to issue such a pardon having been denounced in one of the resolutions at the 1819 meeting at Magdalen Green as 'guilty of the highest species of treason' and having 'deserved dismissal from the office which he so unworthily filled'.

In 1832, the Great Reform Act extended the franchise to approximately one in seven adult males. It was only a fraction of the reform that campaigners such as Kinloch had wanted but it was a significant step along the road to democracy in Britain. Dundee marked the occasion by naming a street, which opened the following year, Reform Street. Reform Street connected the High Street with the area known as the Meadows, which was later to be the site of Albert Square.

Dundee also emerged from the Reform Act with its own Member of Parliament for the first time. The new electors returned George Kinloch. This was his moment of triumph and some of the finer ironies were not lost on him. In 1819, the warrant for his arrest had been signed by the Sheriff of Forfarshire, James L'Amy; now, as Kinloch noted, 'I was, by the same Sheriff L'Amy, proclaimed the chosen representative of Dundee.'

The triumph was short-lived, however, as Kinloch was taken ill with what was described as a fever in March 1833 and died the same month. He was fifty-seven years old. Almost immediately there were calls to commemorate him in Dundee and a committee was formed the month after his death to raise public subscriptions for a statue. Difficulties in obtaining a site for the monument caused a delay of many years. It was not until 3 February 1872 that the statue was unveiled by Lord Kinnaird. The work of John Steell, the man who would later be responsible for the statue of Burns, it was the first statue to be erected in the centre of Dundee and remains the only one of the Albert Square statues to portray a native of Dundee.

Kinloch is still remembered in Dundee but his name deserves to be more widely known. Besides his political activities, he was instrumental in improving the harbour and establishing the Dundee–Newtyle railway line. He will always be best known as a radical politician though, and this is something that is perhaps more, not less, impressive in the light of his background. This was a point he himself once put to his critics in a letter to the *Advertiser* and it sums him up neatly:

Born into the privileged class and with acres enough to make me independent I might have lain on my oars and floated calmly down the stream of life, a useful or perhaps a useless country gentleman, regardless of corruption on the one hand or oppression on the other, but my principles forbade me this inglorious career.

James Carmichael – Engineer

In 1821, while engineers James Carmichael and his younger brother Charles were building the engines for the first steam-driven Tay ferries, Charles is reported to have said to his brother, 'Man, could we not make a boat go backwards as well as forwards?' This was the inspiration for Carmichael to come up with what was then a novel idea – the reverse gear.

Inspecting the invention, Captain Basil Hall R.N. wrote that 'the ingenious reversing gear does its business most perfectly' and was sure that the invention would be 'universally adopted'. There were safety implications too, as the Carmichaels themselves asserted in a letter to Hall:

> The vessel may be moved forwards or backwards, or may be retarded or entirely stopped, at any given moment, by merely turning the handle to the places denoted by the graduations of a dial-plate. No skill is required for this purpose, so that the master himself, or a sailor under his directions, can perform the office as well as the ablest engineer. Thus, the confusion which frequently arises at night in calling out to the engineer below, is avoided and any ambiguity arising from the word of command being transmitted through several persons is entirely prevented.

It would be expected that the Carmichaels would soon be extremely rich as a result of this invention but as Captain Hall noted, the brothers were 'apparently unconscious of having accomplished anything worthy of being made public' and no patent was taken out.

Nor was a patent taken out for James Carmichael's other most celebrated invention – the fan blast, or blowing machine, which provided for the more efficient heating and melting of iron. Indeed, he was said to have freely showed it to anyone in the trade who was interested. At a banquet given in the brothers' honour in Glasgow, James Carmichael was presented with a silver service, which was inscribed:

Presented to James Carmichael Esq., Engineer, Dundee by a
few Friends in the Iron Trade, in testimony of the deep sense of the
liberal manner in which he and his brother have permitted the
unrestricted use of their valuable invention of the
'Fan-Blowing Machine', Glasgow, April 1841

There can be no clearer indication of Carmichael's character. Although he possessed a brilliant mind, he did not have the ruthless business sense to fully exploit it.

James Carmichael was born in Glasgow in 1776. After the death of his father ten years later, he moved to Pentland, south of Edinburgh, where his mother's family lived. Here he was apprenticed to an uncle as a millwright before returning to Glasgow to complete the study of his trade at the cotton spinners Thomson and Buchanan. His younger brother Charles, meanwhile, had found his way to Dundee after an apprenticeship in Loanhead.

In 1810, Charles invited James to join him in Dundee and the two soon acquired a reputation for the quality of the machinery they supplied for the town's flax industry. As well as this and their later work on the steamboats, the Carmichaels also built the engines for Scotland's first steam locomotives in the early 1830s, which operated on the Dundee–Newtyle railway. Charles Carmichael died in 1843, having also served the town as a councillor for a period. James Carmichael died ten years later.

In 1872, a letter appeared in the *Courier* from George Hood, a former employee of the Carmichaels. Signing himself 'An Old Mechanic', Hood called for a public meeting 'so that funds may be got and a suitable memorial be erected in honour of the deceased gentlemen'. Such a meeting was held on 17 July at the Town House and it was proposed that a statue be erected in James Carmichael's memory. The 'Old Mechanic' again wrote to the *Courier*, suggesting that there should also be a statue to acknowledge the contribution made by Charles Carmichael but this was not taken up at an official level.

The statue of James Carmichael in Albert Square

The statue of James Carmichael, designed by John Hutchison R.S.A. and said to be a good likeness of the engineer, was unveiled on Saturday, 17 June 1876. Between ten and fifteen thousand people attended the ceremony. The workers of Messrs J. Carmichael and Co. marched to the ceremony from the nearby Ward Foundry. It was a great occasion but would undoubtedly have been more enjoyable for all those concerned had it not taken place during an unrelenting downpour. As the *Courier* reported, 'No sooner had the veil been lifted from off the statue amidst loud and enthusiastic cheering, than the rain increased and pelted so hard that in a few minutes the effigy itself was dripping.'

Spanish Civil War Memorial

Man's dearest possession is life. It is given to him but once, and he must live it so as to feel no torturing regrets for wasted years, never

know the burning shame of a mean and petty past; so live that, dying,
he might say: all my life, all my strength were given to the finest cause
in all the world – the fight for the liberation of mankind.

This quotation from the Russian writer Nikolai Ostrovsky is to be found
on the small plaque that remembers the Dundonians who died in the
Spanish Civil War. The plaque, containing sixteen names, was unveiled
on 23 February 1975 in a ceremony attended by Dundee veteran Arthur
Nicoll and Lord Provost Tom Moore but boycotted by the Unionist and
Progressive group on the council.

The Spanish Civil War plaque in Albert Square

At the time the plaque was unveiled, General Francisco Franco was still
alive and, though ailing, was still nominally Head of State in Spain. Before
the year was out, however, he would, unlike his former comrades Hitler
and Mussolini, die in his bed.

Franco was the leader of the group of generals whose attempt to seize power from the democratically elected government had precipitated the Spanish Civil War and inspired many from Dundee and the surrounding district to join the British Brigade. As one of the men whose name appears on the plaque, John 'Patsy' McEwan famously said, 'If I don't go and fight fascism, I'll just have to wait and fight it here.' This was in an era when the British government's attitude toward fascism was one of appeasement.

Much has been done in recent years to revive interest in this hitherto forgotten aspect of Dundee's history and it was discovered that the plaque contained two significant errors – it listed John McHugh instead of his brother James and it had also omitted the name of Allan Craig altogether. Money was raised for an additional stone to correct these errors and a re-dedication ceremony was held in October 2008 in the presence of Jack Jones, the former leader of the Transport and General Workers Union who had himself fought in Spain.

The Wallace Stone

Not much evidence remains today to indicate that Dundee once had a castle. Besides the name of Castle Street, the only memorial is a small plaque on the outer wall of St Paul's Episcopal Cathedral, which is built on the remains of the Black Rock on which the Castle once stood. It states simply: 'Site of Castle of Dundee destroyed cir. 1314'.

The plaque is more interesting for the fact that it goes on to mention the exploits of one of Scotland's national heroes: 'Near this spot William Wallace struck the first blow for Scottish independence cir. 1288.'

Tradition has it that William Wallace received at least part of his education at Dundee's grammar school, the forerunner of today's High School of Dundee. The 'first blow' that the plaque refers to was when Wallace killed the son of Dundee's English governor – a youth named Selbie – and had to flee for his life.

The main source for this story is 'The Wallace', an epic poem composed

The plaque that marks the spot of William Wallace's 'first blow for Scottish independence'

around the 1470s by a professional bard named Henry the Minstrel (also known as Blind Harry). Harry was said to have based his poem on earlier writings by a man named Blair who had been a school friend of Wallace's at Dundee and who, after studying for the priesthood in Paris, returned to Scotland in 1296 to become his personal chaplain and confessor. It may even be that Blair had witnessed the events described by Blind Harry when Wallace stabbed Selbie to death.

Perhaps it is because there is no tangible relic of Wallace's time in Dundee that attention has turned to an event that is reputed to have happened as he fled from the town after killing Selbie. He was heading to his maternal uncle's home at Kilspindie and passed through the village of Longforgan. Here he is said to have rested outside a cottage on a 'bear stone' or 'knocking stone', which was a type of hollow stone used for grinding grain. It also had a flat stone lid which could be used as a seat. The woman of the house is said to have sheltered Wallace and given him bread and milk.

Some accounts have tried to combine this incident with one referred to in Blind Harry's poem where a woman aided Wallace by giving him some of her clothes. Wallace, dressed as a woman, then sat spinning while soldiers searched for him nearby. However, this incident, if it happened at all, seems much more likely to have occurred while he was still within the confines of the town when the authorities were in hot pursuit. Some versions add that the woman at Longforgan expressed a passionate love of Scotland, which so impressed Wallace that he told her why he was fleeing, but this has all the hallmarks of a later romantic invention.

The tradition that Wallace rested on the stone at Longforgan is certainly an old one. In 1899, a Broughty Ferry architect and antiquarian, Alexander Hutcheson, was involved in the renovation of the church at Longforgan and it is likely that the story of the stone came to his attention at that time. The next year, Hutcheson wrote a paper for the Society of Antiquaries of Scotland. In the paper he presented an account he had unearthed that had been written about 1760 and was then in the possession of Mr Paterson of Castle Huntly. The account tells first of the killing of Selbie and is presented here as it was written:

> On day when all the Schoolars was at play at the west port of that town Young Selbie found fault with Wallace for having a Suit of short Green Clothes with a belt from thence depended a Durk or Skene. This weapon is still practised in Scotland and is very Dangerous in Close Combat … this Weapon young Selbie wanted from Wallace at anyrate, so that a scuffle inshued between the two young Heroes, four times Wallace threw his antagonist on the ground, at the fifth atack Wallace drew his Skene & stobed young Selbie to the Heart and then fled to a house on the Northside of the Overgate of that town where he was well screened by the female Sex while the English Garishon vended their fury on the inhabitants of the town.

The house on the north side of the Overgate would seem a much more likely venue for Wallace's disguise as a woman. The account goes on to tell of Wallace's visit to the house at Longforgan:

The first halt he made was at a house in Longforgan and sat Down at the Door of said house on a stone which serves for a knocking stone and hear the Hospitall Landlady give him an ample repast of Bread and Milk, from there he proceeded to Killspindie, but his Uncle fearing a Search from Dundie sent our young Hero with his wife over the ferry at Lindors on their way to Dunipce in Stirllingshire where he was safe at that time. But to return, that stone at the house in Longforgan still goes by the name of the Wallace Stone, and what is more remarkable ever since the for-mentioned period of Wallace, the name of Smith from father to son hath been Landlords of this House and how long before is not known, only this on thing among all the Revolutions of time they have been very carfull in preserving this stone as a piece of great Antiquity.

The stone was certainly preserved by the family for at least the next century. In the Statistical Account of Scotland in 1795, the tradition was once again referred to:

There is a very respectable man in Longforgan, of the name of Smith, a weaver, and the farmer of a few acres of land, who has in his possession a stone, which is called Wallace's Stone. It is what was formerly called in this country a bear stone, hollow like a large mortar, and was made use of to unhusk the bear or barley, as a preparation for the pot, with a large wooden mell, long before barley-mills were known. Its station was on one side of the door, and covered with a flat stone for a seat, when not otherwise employed. Upon this stone Wallace sat on his way from Dundee, when he fled, after killing the governor's son, and was fed with bread and milk by the goodwife of the house, from whom the man, who now lives there, and is proprietor of the stone, is lineally descended, and here his forbeers have lived ever since, in nearly the same station and circumstances, for about 500 years.

In 1847, James Thomson was able to report in his *History of Dundee* that the Smith family was still resident in Longforgan and taking good care of the stone: 'When we saw this relic of the days of old so closely associated with the memory of the illustrious hero, we found it carefully laid aside, clean, and as neatly caum-stoned over as the hearth of the very tidy cottage in which it is preserved.' The next year, the *Courier* added, 'It is kept as clean and clear as any dish in the house, and is exposed in as favourable a place for view as if it were a splendid piece of family china.'

By 1869, however, a correspondent to the paper noted that the stone had been gifted to Mr Paterson of Castle Huntly and was 'carefully preserved within the mansion house'. The last male representative of the Smith family, Alexander Smith, was unmarried and had no children. He left the cottage around 1860 and moved to Blackness Terrace, Perth Road, Dundee, with his sisters Rachel and Elizabeth – ending the family's long association with Longforgan. The stone was handed over to Paterson at that time.

The Wallace Stone has since come into the possession of the Dundee Museum. It is an interesting old item in its own right, but could it be that William Wallace really once rested on it? Certainly, the stone is of a type which was used for centuries in rural Scotland but this merely raises both the possibility that it dates from Wallace's time and that it might belong to a later period. Perhaps the conclusion that Alexander Hutcheson reached in 1900 in his paper for the Society of Antiquaries of Scotland still holds true today: 'The Longforgan tradition does not deal with any of the superhuman feats, the hero-myths current in Scotland, many of which have not yet been recorded, but relates to an incident that has all the colour of probability about it.'

Royal Blood?

High on Balgay Hill, in the west most part of the cemetery, there is a remarkable gravestone. It is the gravestone of one Professor Patrick O'Neil who died in 1880. Headstones can often provide a useful source

The gravestone of Professor Patrick O'Neil

of information to people researching their family history but any visiting descendant hoping to glean some useful detail from the inscription on this particular stone would truly have hit the genealogical jackpot. The inscription charts Professor O'Neill's descent from Hugh O'Neil, Earl of Tyrone, who died in 1616.

Hugh O'Neil was a pivotal figure in Irish history, a rebel chieftain who defeated the English at the Battle of the Yellow Ford and sparked a nationwide rebellion, but whose eventual flight into exile – known as the Flight of the Earls – spelled the end of Gaelic Ulster. This left the way open for the protestant plantation of the province and centuries of conflict.

Over the years, the weather has taken its toll on the monument but it is till possible to make out most of what it says:

ERECTED BY PROFESSOR O'NEILL,

TO THE MEMORY

OF

HUGH O'NEILL OF THE RED HAND OF ULSTER CREATED EARL

OF TYRONE BY HER MAJESTY QUEEN ELIZABETH AND

AFTERWARDS ELECTED KING OF ALL IRELAND BY THE

KINGS, CHIEFS AND EARLS AND WITH THE UNANIMOUS

GOOD WILL OF THE COMMON PEOPLE OF HIS COUNTRY

WHO DIED IN EXILE AT ROME ON THE 20TH JULY 1616

AGED 76 YEARS,

HE WAS INTERRED WITH THE RIGHTS AND CEREMONIES OF

HIS CREED, AND ALSO THE POMP THAT HEREDITARILY

BELONGED TO HIS NOBLE NAME AND ROYAL STATION IN

LIFE AND OF HIS FOREFATHERS AND DESCENDANTS,

WHO ARE INTERRED IN DONAGHMORE, COUNTY OF TYRONE,

IRELAND

HE HAD FIVE SONS HUGH, HENRY, JOHN, BRIEN AND CON.

OF

CON O'NEILL FIFTH SON OF THE KING WHO DIED AT

GORTINAGOLLY PARISH OF DONAGHMORE, TYRONE, IRELAND

ON THE 16TH MARCH 1670 AGED 65 AND IS INTERRED IN

DONAGHMORE;

HE HAD FOUR SONS BORN TO HIM AT GORTINAGOLLY,

PARISH OF DONAGHMORE, NAMELY FELIMY, HUGH, SHAN

AND HENRY.

OF

FELIMY O'NEILL, ELDEST SON OF CON, WHO DEPARTED THIS
LIFE ON 15TH AUGUST 1723 AGED 51 YEARS AND IS INTERRED
IN DONAGHMORE. HE HAD THREE SONS BORN TO HIM AT
GORTINAGOLLY NAMELY TURLOUGH, SHAN AND CORMAC.

OF

TURLOUGH BAGHA O'NEILL ELDEST SON OF HUGH WHO
DEPARTED THIS LIFE ON 6TH MARCH 1817 AND IS INTERRED
IN DONAGHMORE
HE HAD FOUR SONS BORN TO HIM AT GORTINAGOLLY
NAMELY CON, SHAN BUIE KNOWN BY THE BY NAME OF
STOUT OR YELLOW JOHN, FRANK AND JAMES.

OF

CON O'NEILL ELDEST SON OF TURLOUGH BAGHA, WHO
DEPARTED THIS LIFE AT ALTMORE ON 23RD DEC. 1841 AGED
51 YEARS AND IS INTERRED IN DONAGHMORE,
HE HAD SEVEN SONS BORN TO HIM AT GORTENDARRAGH
PARISH OF DONAGHMORE COUNTY OF TYRONE IRELAND
NAMELY TURLOUGH, JAMES, SHAN, CHARLES, CON, PATRICK
AND FRANCIS.

NAKED CAME I OUT OF MY MOTHER'S WOMB
AND NAKED SHALL I RETURN THITHER,
THE LORD GAVE,
AND THE LORD HATH TAKEN AWAY
AS IT HATH PLEASED THE LORD SO IT IS DONE,
BLESSED BE THE NAME OF THE LORD.

JOB. I. 21.

OF

JOHN O'NEILL OR SHAN BUIE, KNOWN BY THE BYNAME OF
STOUT THE SECOND SON OF TURLOUGH BORN AT
GORTINAGOLLY PARISH OF

DONAGHMORE TYRONE IRELAND, WHO DEPARTED THIS LIFE
ON 7TH MAY 1857 AGED 77 YEARS AND IS INTERRED IN THE
CONSTITUTION BURYING GROUND DUNDEE
HE HAD FIVE SONS BORN TO HIM AT GORTENDARRAGH AND
ALTMORE PARISH OF POMEROY AND DONAGHMORE NAMELY
PATRICK, TURLOUGH, SHAN, JAMES AND FRANK.
OF
PATRICK O'NEIL, PROFESSOR OF PHYSICK, ELDEST SON OF
SHAN BUIE WHO DIED ON 18TH DECEMBER 1880 AGED 69
HE HAD FOUR SONS BORN TO HIM IN DUNDEE NAMELY
SHAN, CON, JAMES AND JOHN.

So who was this descendant of kings who now lies buried among so many commoners on Balgay Hill?

Patrick O'Neil, if the gravestone is to be believed, was born in County Tyrone around 1815 and came to Dundee in 1833. Despite his royal antecedence, his family was not wealthy. His father John (Shan Buie or Stout or Yellow John according to the inscription) ended his days in Dundee working as a handloom weaver and his grandfather Terrance (Turlough Bagha on the inscription) had been a tailor back in Ireland.

On arrival in Dundee, Patrick O'Neil worked as a hackler in a linen factory and lived in the West Port. He was said to be popular among his fellow workers, being described as a wit and lover of stories. In his early twenties O'Neil married a woman named Alice Goodwin and ensured the continuation of his own branch of the O'Neil family into a new generation with the birth of his son John in 1840.

In the next few years O'Neil's life began to change. It seems that his wife Alice died in the early 1840s and he remarried in 1843, this time to a Bridget Monaghan. Patrick and Bridget had a son James born in 1844. No record appears to exist of the other two sons mentioned on the gravestone – Shan and Con – and it seems highly likely that they did not survive into adulthood. Perhaps the loss of his children was what inspired Patrick to turn to the study of medicine. The fact that he specialised in the area of mid-wifery and childbirth would appear to point to this.

He began attending night classes and around 1847 went to Anderson's University in Glasgow where he attended courses in subjects such as 'mid-wifery and the diseases peculiar to woman and children'. He also spent six months at the Glasgow General Lying-in Hospital in St Andrew's Square (the equivalent of a modern maternity hospital) during which time he, according to one of his certificates, 'attended and had charge of fifty-two cases of childbirth'. His time in Glasgow coincided with the cholera epidemic of 1848–9 and he is said to have distinguished himself in the treatment of its victims both there and back in Dundee. He spent a further year studying at the Dundee Royal Infirmary.

Having completed his studies and going by the title of surgeon-accoucheur (the male equivalent of a midwife), Patrick O'Neil set sail for America in 1852 to undertake a professional tour 'investigating the hospitals and institutions of America'. He took with him a reference from some of Dundee's leading professionals, medical practitioners and

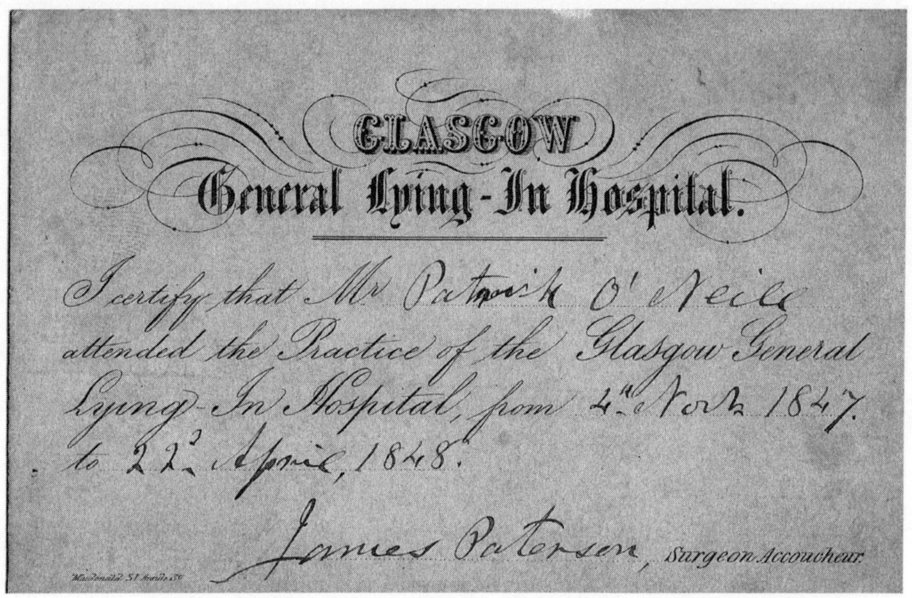

GLASGOW
General Lying-In Hospital.

I certify that Mr Patrick O'Neill attended the Practice of the Glasgow General Lying-In Hospital, from 4th Nov 1847 to 22d April, 1848.

James Paterson, Surgeon Accoucheur.

A certificate marking Patrick O'Neil's attendance at the Glasgow General Lying-in Hospital

clergymen in which they said that O'Neil had 'rendered himself of great service in the practice of medicine in Dundee upon many occasions and particularly during the prevalence of cholera both here and in Glasgow some years ago'.

Patrick O'Neil spent two years in America and returned to Dundee in 1854. Soon after this, he opened his shop at No. 70 Overgate where he sold a wide range of remedies and dispensed medical advice. Perhaps during his time in the United States he had encountered some of the more dubious characters whose peddling of medicine had more to do with showmanship than cure, for he then styled himself 'Professor of Physick' and spelled his surname O'Neile. His new name and title were proudly displayed above the door of the shop in large letters. Dundonians, never easily impressed, simply called him Paddy.

O'Neil was obviously an intelligent man who had done very well for himself considering his humble origins, but his tendency towards over-blown language and outrageous claims for his medicine meant that the local population rarely seemed to take him as seriously as he took himself. The mere mention of his name in a public meeting or courtroom was often enough to reduce the proceedings to laughter.

There were some who questioned whether O'Neil had any medical experience or was just a charlatan altogether. This moved him to publish a list of his qualifications and several impressive testimonials from satisfied customers. Typical of these was one from William McMahon of 18 Kidd's Land, Rosebank, Dundee, whose son had suffered from dysentery for ten weeks and, although attended by a doctor and given various medicines, had made no improvement. McMahon's testimonial concludes, 'My son becoming still weaker, until reduced to a perfect skeleton, the doctor told me he could do no more for him; and when about giving up all hope, a friend of mine advised me to apply to Professor O'Neile, 70 Overgate, Dundee; I have done so and in a few days he has effected a complete cure. This I insert that others may know where they will get proper medicine and treatment.'

It did not help that the author of one of O'Neil's testimonials, Johan Beattie, took him to court for its use in his advertisements but the case was withdrawn when it emerged that her recommendation, like others used by O'Neil, had been given voluntarily and sworn in front of a Justice of the Peace. Nevertheless, the *Courier* used the incident to disparage O'Neil and his use of the title 'professor':

> Now professor has a range of misapplication which often renders it liable to the suspicion of being synonymous with 'pretender' . . . We should not be surprised to hear of a scavenger calling himself 'professor of the sweeping' or of a knife grinder assuming the dignity of a 'professor of friction'. There are 'professors of hair cutting' and last, if not least, Dundee rejoices in the presence of Professor Patrick O'Neile.

O'Neil responded in typical fashion with a letter outlining his qualifications. These looked impressive, if hardly justifying the title of professor. More dubious was his claim as to the 'unfailing efficacy' of his herbal preparations or his claim to cure cancer 'permanently without the use of the knife'. Nevertheless, O'Neil must have been doing something right as he remained in business for over twenty years. Certainly, no one could accuse him of not working hard enough. His shop remained open for consultation between 10am and 10pm every day except Sunday when country patients could visit his private residence, Goschen Cottage, 63 Hospital Wynd, Dundee, between 2pm and 10pm. Visitors were also invited to inspect his 'extensive and unique' collection of coins.

O'Neil also carried out consultations by correspondence. As he himself put it, 'Great numbers of my patients I have never seen but have treated entirely by letter; and often a case may be submitted in that way even *better* than by word of mouth.' His writing was not restricted to letters to patients. A treatise survives which he wrote on the perils of 'onanism'. Anyone who had 'abandoned himself however slightly to this practice' of self-gratification was urged to seek medical attention, which, of course, they could do by post to Professor O'Neil who would send the 'proper remedies' to any place in the United Kingdom on receipt of a Postal Order.

O'Neil was assisted by his wife Bridget – or as he described her in his usual overblown style, 'the celebrated Madam B. Monaghan, Midwife, a lady who . . . has established her reputation not only in this country but also in America and on the continent and is an expert Chemist and Druggist'. She was no doubt a suitable partner for the man who referred to himself as someone 'whose studies and labours in the cause of suffering humanity have given him a wide spread and daily increasing reputation as being one of the most accomplished and skilful practitioners of our time.' Modesty, it seems, was not one of Patrick O'Neil's failings.

O'Neil never read the Sherlock Holmes stories, which did not appear until after his death, but had he done so he would surely have sympathised with the lead character, for just as Holmes had Professor Moriarty so O'Neil had a similarly named arch-enemy – 'Professor' Marriott. Marriott had previously practised under the name 'The Old Army Doctor' and it surely must have been particularly galling to O'Neil when he adopted the title 'Professor', particularly as he had none of the qualifications of which O'Neil was so proud. The two 'Professors' employed teams of billposters who not only posted up their own employer's posters, but also tore down, posted over or painted over those of his rival. The billposters often came to blows and the matter ended up in court on more than one occasion.

The business clearly made O'Neil wealthy. As well as the property at the Overgate, he owned his home at Hospital Wynd (the site of which is located at present day Kinghorne Road near its junction with Bruce Street), together with further property in nearby Hill Street. The scale of the Balgay Hill monument erected at a time when most people could not afford any sort of gravestone also testifies to a wealthy man. Nor was that stone one of a kind. O'Neil had paid for an almost identical one to be erected in the graveyard of his ancestral home of Donaghmore, where an additional inscription reads:

THE ABOVE IS AN EXACT COPY OF THE FAMILY STONE IN BALGAY CEMETERY ERECTED BY PROFESSOR O'NEILL DUNDEE ELDEST SON OF SHAN BUIE OR STOUT OR YELLOW JOHN TO THE MEMORY OF HIS FOREFATHERS WHO ARE INTERRED IN DONAGHMORE, AND TO HIS FATHER AND MOTHER AND FAMILY IN DUNDEE.

His heritage and family tradition were clearly important to Patrick O'Neil, so it is perhaps surprising that he should abandon one thing that definitely linked him to Hugh O'Neil, Earl of Tyrone and all the others listed on the monument – the Roman Catholic religion, the religion that his forefathers had professed and that they and their descendants had gone to great lengths to maintain in the face of the penal legislation in Ireland that followed the Flight of the Earls.

A clue to Patrick O'Neil's conversion is on the gravestone itself where it refers to Hugh O'Neill being buried with the 'rights and ceremonies of *his* creed' – his creed was clearly not the same as Patrick's. It is not clear whether religious conviction or hopes of personal advancement in Presbyterian Scotland motivated Patrick's conversion to Protestantism, but the timescale in which it happened can be narrowed. In 1840 and 1844 respectively his sons John and James each received a Catholic baptism in St Andrew's Cathedral in the Nethergate, yet his marriage to Bridget Monaghan in 1843 was held in the Church of Scotland. At the time of his trip to America in 1852, the signatories to the testimonial he took with him included James Thomson, the Presbyterian minister of St Clement's Church.

When O'Neil's will was published following his death, it contained a clause stating that any beneficiaries should satisfy his trustees that 'they are of the Protestant faith and do not profess or believe in the Roman Catholic faith, providing and declaring that any beneficiary who shall belong to or profess any other than the said Protestant faith shall forfeit all right hereunder'. No Roman Catholic was eligible to be a trustee either. Clearly, O'Neil wanted to control events from beyond the grave.

Other provisions in the will disinherited Bridget if she married again and any beneficiary who refused to use the surname O'Neil also lost their rights.

Due to the lack of documentation, it may never be possible to ascertain whether or not Patrick O'Neil's claim to be descended from the Earls of Tyrone has any basis in fact, yet like O'Neil's claims for his medicines, there may be some truth behind the exaggeration. It does have the ring of an authentic family story – similar, no doubt, to many others that were handed down. The difference is that whereas many such stories were never even recorded, O'Neil became rich enough for his family story to be carved in stone.

Patrick O'Neil was obviously well prepared for his death. The monuments on Balgay Hill and in Donaghmore Graveyard both state that he erected them – presumably during his lifetime. At one time the Balgay monument contained, behind a glass panel, his prescriptions for fighting cholera, which he had bequeathed to the local community but, according to a newspaper report, 'the language in which they were couched was considered so indelicate that the Burial Board ordered them to be removed.' It was also said that O'Neil had his coffin on show in his back shop for many years before his death. He died at his home in Hospital Wynd on 18 December 1880 and was buried on Balgay Hill under the names of his illustrious ancestors.

Later additions to the stone indicate that Patrick's wife Bridget Monaghan died some twenty-seven years after her husband in 1907. She had also outlived her son James, who died in 1893. James had been a boxer in his younger days, described in one report as 'an obstinate looking urchin'. He later received convictions for assault, including one against two of Professor Marriott's billposters. An assessment of James's character is to be found in a note made by solicitor Thomas Thornton, who was preparing for the inquiry into the ill-fated Tay Bridge. James O'Neil had worked on the bridge for two and a half days as a riveter. Thornton noted of O'Neil, who had turned up drunk at his office, '[He] is a son of Professor O'Neil and is a well known bully and fighting man. This is a most disreputable character and it would be a disgrace if he were allowed to appear.'

James O'Neil's daughter Agnes had lived with her grandmother for much of her childhood. She married Alfred Landon in 1892 but the marriage ended in divorce in 1907. Agnes died in 1936 and is also commemorated on the Balgay monument. Her daughter Linda Violet Landon (later Smith) who died in 1963 in Toronto, Canada, is the last person to be commemorated on the stone.

No mention is made on the monument of what became of Professor O'Neil's oldest surviving son John or of any descendents that he might have had – nor is any mention made of the fate of any of his brothers and their families. It is quite possible, therefore, that there are people in Dundee today who can trace their descent from some of those family members and, thanks to Patrick O'Neil and his remarkable gravestone, all the way back to Earl Hugh, the Great O'Neill, himself.

9
The Radical Toun

Is not every day adding a new link in our chains? Is not the executive branch seizing new and warrantable powers? Has not the House of Commons (your only security from the evils of tyranny and aristocracy) joined the coalition against you? Is the election of its members fair, free or frequent? Is not its independence gone, while it is made up of pensions and placemen?

There are many in Dundee today who would find themselves answering 'yes' to some or all of these questions, but in 1793, with the shadow of the French Revolution hanging over Europe, it was considered an offence even to ask them. They are the words of one George Mealmaker, a handloom weaver and one of the founders of the Dundee 'Friends of Liberty'. Despite Mealmaker's admission of authorship, his words led to a sentence of seven years transportation on a fellow member of the Friends of Liberty, the Reverend Thomas Fysche Palmer, an English-born Unitarian clergyman known locally as 'Doddy'. A ninety-foot-high stone obelisk in Edinburgh's Old Calton burying ground now commemorates Fysche Palmer and other early advocates of democracy.

Mealmaker and Fysche Palmer represent a radical strand in Dundee's political outlook, which would later see Chartists, suffragettes and trade unionists flourish in the city. It was this trend that saw Dundee become first a Liberal and then a Labour stronghold in the twentieth century. Not that anyone could take the votes of Dundonians for granted. The Liberal Winston Churchill was rejected in favour of Neddy Scrymgeour, Britain's first (and only) prohibitionist MP in 1922, and in 1974, Dundee East elected Gordon Wilson, giving the Scottish National Party a foothold in what had hitherto been Labour's industrial heartland.

The following stories have a political flavour but perhaps also have something to say about the vagaries of the Dundonian character.

His Darkest Hour? Dundee's War with Churchill

For most people, the name Winston Churchill is not one associated with defeat. For them, he is the man who led Britain to victory in the Second World War, the most famous Prime Minister of the twentieth century and the man voted the greatest ever Briton. He may, indeed, be all of these things but in Dundee in 1922 it looked like his career was at an end. He had represented the city in Parliament since 1908 but now came fourth in the poll.

The newly elected members for the city were Edwin Scrymgeour, Britain's first prohibitionist MP and E. D. Morel, the Labour candidate who had taken a pacifist stance during the First World War. Despite being the sitting MP, Churchill did not even amass as many votes as D. J. Macdonald – his fellow Liberal Candidate for the two-member seat. It had been a fiercely contested campaign and it did not help the Liberal cause that Churchill and Macdonald had both been forced to miss part of it due to illness – in Churchill's case he had his appendix removed.

Churchill did not make a speech at the official declaration. A temporary platform had been erected at the Caird Hall to allow the candidates to address the crowds waiting in Dock Street and he stood at the bottom of it, reportedly with tears in his eyes while Scrymgeour and Morel made their speeches. When Willie Gallagher, the Communist candidate, decided

Churchill during his time as Dundee MP

that he too would make a speech, Churchill and his wife left. They took a taxi from Castle Street back to their hotel to a mixture of cheers and booing.

Later that evening, Churchill addressed a meeting at the Liberal Club in Reform Street where he spoke to party members. He told them how profoundly he would always feel in the debt of Dundee and how his heart was devoid of the slightest sense of regret, resentment or bitterness. All his life, he told them, he would look back with feelings of the deepest regard for Dundee. Then it was over. Churchill left Dundee by train that night. In his own words, he left Dundee 'without office, without a seat, without a party and without an appendix'.

It is difficult to believe that Churchill left Dundee feeling the lack of resentment that he expressed to his supporters. He had been unceremoniously thrown out of what he believed would be a seat for life. Though he never expressed any resentment publicly, he was to enjoy a stormy relationship with the city for the rest of his life. In Dundee, too, there remained a bitterness towards the defeated candidate unlike that reserved for anybody else.

Within a couple of years of his defeat in Dundee, Churchill had found his way back to the Conservative Party after one more election defeat as a Liberal candidate and a victory as an independent 'Constitutionalist'. He had left the Conservatives in 1903 to join the Liberals over the issue of tariff reform. 'Anyone can rat but it takes a certain ingenuity to re-rat' was his comment on his shifting party loyalties.

Back in Parliament, he was made Chancellor of the Exchequer by Prime Minister Stanley Baldwin. An unrelenting opponent of the General Strike and the trade unions in general, his actions at this time hardened the view of many of his former constituents in Dundee that Churchill was a ruthless class warrior.

In 1927, a full five years after Churchill's defeat, Sir Herbert Samuel, the Liberal party chairman, addressing a party meeting in Dundee knew that Churchill was still an easy target in his old constituency. 'Probably Dundee would be especially interested in the doings of the present Chancellor of the Exchequer,' he said to much laughter. 'Dundee was one of six constituencies which Mr Winston Churchill has contested for Parliament and now we watch him as head of his ninth Department of State in the course of his fourth party allegiance.'

In 1929, in the so-called "Flapper Election" (when women under thirty were given the vote for the first time), Churchill attempted to hold on as a Conservative to the seat in Epping that he had won in 1924 as an independent. At a meeting in Epping Market Place during that campaign his wife Clementine gave a vigorous defence of her husband – just as she had in Dundee during much of the 1922 campaign when Churchill was ill. When she had finished her speech, the Labour candidate T. J. Walton Newbold took to the platform. In a clearly pre-arranged piece of showmanship, he was handed a telegram during his speech. It was from the Dundee Labour Party and read as follows: 'Hope you will defeat Winston Churchill, the despised and rejected of Dundee.'

Churchill retained his seat in the 1929 election but the Tories lost over 150 seats. He was still an MP but no longer held government office. He then entered what have come to be known as his wilderness years – devoting much of his time to painting and writing. Surely now, with the defeat at Dundee receding over a decade into the past, his relationship with the city would become a thing of historical interest only. Dundee would surely have no rancour against Churchill the writer.

The publication of Churchill's book *Thoughts and Adventures* in 1932 put paid to any idea of a truce with Dundee. A review in *The Scotsman* pointed out that Dundee would 'resent the imputation of being the most drunken city in the United Kingdom'. This was an understatement. Churchill had referred in the book to 'the bestial drunkenness of Dundee for which it bears an evil reputation and I must admit I have never seen "paralleled" in any part of the United Kingdom'. Not surprisingly, this immediately incurred the wrath of Dundonians. The Lord Provost W. H. Buist was moved to write a letter of complaint to Churchill. In his reply, Churchill said that he was dealing with his impression of the city from nearly a quarter of a century earlier and was not suggesting that they reflected contemporary conditions in Dundee. This was certainly a qualified apology. Nevertheless, he went on to say, 'I need scarcely say that I always retain the strongest regard and respect for the citizens of Dundee and look back with the greatest satisfaction to my long and pleasant association with the city.'

This was not good enough for Buist who, while accepting Churchill's expression of regret, pressed for more, objecting in particular to his claim that drunkenness in Dundee was unparalleled in the United Kingdom and that the offending section should be removed from any future edition. Churchill agreed to do this and again regretted any annoyance caused by his original statement but would not concede the main point saying that his impressions were derived from personal observation.

Churchill surely had a point. At the time he had first arrived in Dundee, drunkenness was a great problem – the police in the city at one time kept a wheelbarrow for wheeling away drunks. A prohibitionist like Scrymgeour was surely unlikely to have been elected in a city with no drink problem. Whether that drink problem was 'unparalleled' in any part of the United Kingdom is certainly open to question – all industrialised cities faced similar problems to some extent – but a visit to the Dundee law courts on a Monday morning in the early years of the twentieth century may have persuaded doubters of Churchill's case. However, Dundonians who may have accepted this criticism from one of their own simply did not want to hear this from Churchill and resented his use of the phrase 'bestial drunkenness'. This phrase is often quoted even today when describing Churchill's attitude to the city.

Throughout the 1930s, Churchill continued to warn of the dangers posed by the rise of Hitler and the Nazis in Germany. The policy of appeasement adopted by Prime Minister Neville Chamberlain began to unravel as Hitler's demands for territory continued to grow. With the German invasion of Poland in 1939 and the start of the Second World War in September of that year, Churchill returned to government as First Lord of the Admiralty, and then in May 1940, at the age of sixty-five, he replaced Neville Chamberlain as Prime Minister. The so-called phoney war was over and the conflict then began in earnest; France was falling further into German hands on a daily basis; the USA was far from entering the war and Britain was isolated. This must surely be a time for reconciliation. Not according to the Dundee press. When he was MP for Dundee, Churchill had clashed with local newspaper proprietor DC Thomson. Now Thomson's *Courier* welcomed Churchill as Prime Minister by saying that he was 'not a reconciling personality'.

Nor was resentment towards Churchill in this period restricted to the local press. In cinemas in Lochee it has been said that during the newsreels, the audience would boo and heckle whenever Churchill appeared. Their cheers, on the other hand, were reserved for 'Uncle Joe' Stalin. Twenty years after his defeat at Dundee, and even as a wartime Prime Minister, Churchill could not, it seems, win the city's respect.

By 1943, the defeat of Rommel's forces in North Africa had made people dare to contemplate the end of the war but they knew that a long and arduous struggle still lay ahead. The country in general seemed to have confidence in Churchill's leadership – or at least to have rallied behind him for the duration of war. It was against this background that a motion came before the Council in Dundee that Churchill should be awarded the Freedom of the City. In any other city at this time, such a motion might have been nodded through without a formal vote – but not in Dundee. The council at this time was almost evenly divided between Labour- and Conservative-supporting councillors and thus both the debate and the vote split along party lines. Labour members objected to the cost ('There will be a casket, luncheon, people coming to the Caird Hall and buses running'), to the timing ('The best course to adopt is to defer the matter until the end of the war') and simply to Churchill ('I don't think the Prime Minister is worthy of the Freedom of our ancient burgh'). Eventually, the proposal was adopted by sixteen votes to fifteen. Labour Councillor Harry Hird suggested that the figures of the vote should be included in the invitation but he was, not surprisingly, ruled out of order. Ten days later, a special council meeting listened in silence as Lord Provost Garnet Wilson read a letter from Churchill's Private Secretary in which Churchill regretted he was 'unable to accept the honour which you have proposed to confer on him'.

The episode had ended in the worst of all possible outcomes for Dundee. The deliberations had been concerned with whether or not to grant the honour to Churchill. The thought that he might decline the offer once made had not even occurred to the councillors. Frantic efforts then went on behind the scenes to take the edge off of the rejection. Dundee's MPs, Dingle Foot and Florence Horsburgh, hoped that they might be permitted to say that it was only the narrow nature of the vote that prevented Churchill accepting the honour and that it was nothing to do with past political history. When this idea was put to Churchill in a memo from his Private Secretary John Martin he responded with a terse one-line reply saying that he had nothing to add to the reply that had already been sent. The implication was clear – it *did* have to do with past political history. Despite the fact that more than two decades had passed since his defeat at Dundee and that he was now Prime Minister, it seems that the botched Freedom offer had brought Churchill's resentment to the surface once more – though, in truth, no one could blame him for rejecting so half-hearted a gesture.

In 1945, Churchill suffered a rejection much greater than that at Dundee in 1922. As the war ended, the people of Britain went to the polls and threw out the hero of the Second World War and elected the Labour Party under Clement Attlee by a landslide. While in opposition, Churchill surrounded Dundee with accepted Freedom awards. In 1942, he had been made a Freeman of Edinburgh; in 1946, he received the Freedom of Aberdeen and in 1948, he travelled to Perth to accept the Freedom of the Fair City. He had no particular connection with any of these places – the only place in the vicinity he enjoyed a long association with was Dundee. At the ceremony in Perth, he recalled that association and said that it was not at his wish that it was broken. He remembered as a child being told of the Tay Bridge disaster – later on, he joked, he had had a minor Tay Bridge disaster of his own – but he carried away nothing but agreeable souvenirs of his long association with the city of Dundee.

Churchill was returned to Downing Street for one last time in the General Election of 1951, despite losing the popular vote. Now seventy-six, he was, unknown to the general public, ill for much of this period of office having suffered a series of strokes. In 1952, there was a by-election in Dundee, just like the one in 1908 that had delivered the seat to Churchill. The victor this time was the Labour candidate George Thomson, returned with a significant increase in the Labour majority. In Thomson's introduction to Tony Paterson's account of Churchill's time in Dundee, *A Seat for Life*, he recalled taking his seat in Parliament:

As I walked up the Floor of the House to be introduced, the Labour benches erupted. They shouted across at the Prime Minister – 'Resign! Resign! It's the voice of Dundee.' Winston, by this time a deaf old man . . . began an elaborate ritual of fumbling with his hearing aid, removing it, and tucking it in his waistcoat pocket.

Churchill had succeeded in upstaging the new MP by literally turning a deaf ear to the 'voice of Dundee'.

Churchill retired as Prime Minister in 1955 but remained a backbench MP until 1964. He died in January 1965. In April that year, members of the Dundee Council passed a motion by eighteen votes to fifteen saying that they did not agree to the use of public money for contributions to the Churchill Memorial Fund. They could not, they felt, use ratepayers' money for a fund with which they might disagree.

Churchill despised Dundonians; he was a sham; he said he hoped grass would grow over the streets of Dundee. These were sentiments expressed in the letters page of DC Thomson's *Evening Telegraph* – not during his time as MP or after his defeat in 1922 but in 2006, when it was proposed that the city should have a statue of Churchill to mark the association. Clearly, bitterness against their former MP was still present among Dundonians in the twenty-first century. A telephone poll in the paper found 80% against the idea of a statue.

The idea that Churchill had said something to the effect that the grass would grow green on the streets or around the mills of Dundee if he was not elected is one that occurs again and again in the reasons given as to why he should not be commemorated in Dundee. It is one of the facts that everybody seems to know about Churchill's time in Dundee. It is not clear, however, whether or not he actually said it. If he did say it, it was certainly one of Churchill's less original utterances. Jefferson Davis, President of the Confederate States, had used a similar phrase at the time of the US Civil war: 'Grass will grow green in the northern cities,' and another American, William Jennings Bryan, Democratic Party nominee for President of the

United States, said in a famous speech in 1896: 'Destroy our farms and the grass will grow green in every city in the country.'

Had Churchill not gone on to be wartime Prime Minister and thus the most famous holder of that post in history, it is most unlikely that there would be any move to commemorate him in Dundee. On the other hand, denying him a commemoration sometimes seems to perpetuate a grudge from decades ago. The irony is that many of those who now want to mark Churchill's time in Dundee might not have voted for him in 1908 were they around then and many of those opposed to the idea might have given him their vote were they entitled to one. In truth, there are many Churchills. In Dundee's collective mind it seems that the architect of the Gallipoli disaster, the Tory Prime Minister, the ruthless anti-trade unionist and the man who said there would be a Gestapo in Britain were Labour elected have obliterated the young radical that they elected in the first place.

In May 2008, a century after he was elected as MP for the city, Churchill's eighty-five-year-old daughter Lady Mary Soames unveiled a bronze plaque at Dundee University, later to be displayed at St Paul's Cathedral.

'I first visited here over eighty years ago as a baby of only seven weeks old. A newspaper at the time ran a picture of me in my mother's arms in Dundee and had the caption Churchill's wife and "her un-baptised child"!' said Lady Soames. 'It's nice to return all these years later and have my father fondly remembered.'

Dundee's Lord Provost John Letford said that the day meant so much to so many and that the view that the people of Dundee did not care about Churchill had been proved wrong.

One hundred years after his election at Dundee, was this a reconciliation – the end of the ongoing animosity between the city and Churchill? Previous history shows that feelings run deep and the matter has flared up from time to time across the decades. Perhaps, as Churchill himself said in another context, 'It is not the end. It is not even the beginning of the end. But it is, perhaps, the end of the beginning.'

George Nicoll Barnes: Labour's Forgotten Leader

Ask anybody to name a Scottish-born leader of the Labour Party and the chances are that they will mention Gordon Brown (born in Giffnock) or Tony Blair (born in Edinburgh). Those with longer memories will mention the late and much lamented John Smith (born in Damally, Ayrshire). The more historically minded might mention Labour's first Prime Minister Ramsay MacDonald (born in Lossiemouth) or the party's first leader Keir Hardie (born in Newhouse, Lanarkshire). Few, if any, though, will mention George Barnes from Lochee, Dundee.

George Barnes's paternal family roots, certainly, did not run deep in Dundee. His father, James, was originally from Leyland in Lancashire and worked in various places in the north of England before coming to Dundee with an engineering firm from Darlington (most probably the firm started by Dundee's future provost Charles Parker who made such a move in 1849).

James Barnes met a local woman named Catherine Langlands whom he married in the United Presbyterian Church in Tay Square in 1855. George Nicoll Barnes was the couple's second son, and was born in Lochee High Street, four years later. A plaque has recently been added to the refurbished Lochee Library to mark Barnes's birthplace but the family did not stay there long. They soon moved to Cobden Street, then known as Union Place.

Union Place was not a permanent arrangement either and they had moved to Kerr's Lane at South Road by the time Barnes was four or five years old. His earliest memories, he later recalled, were of this low-lying marshy area known as 'the bog', which at the time was home to several small cottages where the householders kept pigs. In his later years he still remembered summer evenings with the cottage holders gossiping among the squealing and grunting of the pigs. This semi-rural idyll was also short-lived, however, as when Barnes was seven years old, his father – who he said was 'of migratory habits' – took the family to Liverpool and soon after to Ponders End in Middlesex.

By his own admission, Barnes was a poor scholar in his youth. He left school when he was eleven years old and started work. At thirteen, he was working in the same engineering plant in London as his father. The adolescent Barnes fell in love with London, which he called the 'best place on earth', so he must have been bitterly disappointed in 1872 when his parents told him that they were returning to Dundee.

This time the family settled in Mortimer Street and George began an apprenticeship in Parker's Foundry. It was while working at Parker's that Barnes experienced his first political meeting when the Liberal Edward Jenkins came to speak at the factory gates during the 1874 election campaign. Young Barnes was captivated by the speaker's oratory and liberal ideas and thought he would go far in politics. Barnes later laughed at his own credulity – Jenkins' political career, in fact, turned out to be unremarkable and he later became a Tory.

When he had completed his apprenticeship, Barnes left Dundee to go to Barrow-in-Furness where he worked in the shipyards. This time the rest of his family did not follow. His parents' travelling days were over and they stayed in Dundee for the rest of their lives, living in Rosebank Street and running a Post Office and stationers.

After his time in Barrow, Barnes made for London. He settled in Fulham where he eventually married and raised his family. It was there, too, that he first became involved in trade unionism and labour politics, becoming an active member of the Amalgamated Society of Engineers.

On 13 February 1887, he attended a demonstration in Trafalgar Square, which turned into the riot known as Bloody Sunday. He retained a memento of this occasion all his life, he said, in the shape of deformed toenails where the hooves of a mounted police horse had trod on him.

In 1889, Barnes became a member of the union's Executive and undertook a punishing schedule of nightly meetings in addition to working at his trade during the day. By 1896, though, he had given up his day job altogether to become the union's General Secretary.

Barnes had stood unsuccessfully at Rochdale in 1895 as an Independent

Labour Party candidate. He became convinced trade unionists needed a voice in parliament. He was one of 120 delegates at the meeting in Farringdon Street, London, on 27 February 1900, where Keir Hardie's motion in favour of a 'distinct Labour Group in Parliament', with its own whips and its own policy, was presented – in effect the birth of the modern Labour Party.

Barnes was also interested in the idea of pensions and formed the National Committee of Organised Labour for Old Age Pensions in 1902. His high profile on this issue was one of the things that helped take him to parliament in the 1906 General Election. Two years later, the Liberal Government passed the Old Age Pensions Act – influenced, in part, by Barnes' pressure. He maintained, nonetheless, that the rates introduced were too low.

Around this time Barnes believed that the Labour Party was wasting too much time on what he saw as side issues, such as votes for women, and not enough on 'questions more akin to labour reform'. He became Chairman of the Parliamentary Labour Party (the equivalent of the modern party leader) in 1910 and tried to refocus the party – but it would be international events that were to dominate the next few years.

When war with Germany came in 1914, Barnes was certainly not on the pacifist wing of the Labour Party. Germany, he wrote after the invasion of Belgium, had challenged the world: 'She has trampled on a small people that we were Treaty bound to protect.'

He was to pay a high personal price for his support of the war. His son, Henry – known to the family as Dick – who was a Second Lieutenant in the Gordon Highlanders, was killed in action on 25 September 1915 at the Battle of Loos. This was the battle that also claimed the lives of many men from Dundee – members of the 4th Battalion of the Black Watch known as Dundee's Own. Every year on 25 September, the beacon on Dundee's Law War Memorial is lit in their memory.

George Barnes joined the cabinet in 1916 in Lloyd George's coalition government, becoming Pensions Minister. He was later Minister without

Portfolio. Two years later, in 1918, when the Labour Party decided to quit the coalition, Barnes stayed put and instead quit the Labour Party. Many saw this as a betrayal, but Barnes thought it was his duty. He said at the time, 'Having been put into the Government to help win the war and until the peace was signed, I am going to stick to my mandate.'

Barnes did see the peace process through to the end, taking particular interest in the creation of the International Labour Organisation. On 28 June 1919, he was part of the British delegation that signed the Treaty of Versailles, bringing to an end the Great War which he had supported so strongly and which had cost him so dearly in personal terms.

It was his support for the war, too, which had, in effect, ended his involvement with the Labour Party. His attempts to regain party support, after the Peace Treaty was signed and he had resigned from the Government, came to nothing. 'I have no desire to be in public life if I am opposed by

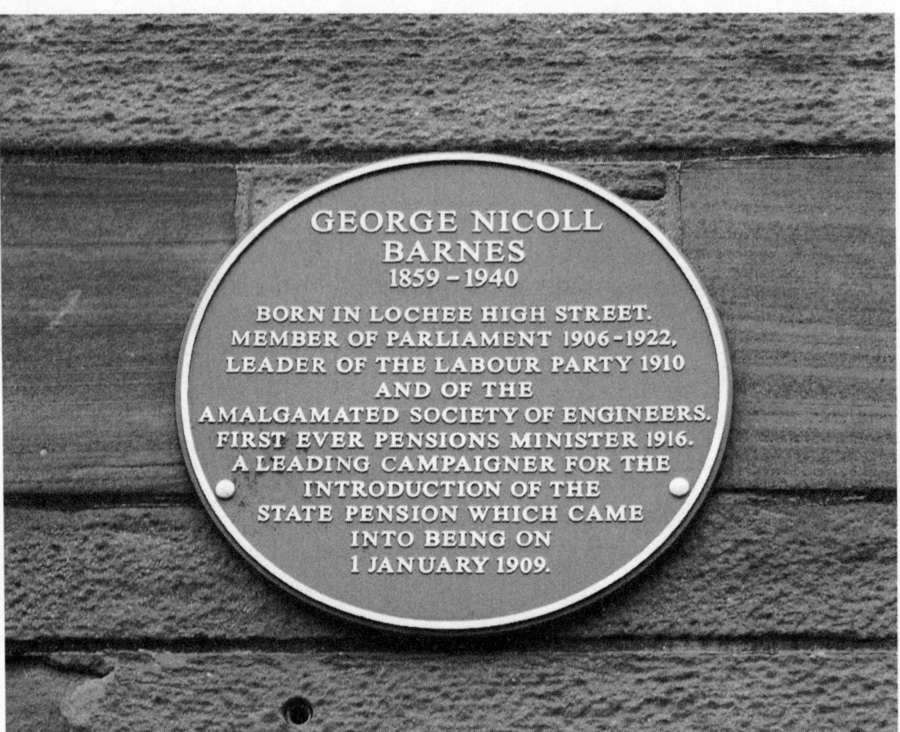

The plaque commemorating George Nicoll Barnes

Labour,' he once wrote. When Labour decided to put up a candidate against him in his Glasgow constituency, he was as good as his word and retired from public life.

By the time George Nicoll Barnes died in 1940, the peace that he had helped build was in tatters as the world was once again plunged into war. The provisions of the Versailles Treaty, far from securing the peace, were blamed by some for sowing the seeds of this new conflict. Whatever the truth of this, the Treaty remains one of the key documents of twentieth-century European history. It is extraordinary to think that it bears the signature of a man from Lochee.

The Rebel Sisters

In April 1966, two elderly sisters, Kathy and Lena McDonald, flew into Dublin on a plane from New York. They were guests of honour in the Irish capital during the celebrations to mark the fiftieth anniversary of the Easter Rising in 1916. The McDonald sisters were given places of honour at official ceremonies and attended a party in the Mansion House held by the Lord Mayor of Dublin, Eugene Timmons. At a state reception they were special guests of the President of Ireland Eamon de Valera himself. De Valera was no stranger to these women, though. Many years earlier, when the man who was in 1966 a head of state was a fugitive from the British, he had been given refuge in the McDonalds' house in Brook Street, Dundee.

The rebellion of 1916, which the sisters had come to commemorate, could not be considered a military success. Almost entirely confined to Dublin, the rising was suppressed within a week by the British forces and its leaders were executed – among them the Edinburgh-born James Connolly who, badly injured, was shot whilst tied to a chair. The outrage that followed the executions, though, rallied people in Ireland and around the world to the cause of Irish independence. There would have been much sympathy in Dundee, which had seen substantial Irish immigration in the previous century and now was home to a large number of people who were Irish by birth or descent. Some may even have known James Connolly personally. He had lived in Dundee for a time in 1889, staying with Owen Boyle, his aunt's brother, at 9 St Mary's Street. It was in Dundee, too, that he first became actively involved in politics, joining the Socialist League there.

One of the areas in Dundee which had a particularly high concentration of Irish people and where events in Ireland would have been followed most closely was the Scouringburn area. This was the area in which the McDonald sisters were born and raised. The elder sister Kathy – Catherine Ann McDonald – was born in 1893 at 8 East Henderson's Wynd and her sister Mary Helen Higgins McDonald – known throughout her life as Lena – was born at the same address in 1897. Their father Peter worked as a groom and later as a carter. Although he lived until 1942, Peter McDonald does not feature much in his daughters' story. It seems that he separated from their mother, Helen, while the girls were still young. A bigger influence was surely their Irish-born grandmother Bridget Higgins, in whose home they were brought up. The girls were also said to have become radicalised after a holiday in Ireland. Whatever the reason for their developing interest in Irish politics, the sisters took things further than many of their contemporaries who merely sympathised with the Irish cause and became actively involved.

The McDonalds became gun-runners, buying their first gun for 3s 6d. By this time, they lived with their mother in the heart of the Scouringburn area – now renamed Brook Street. Their house at number 31 became the unofficial headquarters of the Irish republican movement in Dundee. They also ran a greengrocer's shop on the other side of the street and this provided useful cover for their activities. Arms were smuggled into the shop in all sorts of packaging and stored in the back. Lena later recalled bullets being smuggled in the papers of fish and chips.

It was another type of packaging – egg crates – that was to provide a problem for the sisters in April 1921. Sean O'Doherty, a leading member of the Sinn Féin movement in Dundee, had acquired some service rifles and revolvers but was growing nervous about storing them in the house he shared with his widowed mother in Rosebery Street. When IRA men Sean Healy and D. P. Walsh arrived in Dundee, it was decided that a meeting would be held in the back of the McDonalds' shop to decide what to do with the weapons. The lorry, which would usually have taken them to Glasgow, had recently been captured by police. Walsh decided that they should be transported in egg crates and Lena managed to find some that were suitable on the premises. There was not enough space in the back room to pack the crates and so they brought the weapons through to the shop and began to pack them in the space behind the counter. Then there was a knock at the door.

The gang crouched behind the counter among the guns, straw and packing crates while Lena answered the door to find two policemen standing there. They had noticed the shop lights were still on and had come to investigate. Lena assured them that she was working late, catching up on her accounts. Satisfied with her explanation, Lena watched as the officers carried on their way, each clutching an orange that she had given them for their trouble.

The egg crates were addressed to a provision merchant James McGlinchey of Ingram Street, Glasgow, and it was arranged that Sean Healy and D. P. Walsh would travel there to warn him to expect a delivery. Healy and Walsh took a detour to Edinburgh, however, where they stayed overnight to collect some more weapons and McGlinchey was faced the next day with the arrival of not only the egg crates, but also the police, who promptly arrested him.

Stories vary as to how the plan was uncovered. Sean Healy was told that the lorry hired to take the eggs from Brook Street to the railway station had been followed by police who recognised some of the men on board. Newspapers at the time, however, reported that it was railway officials who had found the guns in the egg crates. In any case, the police allowed the cargo to proceed on its way to Glasgow, exposing McGlinchey to arrest.

Five arrests were made in Dundee. As well as Lena McDonald and Sean O'Doherty, shipyard worker James Kimmet, barber James Devaney and James Malloy, a french polisher, were charged with contravention of the Explosive Substances Act 1882 and the Firearms Act 1921. Malloy was later released but the others were held in custody awaiting trial. Requests that James Devaney and Lena be released on bail were turned down.

At the trial in Edinburgh in August 1921, O'Doherty and Kimmet pled guilty to all charges and were each sentenced to three years penal servitude. As he was led away, O'Doherty raised his right hand in a salute and, facing Lord Chief Justice Scott Dickson, shouted, 'God save Ireland!' James Devaney, who had a lesser role in the affair, was sentenced to eighteen months imprisonment. The case against Lena McDonald, however, was dismissed.

A large crowd of supporters had gathered outside the High Court and Lena was presented with a bunch of flowers. This was nothing, though, in comparison to the welcome that awaited her in Dundee. A crowd carrying flags and banners had gathered outside the Tay Bridge railway station, entirely blocking Union Street. A large welcome-home banner was strung across the station entrance. When her train arrived, she was cheered and presented with chocolates and flowers. More cheers and flag waving followed when she got into a waiting car and people followed behind singing the 'Soldier's Song'. Later, there was a celebration in her honour at the Blackness Hall. Not everybody in Dundee was so enthusiastic about Lena's release, though. She later recalled that some of her neighbours were furious and thought that she should have been executed.

Gun-running was not the McDonald sisters' only contribution to the Irish cause. Their home became a place of refuge for many leading lights of the republican movement. Indeed, it is no exaggeration to say that some of the most important figures in twentieth-century Irish history were accommodated at 31 Brook Street, Dundee. Furthermore, the list is almost certainly incomplete given the shroud of secrecy that necessarily surrounded these matters.

Eamon de Valera is undoubtedly the most famous of the sisters' house-guests. De Valera had been involved in the rising of 1916 and had originally been sentenced to death. Only the fact that he had been born in the United States saved his life. The executions of his comrades left him in a leading position in the movement and he was elected leader of Sinn Féin on his release from prison in 1917. De Valera became the dominant figure in twentieth-century Irish politics, founding the Fianna Fáil party and becoming Taoiseach (Prime Minister) on three separate occasions between 1937 and 1959 and President of Ireland from 1959 to 1973. De Valera is known to have visited Dundee in 1926 when he addressed a meeting. Newspaper reports in 1966 state, however, that he had used the McDonalds' home on several occasions and there is at least the possibility that he hid there for part of the time after his escape from Lincoln Jail on 3 February 1919 and before his return to Dublin on 20 February.

To have had one future President of Ireland under their roof would have been remarkable enough, but Kathy and Lena McDonald also played host to Sean T. O'Kelly who held that position from 1945 to 1959. A close associate of de Valera's, he helped to found the Fianna Fáil party in 1926. The sisters were reunited with O'Kelly as well as de Valera on their visit to Dublin in April 1966, three months before O'Kelly's death.

Ireland's most famous trade unionist, James Larkin, was another visitor to Brook Street. A native of Liverpool, he founded the Irish Transport and General Workers Union and together with James Connolly formed the Irish Labour Party. In 1913, he led a famous lockout in Dublin over union membership. The lockout ultimately collapsed in 1914 and Larkin left for the United States where he ended up in prison during a period of anti-communist panic known as the Red Scare. On his release he returned to Ireland, where he worked as a communist activist before ultimately returning to the Irish Labour Party. His statue stands today in Dublin's O'Connell Street.

It is fitting that as women activists in a male-dominated world, the McDonald sisters should also have provided refuge for two of Ireland's most remarkable female figures – Mary MacSwiney and Constance Markiewicz.

Mary MacSwiney was born in England to an Irish father and English mother but the family returned to Cork when she was six. Unusually for a woman at the time, she trained as a teacher at Cambridge University. She was a founding member of the women's paramilitary organisation Cumann na mBan and was imprisoned after the 1916 rising. Her brother Terrance, the Lord Mayor of Cork, died after seventy-four days on hunger strike in Brixton Prison. Like her brother, Mary MacSwiney remained a staunch and uncompromising republican to the end.

Constance Markiewicz visited Dundee in 1923 and probably stayed with the McDonalds on that occasion. Born Constance Gore-Booth in 1868, her background could not have been more different to that of Kathy and Lena McDonald. The wife of Count Kazimierz Dunin-Markiewicz, she came from a land-owning family and had been presented to Queen Victoria as a debutante. By the time she met the McDonalds, however, she had become a republican and a campaigner for women's rights. She had also taken an active part in the 1916 rebellion against British rule in Ireland when she was second in command to Michael Mallin at St Stephen's Green, Dublin. Just as de Valera's place of birth had prevented his execution, it was only Constance Markiewicz's gender that saved her from the firing squad. She later became the first woman ever elected to the British parliament (though she did not take her seat) and one of the first women cabinet ministers in Europe.

In later years Kathy and Lena McDonald worked as maternity nurses in Dundee alongside their mother. They emigrated to Canada and the United States but both ended up working in the same nursing home in New York. To many people, and certainly to the British authorities, the McDonald sisters were guilty of criminal acts, but in the Irish Republic in 1966 they were officially recognised as heroes. They received medals in recognition of their 'bravery, nobility and sacrifice during the independence struggle' and were each awarded war pensions. Asked by an *Evening Telegraph* reporter if they would change anything, Lena replied, 'Well, when I look back on it now I think we must have been mad to do some of the things we did. But it was an exciting time. We have no regrets.'

Vote for Shackleton

Polar explorer Ernest Shackleton's links with Dundee are well known. He was a member of Captain Scott's Antarctic expedition on the Dundee-built, *Discovery*, which began in 1901. In 1914, Shackleton's own expedition on the *Endurance* was in part financed by Dundee's Sir James Key Caird, the jute manufacturer who gave the city the Caird Hall and Caird Park. Shackleton said that Caird's 'munificent' donation of £24,000 had relieved him of all anxiety about financing the expedition. He later named Caird Coast in Antarctica in Sir James's honour.

One of the *Endurance*'s lifeboats was also named after Caird and the *James Caird* was to play a vital role in the expedition when Shackleton used it for an incredible seventeen-day, 800-mile journey in freezing conditions from the desolate, uninhabited Elephant Island (where he and his men had landed after the loss of the *Endurance*) to South Georgia Island. This journey was instrumental in the expedition returning without the loss of a single life and is generally considered to be one of the greatest small-boat journeys ever undertaken.

Had the electors of Dundee felt differently in 1906, however, it might never have happened. Shackleton was persuaded to stand for election to Parliament by the Liberal Unionist Party in Dundee. The Liberal Unionists had originally split from Gladstone's Liberal Party in 1886 over the question of Home Rule for Ireland and would eventually merge with the Conservative Party in 1912 to form the Conservative and Unionist Party. Shackleton was unanimously adopted as their candidate at a meeting in January 1905.

Addressing the meeting, Shackleton tried to counter those who said that he was a stranger to Dundee, saying that he had lived in Dundee for some time and had done a good deal of work there and he felt that he was more allied to Dundee than to any other part of the United Kingdom.

This was the first of many meetings that Shackleton was to address over the next few months in Dundee. These meetings were generally busy and Shackleton showed himself to be adept at answering questions from the floor. In response to being called an Irish landlord, he said that he only owned enough land to hang his washing on. When asked about votes for women, he prefaced his positive answer by saying that his wife was present. He did not shy away from controversial issues either, stating that, as a patriotic Irishman, he was against home rule for Ireland. He also rejected prohibition saying that he would not deprive people of getting a drink if they wanted it.

Shackleton also took time to venture into areas where the Liberal Unionist message was not guaranteed to go down well. He addressed meetings at factory gates and dockyards and in areas with a large Irish population such as Lochee. On these occasions, Shackleton would face sustained heckling but his good-natured replies and attractive personality made it difficult for his opponents to genuinely dislike him. A 'Working Man' wrote in a letter to the *Courier* that Shackleton had 'won friends in Dundee whose opinions are as far apart from him as are the poles'. Personal popularity did not translate into votes, however. As Shackleton himself put it, 'I got all the applause and the other fellow got all the votes.'

Shackleton secured some 3865 votes, finishing in fourth place. Dundee elected as its two Members of Parliament Alexander Wilkie, the city's first Labour Party representative, and the Liberal Edmund Robertson, whose elevation to the peerage as Lord Lochee in 1908 was to cause the by-election that brought Winston Churchill to Dundee. Shackleton, meanwhile, took his defeat well and soon turned his attentions to preparing another trip to Antarctica in what was to become the *Nimrod* expedition of 1907–9.

On 1 February 1910, Sir Ernest Shackleton, knighted the previous year by King Edward VII in the wake of the *Nimrod* expedition, returned to

Ernest Shackleton, circa 1910

Dundee to give a lecture to the Dundee Branch of the Royal Geographical Society. Receiving a warm welcome, Shackleton said that he was renewing his friendship with Dundee after four years. The last time he was on the very platform on which he then stood, he said, he had spoken very well,

he thought, for twenty minutes. He had then been heckled for forty minutes. These days were dead and gone for him, he added, and he knew that
there would be no heckling at the end of that particular meeting. For Sir
Ernest Shackleton, his days as a would-be politician were at an end but
some of his greatest adventures still lay ahead.

10
Passing Through

From the earliest times, Dundee has attracted visitors. Some, such as King Edward I of England in 1296 and 1303, arrived intent on destroying the place. Others, such as the poet Hugh MacDiarmid, launched only verbal assault, calling the city 'a grim monument of man's inhumanity to man'.

There were other visitors, of course, who took a more favourable view. Daniel Defoe, the author of *Robinson Crusoe* and one-time English spy, wrote that Dundee was 'a pleasant, large, populous city, and well deserves the title of Bonny Dundee'.

For Mary Shelley, who spent time in the city as a young woman, Dundee provided inspiration. In the 1831 introduction to her novel *Frankenstein*, she wrote, 'My habitual residence was on the blank and dreary northern shores of the Tay, near Dundee. Blank and dreary on retrospection I call them; they were not so to me then. They were the eyry of freedom, and the pleasant region where unheeded I could commune with the creatures of my fancy.'

Dundee also had its share of Royal visitors, some exhibiting a more stately progress than others. Among them was Robert the Bruce, who had been proclaimed King in Dundee in 1309, and who marked his first visit a few years later with the destruction of the town's castle, to prevent it falling back into English hands. Mary, Queen of Scots, paid four visits to the town in the 1560s and each of the first six Kings of Scotland named James also passed through at one time or another. Jacobites would add another, James VIII, known to Hanoverians as 'the Old Pretender', who stayed in the town in early 1716. This was to be the last such visit until that of Queen Victoria in 1844. Since then, though, every British monarch has visited the city, though not necessarily during their reign.

Edward VIII did not visit the city during his short period as King, but as Prince of Wales in 1923, when he formally opened the city's biggest entertainment venue, the Caird Hall. Dundee had always attracted travelling entertainers – some even speculate that William Shakespeare visited the town with the Laurence Fletcher Company in 1601. This new hall, though, firmly established the city on the touring circuit for major stars – among them Gracie Fields, Mario Lanza, Paul Robeson, Duke Ellington, Frank Sinatra, Bob Hope, the Beatles and the Rolling Stones. Similarly, Dundee's major theatre, the Rep, has played host over the years to Richard Todd, Jill Gascoigne, Joanna Lumley, James Bolam, Arthur Lowe and David Tenant among others.

The following pages look at some famous and some unusual visitors to Dundee.

Charles Dickens (1858)

On Tuesday, 28 September 1858, the following advertisement appeared in the Dundee press heralding the arrival of the greatest literary figure of the age:

MR CHARLES DICKENS
Will read at the NEW PUBLIC HALL, Bank Street, Dundee,
On FRIDAY evening, October 1st his
CHRISTMAS CAROL;
And on SATURDAY'S Evening, October 2,
THE POOR TRAVELLER;

BOOTS AT THE HOLLY TREE INN; and
MRS GAMP;
To commence each evening at half past eight o'clock.
Doors open at half past seven
Places for each Reading – Stalls, Numbered and reserved, 4s each;
Family Cards, to admit Four, 12s; Unreserved Seats, 2s 6d each;
Back Seats, 1s each.
Tickets to be had, and Plans of Reserved Seats to be seen at
Mr CHALMERS, Bookseller, Castle Street; or
Mr METHVEN, Musicseller,
Nethergate.
On Friday Evening, SPECIAL TRAINS will be despatched at the
Conclusion of the Reading to Perth and Arbroath, stopping at the
Intermediate Stations; also, a Boat to Newport.

Charles Dickens was in Dundee as part of a provincial reading tour that had begun at the start of August and would continue to mid-November, rounding off a difficult year for the author, which had seen a very public separation from his wife. The tour was the first time he had read for profit rather than charity, although at Dundee he was to give half his profits towards the new hall's Decoration Fund. His visit created much excitement as people flocked to catch a glimpse of the man responsible for so much of their entertainment.

Dickens described Dundee as 'an odd place, like Wapping with high rugged hills behind it'. He seemed to be more impressed with the venue at which he was to perform, viewing it as 'something between the Crystal Palace and Westminster Hall', although he noted that it had not yet been used for public speaking.

People began to crowd into the 'New Public Hall' in Bank Street (later known as the Kinnaird Hall – later still as the Kinnaird Cinema) as soon as the doors opened at 7.30pm on the evening of Friday, 1 October 1858. The house was packed to capacity when Dickens came on stage around

A depiction of Charles Dickens giving a reading

one hour later to tumultuous applause. He told the audience that he hoped the event would be like a 'family party' and that they would 'not restrain themselves in the slightest, but give free-vent to whatever emotions, risible or otherwise, the little ebullition of feeling would not interrupt him, but rather be agreeable'. Dickens read from *A Christmas Carol* – already much loved even though it was only fifteen years old at this point. When he had finished, he left the stage to more loud applause.

The audience was less enthusiastic about the new hall, though. A correspondent to the *Advertiser* adopted the persona of Sairey Gamp from *Martin Chuzzlewit* to write, 'When my respected friend Mrs Harris told me she had paid four shillings for a ticket for the stalls in Lord Kinnaird's fine new hall, I thought that I was sure of getting a seat with a velvet cushion. You will conceive my feelings then in having to sit two hours upon one of the hardest planks my poor old bones ever did sit upon.'

There were also complaints about the acoustics. A *Courier* reader complained, 'I could *see* from the working of his features that he was evidently giving the feeling of his text, and regretted on this account the more that I was deprived of the pleasure of *hearing* him.' The same reader reported that at least 200 people who were seated at the back of the hall left at the interval and did not return.

It was perhaps for this reason that the attendance – though still large – was down for the reading on the Saturday night when Dickens read 'The Poor Traveller', 'Boots at the Holly Tree Inn', and 'Mrs Gamp'. Whatever the problems with the venue, some would simply treasure the memory of having seen the great man in the flesh. The Dundee merchant and humorist D. M. Nicoll recalled almost forty years later, 'Can we forget the alert bird-like look of the piercing black eyes and the natty way in which he was dressed and, above all, the delightful, masterly way, marked by faultless elocution in which he rendered his own immortal productions. Take him for all in all, we shall not look upon his like again.'

In a way, Dundee did 'look upon his like again'. In 1889, nearly twenty years after Dickens' death, his son Charles gave readings from his father's works *David Copperfield* and 'Bob Sawyer's Party' from *The Pickwick Papers* in the Gilfillan Memorial Church in Whitehall Street. He was, according to the *Dundee Advertiser*, almost as good as the real thing – Mr Dickens 'has the involuntary facial mannerisms of the father: the knitted eyebrows have the same expression, their sudden arching conveys the same meaning, and there are cadences in the voice that recall the tone of the father'.

Ulysses S. Grant (1877)

Following the end of his second term in the White House, the eighteenth President of the United States and the hero of the Union Army in the American Civil War, General Ulysses S. Grant spent over two years travelling the world with his wife. Included on his itinerary in Britain was the latest Victorian engineering marvel – the Tay Bridge. The bridge was almost completed but had not yet been opened to the public and the first train had not yet crossed it. Even so, Grant was not the first celebrity to visit the bridge – Emperor Pedro II of Brazil had made a flying visit in July.

Grant arrived in Tayport from Edinburgh with his wife and son Jesse on the morning of Saturday, 1 September 1877. A crowd had gathered hoping to catch a glimpse of the former President. Grant's party, including Lord Provost Falshaw of Edinburgh and ex-Lord Provost Cox of Dundee, boarded the steamer *Excelsior* to view the bridge. They also stopped off on the training ship *The Mars* where the boys treated them to a performance of 'The Canadian Boat Song' and demonstrated their fire drill and climbed the rigging.

Grant then visited the construction offices where he viewed various models and diagrams of the bridge. The former president walked out a short way onto the south side of the bridge. After lunch it was back aboard the *Excelsior* for a tour round both sides of the bridge. Arriving on the Dundee side to loud cheers from a waiting crowd, the party walked along the bridge from the north side. Grant was presented with an album of photographs of the bridge under construction. He left by means of steamer and special train from Tayport.

Not long after Grant had left Dundee, rumours began to circulate that he would return to the city. He would be back within the week it was said, on his way from a trip north. A visit to a jute mill was proposed. At a meeting of the magistrates, Provost Robertson said that in view of the long and important business relationship between Dundee and the United States and the valuable services that the former President had rendered his country, it would be fitting to offer him the Freedom of Dundee. A telegram was dispatched to Dunrobin where the president was staying.

In the days that followed, however, Grant was inundated with requests from towns wishing to bestow civic honours upon him – Edinburgh, Glasgow, Aberdeen, Inverness, Elgin and Paisley among them. It was clear that he could not accept them all. No return visit to Dundee was made. Provost Robertson received a telegram saying that the General was very much obliged to the Provost and Magistrates for the compliment paid him in offering him the freedom of the town, but that his engagements would prevent him from visiting Dundee.

John Rowlands (1890)

John Rowlands received the Freedom of Dundee in June 1890 at a ceremony at the Kinnaird Hall in Bank Street. He was warmly welcomed and he praised 'the bounteous hospitality' that he had received in Dundee and expressed his gratitude for the 'precious souvenir' of his visit.

Rowlands was born on 29 January 1841 at Denbigh, Wales, to unmarried parents. He spent part of his childhood in a workhouse. He ran away to sea at seventeen. He fought on both sides in the American Civil War. He worked as a journalist. He was an explorer. He was a colonialist with the dubious distinction of helping Leopold II of Belgium develop his interests in the Congo. He was a writer of both fact and fiction. He was a lecturer and a Member of Parliament.

Any one of these facts would be enough to make his life notable but he is chiefly remembered these days for four words, which some claim he never actually spoke. Nor is he remembered by the name John Rowlands but by that of his employer in New Orleans, which he adopted as his own – Henry Stanley. As for the four words, here is his own account:

I would have run to him, only I was a coward in the presence of such a mob – would have embraced him, but that I did not know how he would receive me; so I did what moral cowardice and false pride suggested was the best thing – walked deliberately to him, took off my hat, and said: 'Doctor Livingstone, I presume?'

Arthur Conan Doyle (1893)

There was a large turnout at the Kinnaird Hall on Saturday, 25 November 1893, when the creator of Sherlock Holmes, Arthur Conan Doyle, delivered a lecture entitled 'Facts about Fiction'. *The Advertiser* reported: 'The fame of "Sherlock Holmes" is in everybody's mouth, and for the audience which assembled last night to see and hear him has seldom been exceeded in magnitude in Dundee. Long before the hour was fixed for the lecture every available seat was occupied, and the main door had to be closed upon several hundreds of persons disappointed in obtaining a seat.'

Sherlock Holmes may have been 'in everybody's mouth' at the time, but Conan Doyle himself had had enough of him, writing around this time: 'I am weary of his name.' The next month's edition of *The Strand Magazine* would see the publication of 'The Final Problem' in which Holmes would be killed off, apparently plunging to his death with Moriarty at the Reichenbach Falls in Switzerland. Doyle wished to devote his time to what he saw as more worthwhile work but the public demand for Holmes was such that he eventually relented and brought back the detective in 'The Adventure of the Empty House' in 1903.

Dundee itself features in two Sherlock Holmes stories. In 'The Five Orange Pips', first published in 1891, the city is the point of origin of one of the eponymous pips and a major clue to the solving of the mystery. In 'The Adventure of Black Peter' (1903), the murder victim Peter Carey is the former master of the *Sea Unicorn* of Dundee. The setting for Doyle's non-Holmes short story 'The Captain of the Polestar' (1880) is a Dundee whaler and is written from the point of view of a medical student. Ten years previously, while in the third year of his studies, Doyle himself had served as ship's doctor aboard the Peterhead whaling ship *Hope*.

The mention of Dundee in his work did not betray any fondness for the city from Conan Doyle, however. When John Boraston, the Secretary to the Liberal Unionist Council, asked him in 1900 if he would consider standing as the party's candidate for the city at the general election, Doyle wrote to his mother, 'I am inclined to stand but not for Dundee – an odious place with every disadvantage.' He later unsuccessfully stood for his home-town of Edinburgh.

Tommy Burns (1897)

Tommy Burns visited Dundee in 1897. This was not, of course, the late Celtic football player and manager (he was to visit Dundee many times, attending venues on either side of Tannadice Street, the best part of a century later). This Tommy Burns was from Liverpool and advertised himself as:

> Champion all Round athlete of the World at Diving, swimming, walking, running, Boxing (Marquess of Queensberry), Pole Jumping, Horizontal bar etc. etc. etc. Can accept engagements to compete against any artistes engaged on piers promenades baths bridges pontoons stages dramatic or musical . . . Is open to compete against the world.

In another age he might have been able to devote his time to his sport alone but to earn a living in the later years of the nineteenth century, Tommy Burns had to use his sporting gifts in Music Hall and circus shows. He would walk a mile on stage in under eight minutes and run a mile in under five. He would dive from a great height, expertly landing in a water tank. It seems that what Tommy loved most of all, though, was a challenge.

In 1889, for a bet, he successfully undertook the challenge to dive off the Runcorn Bridge, swim up the Mersey to Liverpool, walk from Liverpool to London where he would dive off London Bridge, and then walk back to Liverpool and swim back up the river and dive off the same bridge, all within nine days.

His jumps from bridges and public buildings became legendary. He successfully dived from the Jamaica Bridge in Glasgow, the Forth Bridge and the roof of the Royal Aquarium in London among many others. Few, if any, of these jumps had the approval of the authorities and arrest was an occupational hazard. He was arrested on numerous occasions either after diving or before making his attempt. He went to increasingly greater lengths to try to avoid arrest. When apprehended at Earlestown in Merseyside he was dressed as a collier. At Trafford Bridge in Manchester he was dressed as a woman. He also found another way of getting on railway bridges: buy a ticket and jump from the moving train. This was the method he used when he visited the Tay Bridge in 1897.

This was not Burns's first visit to Dundee. A programme still exists from a Grand Carnival at West Craigie Park in 1895 where 'High Diving by Tommy Burns, Champion High Diver of the World' was one of the attractions. It was while he was appearing at West Craigie Park that he made his first attempt to dive off the Tay Bridge. Burns was supremely confident, saying that jumping off the bridge would be 'a mere schoolboy's dive'. Before he could even make the attempt, however, he had to get onto the structure without the knowledge of the railway officials. Only a few of his friends and accomplices knew of his plans – or so he thought.

His starting point was to be the North British Railway Company's Esplanade Station, which was situated in close proximity to the bridge, but when he arrived he found it heavily policed by railway officials who obviously had an inkling of his intentions. He made a desperate run for the bridge but was quickly apprehended before he could reach his target.

Undeterred, Burns and his accomplices rowed out to the middle of the river. He was presumably intending to climb the bridge and then dive off but the railway company stationed men on the bridge who followed the movements of his boat and would have been in place to capture him had his climb been successful. After around half an hour of this cat and mouse game, he gave up. He told a *Courier* reporter, though, that he would 'do it some other day'.

That 'other day' was to be Friday, 29 January 1897. Word that Burns would make an attempt to dive off the bridge had again leaked out and a crowd had gathered at the Esplanade. Burns and his accomplices boarded the 10.45am train from Tay Bridge Station. They had a third-class carriage to themselves where Burns stripped down to a bathing costume. He then clambered out of the open door of the train just as it was beginning the crossing of the bridge and hoisted himself on to its roof with a rope. After steadying himself, he dived, 'straight as an arrow' according to one report, into the icy waters of the Tay. Burns was in trouble, though, as the boat that had been arranged to pick him up was too far away. Some workmen on the bridge threw railway sleepers to him. One of these actually struck him, causing him a slight injury, but he managed to grab hold of one and float on it until he was picked up by the steam launch *Incholm*.

He was handed over to the police at Bell Street but after holding him for a while they did not seem to know what to do with him. When one of his supporters inquired as to what was to happen to Burns, one of the policemen said jokingly, 'We are no' sure yet whether we'll send him to Botany Bay or Peterhead but we'll no hang him if we can help it.' He was released after two hours. The authorities at Leith were not so lenient in April of that year when he was given a heavy fine of £7 10s for diving from a tenement building into the Water of Leith.

Burns's dive caused much excitement in Dundee. Some criticized the foolhardy nature of his exploits but many had a secret admiration for him. The *Piper o' Dundee* published a McGonagall-esque poem in his honour:

> Tommy Burns took a dip,
> From the Bridge he did skip,
> In the water had a dip,
> But there must have been a slip
> For he couldn't see a ship

> So he had to take a grip
> Of a floating sleeper's tip,
> Had Tommy Burns
>
> Now the Tay is somewhat cold,
> So, at least, I have been told,
> And poor Tommy he was sold,
> But he kept visage bold,
> Like a miner after gold,
> And an unrelaxing hold,
> Of the stick that past him rolled,
> Did Tommy Burns
>
> He was looking very pale,
> So he had a glass of ale,
> But his explanations fail,
> Are at least of no avail,
> For they took him to the gaol,
> But they've let him out on bail,
> So we'll all cry out 'All hail'
> To Tommy Burns

Burns was back in the city in June 1897, a few months after his Tay Bridge dive, when he attended the gala of the Wallace Swimming and Humane Society at the Public Baths. He also gave a demonstration in the Open Air Bathing Station at the east of the Esplanade. As always he got an enthusiastic reception from the Dundee public. A rumoured dive from the Royal Arch did not take place on this occasion but Burns was keen to do this at some stage in the future.

The next month Tommy Burns went to Rhyl where he was to attempt a 'sensational high dive of 100 feet'. It was to be his last dive. He had always known that each diving attempt had the potential to result in his death.

He had been hospitalised in the past when things had gone wrong but he always remained fearless. Some people watching at Rhyl thought that Burns did not look well enough for the task and there were rumours that he had been drinking. He had kept the crowd waiting three quarters of an hour and had not completed the run that was part of his engagement. Whatever the cause, when he did finally dive, Burns twisted awkwardly in the air and landed heavily on his back. He surfaced but later had to be rescued from the water. All attempts to revive him failed.

Tommy Burns was thirty-one years old. His widow was said to be left penniless. A benefit was held for her that, perversely, featured another diver, 'Professor' Ted Heaton, diving from the platform where Burns had died.

Carry A. Nation (1908)

In the summer of 1908, Dundee's relentless campaigner for the prohibition of alcohol and future Member of Parliament, Edwin 'Neddy' Scrymgeour, was in Columbus, Ohio, at a Prohibition Convention. He was there on a fact-finding mission but took the opportunity to invite one of the best-known figures in the American temperance movement to Dundee. Carry Nation was a woman with a fierce reputation as a 'saloon smasher'. This was not just a nickname either. Carry Nation literally smashed saloons, often with a hatchet.

Carry Amelia Moore was born in Kentucky in 1846. Her first husband, Charles Gloyd, who died in 1869, had been an alcoholic and this was what inspired her campaign against alcohol. Her second husband, a lawyer, David Nation, gave her the name by which she became famous – Carry A. Nation – which had the advantage of also sounding like a slogan.

In 1880, when the State of Kansas prohibited the sale of alcohol, she and like-minded women from the Women's Christian Temperance Union would go and sing hymns in saloons where the law was being broken. By 1900, however, she had opted for more direct action, smashing up saloons in Kiowa with rocks. She would later famously employ a hatchet to break saloon fixtures and alcohol supplies. Not surprisingly, she was arrested and imprisoned many times as a result of what she termed her 'hatchetations'.

In late November 1908, Carry Nation sailed from New York to begin a tour of Scotland and England. Dundee was the first venue on her itinerary where she was booked to address a meeting in the Kinnaird Hall. It was not known, however, if she would attempt to take her hatchet to any of the local hostelries.

Arriving in Dundee on Saturday, 5 December, Nation first had a meeting with Lord Provost James Urquhart where she asked him what reason he had for allowing saloons to be run in the city. Urquhart said that he had no ability to make or alter the laws of the land. There was a demand for alcoholic refreshment and the law of the country said it should be met.

Having failed to persuade the Lord Provost of the need for prohibition, Nation later decided to take her case directly to Dundee's pubs. Accompanied by Edwin Scrymgeour, she made her way to one of the city's better class of drinking establishments, the Bodega at No. 3 Murraygate. Here, she approached a table of five men and told them to give up drinking and go home to their wives. The men were good-natured in their replies but unsurprisingly, her pleas did not meet with any success. She then turned on the barmen but the manager asked her to leave. 'Is this not a place fit for a woman to be in?' she retorted.

Out in the Murraygate a crowd had gathered and proceeded to accompany Nation to her next port of call, The Buffet, which was on the ground floor of the Royal British Hotel in the High Street. Here she was horrified to see barmaids employed. She berated the women and told them that they should be ashamed of themselves for sending young men to Hell. The manager here also ushered her out the door but she continued to verbally attack the barmaids as she went.

The crowd was by then said to be so large that the trams were stopped. Supporters came up to shake her hand and offer words of encouragement. She also occasionally stopped to pat a child on the head and warn them against the evils of drink.

Scenes from Carry Nation's visit to Dundee

In the Overgate, the first pub she went into had been virtually empty but soon became filled with the people who were following her. They stood on the benches to watch her harangue the unsuspecting barman. It was in the Overgate, too, that she saw something that particularly appalled her – a woman with a child in her arms going into a public house. She shouted at the woman but was ignored.

She got a better hearing when she addressed supporters at the Kinnaird Hall. The place was said to be filled to overflowing, with people who had been unable to get in hanging about the entrances just to catch a glimpse of her. She gave a speech denouncing the liquor trade in her usual vehement terms and took questions from the audience. At the end of the meeting Scrymgeour led the singing of a song that had been written in her honour, 'Carry and her Axe'. Nation said that she was leaving Dundee 'with the kindest and most affectionate feeling towards all' before being bundled out a back door to avoid the large crowds.

There had been no appearance from Carry Nation's famous hatchet during her time in Dundee and no actual saloon smashing. One publican, though, had been moved to report her actions to the local police. After she had gone, normal service quickly resumed in the city's bars although some publicans may have felt inclined to invest in a copy of the famous American bar sign 'All Nations welcome except Carry'.

Carry A. Nation died in 1911 but the calls for prohibition continued in Dundee, culminating in 1922 in the election of Edwin Scrymgeour as Britain's only prohibitionist Member of Parliament. It is doubtful that even then there was a majority in the city for the banning of alcohol sales. Three local polls were held on the subject in the 1920s and each returned a majority of more than 2:1 in favour of no change in licensing laws. The coalition of voters that secured Scrymgeour's victory had many motives – not least the defeat of sitting MP, Winston Churchill. Attempts by Scrymegour to get his Liquor Traffic Prohibition Bill onto the statute book never really stood any chance of success.

There is one more story from Carry Nation's time in Dundee that was reported at the time but which may well be apocryphal. On her tour of Dundee's pubs, she is supposed to have entered a temperance establishment and said to the manager, 'Young man, do you sell drink here?'

'No,' came the reply, 'but you can get what you want next door.'

Harry Houdini (1909)

The world famous escapologist Harry Houdini visited Dundee in June 1909. His visit had been heralded by a large teaser poster, which appeared in the centre of town bearing only his surname. To this were later added much smaller posters with the words 'is coming' and 'where'. The 'where' was the Kings Theatre and Hippodrome in the Cowgate where Houdini was to appear at 'enormous expense' twice nightly.

Houdini was described in the publicity material as 'the original handcuff king and jail-breaker' and 'the only living being who ever escaped from the Siberian Transport Van in Russia and who has also escaped from the strongest prisons in all parts of the world'. Those attending were promised sight of Houdini's latest invention, a trick he had first performed at the Columbia Theatre in St Louis in January 1908 and which involved 'escaping out of an air tight galvanised iron can filled to the brim with water and locked with six padlocks'. The audience were invited to bring their own padlocks.

For those who were unable to attend any of the performances at the Kings there was another way to see Houdini. In a stunt similar to ones that he performed at several other venues on his tour, Houdini made a very public appearance. Having been refused permission to jump into the river from the Tay Bridge, Houdini turned up at Earl Grey Dock in a motor car – itself a rare enough site on the streets of Dundee in 1909 – and proceeded to jump off of the dock's swing bridge with his hands manacled behind his back. After an anxious wait, he resurfaced to cheers from the waiting crowd. Houdini slipped away in his car soon afterwards but two of his assistants were held by police, although they were later released.

Some reports state that Houdini also jumped chained and manacled from the bridge of the pleasure steamer *Marchioness of Bute* into the Tay, returning to the surface within thirty seconds to the cheers of the hundreds of people who lined the esplanade.

Dame Nellie Melba (1922)

The great Australian soprano Dame Nellie Melba's entry in December 1922 is the first in the brand new Caird Hall's autograph book. As well as wishing everybody a Merry Christmas, she praised the new hall and said that Dundee should be very proud to possess it. This was not the only time that she played a concert in the city and her connection with Dundee and the surrounding area went far beyond that.

Nellie Melba was born Helen Porter Mitchell in 1861 in Richmond, Melbourne. Although her parents had met and married in Australia, they were actually both Scottish. Her father, David Mitchell, was born on a farm at Inverarity, Forfarshire, and her mother Isabella (née Dow) was born in Dundee itself and as a girl had lived in the West Port. Dame Nellie reputedly sang 'Home Sweet Home' at the 1922 concert in tribute to her mother.

Nellie Melba is not the only person of note whose mother was a native of Dundee:

- Daley Thompson, whose mother Lydia was born in Dundee in 1927, won two Olympic gold medals in the decathlon and is surely Britain's greatest ever all-round athlete.
- The poet Robert Browning's Dundee connection came to light when, at an event to mark the tercentenary of Edinburgh University in 1882, he remarked that he was deeply interested in Dundee as his mother – Sarah Wiedemann – had been born there. The Wiedemann family originally had come to Dundee from Holland in the middle years of the eighteenth century to run a sugar refinery. It was this factory that gave Sugarhouse Wynd (which runs between

the Cowgate and the Seagate) its name. Sarah Wiedemann was born in 1772 and a plaque in the Seagate marks her birthplace. She left Dundee around 1787 and went to London where she met and married the poet's father – also named Robert. She died in 1849.

- Margaret Sinclair, the Edinburgh factory worker whose case for sainthood is being considered by the Vatican, also had a Dundee mother. Elizabeth Kelly was born in the Hilltown in 1874 to Irish parents and worked as a spinner in a jute mill. She was living in Blackness Road when she married Andrew Sinclair at St Joseph's Church in Wilkies Lane in 1896. By 1900, they had moved to Andrew's native Edinburgh where Margaret was born. Margaret started work as an apprentice French polisher and later worked in a biscuit factory. She was also an active trade unionist. In 1923, she entered the convent of the Poor Clares in Notting Hill, London. She died of tuberculosis in 1925 at the age of twenty-five. Her quiet devotion in her ordinary life and in her final illness inspired people and calls for her canonisation began soon after her death. Hundreds of people visit her shrine in St Patrick's Church in Edinburgh's Cowgate each year. In 1978, she was declared by Pope Paul VI to have 'practised the Christian virtues to a heroic degree' and was given the title Venerable.

The Silver Fleet (1942)

In the middle of the Second World War, the Nazis had control of part of the Dundee Docks. Although several members of the public reported this to the authorities, no action was taken. Thankfully, the men spotted at the docks were not real Nazis. They were actors in the film produced by Michael Powell and Emeric Pressburger, *The Silver Fleet* (1943), which told the story of a Dutch resistance hero. It was inspired by the true story of a U-boat that had been hijacked by dockyard workers in the Netherlands and handed over to the Allies.

Somewhat overshadowed by other Powell and Pressburger films such as *The Life and Death of Colonel Blimp* and *A Matter of Life and Death* in which they had more direct involvement, *The Silver Fleet* is still worth a viewing today. It was the first production for the duo's film company 'The Archers' and features strong performances from the leads Ralph Richardson and Googie Withers – although Pressburger was unhappy enough with the film to have his name removed from the writing credits.

The Silver Fleet also features an amazing performance from Esmond Knight where the actor manages to convincingly disguise the fact that he had been totally blinded while on active service. He later regained some sight.

Dundee's own starring role extends only to the outdoor scenes doubling for the docks in occupied Holland. The rest of the film was completed at Denham Films Studios in Buckinghamshire.

Syncopating Sandy (1952)

Premierland Stadium in William Lane Dundee had played host to hundreds of boxers and wrestlers since it opened its doors in 1932 but the contest that took place in October 1952 was one of the most gruelling. It involved only one competitor – a piano player from Bolton in Lancashire known as 'Syncopating Sandy' Strickland. Strickland was trying to set a new world record for non-stop piano playing. In 1951, he had heard that a German by the name of Heinz Arntz held the record of 198 hours. Strickland's first attempt ended in failure just a few hours short of that record. It was the beginning of a rivalry that would last for the next decade or more. The German was reported to have applied different rules regarding breaks being allowed. It seems that they were not, so to speak, playing from the same hymn-sheet.

By the time he arrived in Dundee, 'Syncopating Sandy' was claiming a world record of 176 hours for non-stop piano playing. People crowded into Premierland throughout the ensuing days and nights as he worked his way through a seemingly endless repertoire. Signs and blackboards outside kept the public informed of his progress. He was sustained by glucose and chocolate and endless cups of tea. His assistants massaged his neck and hands and a doctor looked in on him from time to time to pronounce him fit to continue. None of the doctors who looked in on Sandy throughout his marathon piano-playing years in the 1950s seems to have been unduly perturbed by his hundred-a-day cigarette habit.

Newsreel footage of Strickland's 1951 world record attempt shows him being shaved and eating but, says the voice-over coyly, 'We don't have the answer to any other questions that may occur to you.' In fact, when Sandy did feel a call of nature he is said to have started playing 'Lady of Spain' and a curtain would be drawn across. Quite how things were achieved behind the curtain while still playing the piano (perhaps thankfully) remains a mystery.

After seven and a half days of playing non-stop, 'Syncopating Sandy' had beaten his previous record by playing for 180 hours. Thousands crowded into the streets round Premierland and they cheered as Strickland was carried shoulder-high to a waiting taxi.

More world record attempts and other marathon piano-playing events were to make Sandy Strickland a good living throughout the 1950s. His efforts so impressed a young Gerry Rafferty that he wrote and recorded a song on his 1980 album *Snakes and Ladders* in honour of 'Syncopatin' Sandy'.

Eddie Cochran and Gene Vincent (1960)

When rock'n'roll music exploded onto the scene in the mid-1950s, it could not have been guessed that the interest would be worldwide – nor that the 'craze' would last. It is not surprising, therefore, that the pioneers of this new music gave little thought in that first flush of success to touring in Europe – indeed the King of rock'n'roll himself, Elvis Presley, never did. Of those who made it to the UK – like Buddy Holly and the Crickets in

1958 – Dundee did not feature on their itinerary. Home-grown rockers like Tommy Steele and Marty Wilde had visited the city, but Dundee had to wait a long time for a genuine US rock'n'roll legend to come to town – though when it did eventually happen, two came along at once.

Rock'n'roll was said to be in decline in the United States when Eddie Cochran and Gene Vincent arrived in Dundee as part of their UK tour on Saturday, 20 February 1960. Buddy Holly had been killed in a plane crash, Elvis had been drafted into the US army and a new brand of clean-cut teen idol was said to be taking the place of the rough and ready rockers in the American charts. In Dundee, however, enthusiasm for the type of music offered by Cochran and Vincent showed no sign of abating.

The Caird Hall show was scheduled to begin at 8.45pm. The atmosphere was fevered. During Eddie Cochran's set, two men and a girl had fainted. Near the end of Gene Vincent's act at around 10.30pm, a girl had jumped on stage and kissed him. Dozens of others began to follow and invade the stage.

Cochran and support act Vince Eager joined Vincent on stage to sing a final number and help to calm the atmosphere but this, in fact, had the opposite effect and the stage was overrun. The police were summoned but by that point some fans were beating on the door leading to the dressing rooms while others were diving off the stage landing on top of people still in the auditorium. Fighting broke out and girls fainted, an attendant had the sleeve of his jacket ripped off, fittings and fixtures were damaged and, as if to signify the end of the old order, a bust of Sir James Caird himself was toppled. Rock'n'roll had certainly arrived in Dundee.

Eventually, the police managed to clear the hall and restore order but hundreds congregated in the vicinity of the City Square hoping to catch a glimpse of their heroes as they left. When their car finally emerged into Crichton Street from the underground car park, people were banging on the doors and trying to open them.

The hall manager Charles Macdonald, who himself had been pulled off of the stage and attacked during the fracas, was quoted the next day as saying that this kind of concert had been given a fair try in Dundee to let

Gene Vincent on stage at Caird Hall

the teenagers enjoy themselves but last night was 'the last straw' and must be the finish of rock'n'roll as far as the Caird Hall was concerned.

Two men were later fined £20 each at Dundee Sheriff Court for their part in the disturbance. When one solicitor suggested that his client had been carried away with the singing of Gene Vincent, Sheriff Inglis asked, 'What does Gene Vincent sing to incite these people? I don't see why he should get the blame of all this ... I'm sure Mr Vincent doesn't want them to kick the police.' Bailie John Stewart took a different view. Handing out a £5 fine at the Police Court for breach of the peace, Stewart referred to the music as 'caterwauling which causes mass hysteria'.

Two months after the Dundee concert, Eddie Cochran was dead, killed in a car crash in Wiltshire. He was twenty-one years old.

The Sex Pistols (1976)

If there was a defining moment when punk rock came to national prominence, then the Sex Pistols' foul-mouthed appearance on the *Today* show of

1 December 1976, with interviewer Bill Grundy goading them on, would have to be it. This – or rather the later nationwide press coverage of the London-based show – was the moment when what had been a grass roots movement became familiar to the British public at large. Many did not like what they saw and read. Bill Grundy was suspended and later dropped and the *Daily Mirror* in a famous headline railed against 'the Filth and the Fury'. Grundy's career may have never fully recovered but the Sex Pistols' legend was secure from that moment on. Their appearance on the show had been a last-minute decision as they were supposed to have been somewhere else that night. They were supposed to have been in Dundee.

The band had already stopped in Dundee on 12 October – playing their first ever Scottish gig in the room at the Technical College known locally as the 'Bowling Alley'. John Lydon told the *News of the World* in 2007, 'I can't remember anything about it. Except I might have taunted some local hooligans . . .'

The band had signed to EMI four days before their Dundee gig. Their single 'Anarchy in the UK' was released on 26 November. A return to Dundee – this time to the Caird Hall – was scheduled for 1 December as part of the tour to promote it. However, the lure of the publicity afforded by an appearance on the *Today* show, which became available when Queen pulled out, was too much and the show was rescheduled for 16 December.

The Sex Pistols could hardly have anticipated the publicity they did get. The rescheduled Dundee gig, ironically, was one of those that fell victim to the wave of outrage that followed the show and was cancelled.

Grace Kelly (1981)

Grace Kelly, by then Princess Grace of Monaco, together with her husband Prince Ranier visited Dundee on 30 September 1981. The couple went to Tannadice Park where Dundee United were playing Monaco in the first round of the UEFA Cup. United had played well at the first leg, defeating the principality team 5-2 but they lost this leg 2-1. Sadly, Princess Grace's verdict on the renowned Tannadice pies was not recorded.

Tony Benn (1981)

The Labour politician visited Dundee on Friday, 19 November 1981, to attend a rally at the Marryat Hall and to open a lounge that had been named after him at one of the local Labour Clubs. A prodigious diary-keeper, Benn's entry for that day includes his positive thoughts on the city: 'There is a special warmth about Dundee unparalleled anywhere else. Glasgow is very friendly, but Dundee is smaller and more compact and the labour movement there is very strong.'

He also describes the young secretary of the Dundee Labour Party, one George Galloway, as 'the rising star of the Scottish labour movement'.

U2 (1983)

It is hard to imagine U2 kicking off the European leg of a world tour with a visit to the Caird Hall but that is what happened on 26 February 1983 as part of the tour to promote the album *War*. Three tracks from *War* got their first public airing that night – 'Seconds', '40' and the forthcoming single 'Two Hearts Beat as One'.